W9-BSC-499

By the authors

*Anger Kills: Seventeen Strategies for Controlling the Hostility
That Can Harm Your Health*

By Virginia Williams, Ph.D.

*Surrealism, Quantum Philosophy, and World War I*

By Redford Williams, M.D.

*The Trusting Heart: Great News About Type A Behavior*

*Lifeskills*

# Lifeskills

*Eight Simple Ways to Build
Stronger Relationships,
Communicate More Clearly,
and Improve Your Health*

Virginia Williams, Ph.D.,
and
Redford Williams, M.D.

THREE RIVERS PRESS
NEW YORK

Copyright © 1997 by Virginia Williams, Ph.D. and Redford Williams, M.D.

All rights reserved. No part of this book may be reproduced or transmitted
in any form or by any means, electronic or mechanical, including
photocopying, recording, or by any information storage and retrieval
system, without permission in writing from the publisher.

Published by Three Rivers Press, New York, New York.
Member of the Crown Publishing Group.

Random House, Inc. New York, Toronto, London, Sydney, Auckland
www.randomhouse.com

THREE RIVERS PRESS is a registered trademark and the Three Rivers
Press colophon is a trademark of Random House, Inc.

Originally published in hardcover by Times Books in 1997.
Originally published in paperback by Times Books in 1998.

Permissions acknowledgments appear on page 345.

Printed in the United States of America.

Book design by Susan Hood

Library of Congress Cataloging-in-Publication Data

Williams, Virginia Parrott
Lifeskills / Virginia Williams, Redford Williams
Includes index.
ISBN 0-8129-3196-3
1. Interpersonal relations.   2. Interpersonal relations—Health aspects.
3. Family.   4. Social networks.   I. Williams, Redford B., 1940—   .
II. Title.

HM132.W543      1998
302—dc21      97-28464

ISBN 0-8129-3196-3

10 9 8 7 6 5 4 3 2

# Dedicated to
# Lloyd Pinckney Parrott
## (1907–1996)

Lloyd Parrott, Virginia's father, was born on a farm. His mother died of tuberculosis when he was two years old. He was close to his father and helped him in the fields. When he grew up, he went away to college, never again to live on a farm.

Lloyd started a garden soon after his marriage to Elva, beginning by planting tomatoes. When they moved into a house several years later, he added lima beans, squash, green beans, corn, and peppers. He hoed and weeded contentedly, perhaps reminded of his beloved papa.

When Lloyd and Elva moved again, he planned his final garden, including fruit trees, turnip greens, cabbage, and broccoli. He later added strawberries, cantaloupe, watermelon, squash, pole beans, asparagus, raspberries, pecan trees, and an especially delicious variety of Fordhook lima beans. Seeds from the sweetest, juiciest cantaloupes got saved for next year's planting. His produce was the best.

By now Lloyd was feeding not only his own family but all of his neighbors, with occasionally enough for others in town as well.

Though Lloyd and Elva had become affluent, they still lived modestly, except where opportunities for their two daughters were concerned. Despite Lloyd's becoming a pillar in his community, his natural humility continued, reinforced by his deep practice of his religion. He continued to enjoy putting on his work clothes and shoveling dirt. He would shell his pecans before giving them to his daughters.

Lloyd grew older. At age eighty, the year he retired, he purchased a gas-powered rotary tiller to help with the deep hoeing. He dug up the peach trees and planted new fig trees to replace old ones.

Elva developed osteoporosis, requiring him to assume much of the housework and to care for her.

"Maybe I won't have a garden this year."

"Oh?"

"It depends on how your mother is feeling."

"Well, maybe you could put in a tomato plant or two."

Elva got out of bed and Lloyd put in a full garden. Though he was almost eighty-nine years old, his rows still were straight. Like all his other relationships, his garden was well cared for.

On the way out to work in his garden one late spring afternoon, he chatted briefly with his neighbor, commenting that he was feeling fine. He tilled the patches that needed it, and then started to push the tiller back to the shed. Just out of his garden, he fell beside his fig tree, dying apparently three to four minutes later, with eyes closed.

# Acknowledgments

We gratefully acknowledge the help of the following people:

Many, many workshop participants, for their commitment, particularities, and insights;

Dolph Adams and Jim Lewis, for helping us understand how events at the cellular and molecular levels can mediate the impact of psychosocial factors on disease processes;

John Barefoot, for his work and insights on the clustering of psychosocial risk factors;

The Behavioral Medicine group at the University of Miami, for advice on workshop exercises—especially Mike Antoni, Gail Ironson, Pat Saab, and Neil Schneiderman;

Barbara Berryman, for sending numerous newspaper clippings and copies of some key cartoons;

Jim Blumenthal, for helping us do a better job of teaching Lifeskills in the real world;

Reid Boates, our faithful agent, for always being there for us in many, many ways;

James Boice, for pointing out the biblical reference to the fig tree;

Susan Boos, for helping us prepare the manuscript;

Cathy Burkette, Alan Herosian, Brad Markoff, Bob Taber, and Ken West, for their help translating our workshop for teaching Lifeskills into a package that can be used in a wide range of settings;

The Center for Epidemiological Studies at The National Institute of Mental Health, for allowing us to use the CES-D depression scale;

Margaret Chesney, for her constant moral and concrete support;

Sheldon Cohen, for allowing us to use his questionnaire on social support;

Morris Davis, for helping with the section on astronomy;

Patrick Davis, water resource director, Triangle J. Council of Government, for reviewing the information on the water and sewer commission and suggesting numerous changes;

Elizabeth Delman, for describing the items on the list about pillars from the bedside of Mildred Barnes;

Martha Fairbank, for the Russell Baker newspaper article;

Frank Keefe, for helping us understand the problem-solving skill;

Cindy Kuhn and Saul Schanberg, for helping us understand the profound effects that lack of nurturing can have on developmental processes in young animals;

Lynn Underwood Gordon, for pointing us to an important article on religion;

David Handler, for providing additional materials on children;

K. Jalalluddin, for sending us a copy of The Holy Qur-An;

Arlene Lukas, for the story about the Seattle Special Olympics;

John Martin, for suggesting the "I AM WORTH IT!" mnemonic;

Sal Monaco, for sending us an article on humor;

Karen Moorman, for critiquing the section on ACME;

The Massachusetts Mutual Life Insurance Company, for sending all of their reports from 1989 onward, documents which have been extremely helpful;

Mary Nada, for articles on modern ennui;

John Rambow, for help with permissions;

Ilene Siegler, for allowing us to use her questionnaire on strain at work and home and for showing how risky health behaviors cluster in certain individuals;

Chip Spann, for the Martin Luther quotation;

Ed Suarez, for his insights on the biological mechanisms whereby psychosocial risk factors can cause disease;

The University of Michigan Institute for Social Research, for providing materials on drug use among young people;

Karen Weeks, for a helpful book on the philosophical underpinnings of mental health.


A special thanks to two people:

Margaret Ann Harrell, for carefully reading and improving the entire manuscript;

And Betsy Rapoport, our hardworking editor, for having the insight to see major revisions needed in the original manuscript, and then for having the courage to tell us that.

# Contents

*"In my practice, I prefer to treat the whole hog."*

© The New Yorker Collection 1996 Leo Cullum from cartoonbank.com. All Rights Reserved.

# Introduction

I am only one; but still I am one. I cannot do everything, but still I can do something; I will not refuse to do the something I can do.

*Helen Keller*

Deeds shape the doer.

*Anonymous*

Good relationships enhance health and well-being. We have written *Lifeskills* to help you achieve this. Our approach grows out of both professional and personal experiences.

Years ago, we developed a workshop to try out the strategies for controlling hostility that we eventually included in our last book, *Anger Kills*. Since then we have been heartened by the accounts of improved lives from now thousands of people—both workshop participants and *Anger Kills* readers. As we listened to them, we learned that the Lifeskills we taught had proven useful not only for controlling hostility but also for building better relationships.

Indeed, many* have taken our hostility control workshops because a relationship was troubling them:

*Susan, computer programmer from Massachusetts:* "Since my husband and I sought counseling we're getting along a little better. But I'm still worried that one or two slips, and we'll be heading for the divorce courts."

*Amanda, a designer from Georgia:* "I don't even like my son any more. Until he was thirteen years old, we hiked and camped as a family. He sometimes told us secrets. Now we're strangers."

---

*We have changed the names and identifying details of all workshop participants throughout the book.

*Colleen, a physician from Utah:* "I am thirty-five years old, with a successful practice. Why can't my parents realize I'm grown? They still treat me like a teenager. I feel demeaned. Sometimes I just shut them out of my life. But deep down, I still care."

*Frances, a university professor from Virginia:* "Mark came to me and asked if I wanted to work on this grant with him. I did, contributing about half the ideas. When we finished—it took many, many hours over a number of weeks—I felt good about the proposal. Then he gave it to our secretary to type, sending it in before I saw the final copy. The next time I saw it, his name—but not mine—was listed as principal investigator."

We were able to help all of these people develop the Lifeskills they needed to cope with their problems:

Susan and her husband turned the corner by learning to speak up when a problem first begins to develop—and to listen, in turn. No longer are they considering divorce.

Amanda and her husband Ted improved their relationships with their son, once they decided to set fewer rules and enforce them energetically. They now feel less uptight about how well they are handling his adolescence.

By speaking up and setting limits, Colleen is finally getting across to her parents that she is a grown, successful, independent woman who still values their blessings but needs to be left alone about how she chooses to live her life. Actually, she has more contact with them than before.

Frances will never again make a mistake about whose names appear on the grant proposal, even without the workshop. But relationships with all work colleagues, she thinks, are now more equitable. By being assertive, she has stopped playing the easy-target martyr.

We could recount numerous other odysseys of people who have built better relationships through Lifeskills. Learning to clarify their options and adjust their behaviors as needed has made a big difference.

Once you develop these skills, you'll find them useful beyond the relationships you've targeted for improvement. You'll find that getting along with yourself, your family, your coworkers, and outsiders all gets easier.

As we have helped others to change, they have aided us. Over the years, as we have led workshop after workshop and spoken to one group after another, we have sharpened our focus. Originally, we advocated the seventeen skills that appear in our earlier book. As readers and workshop participants told us what proved most effective and as we observed what worked best during workshops, we began to winnow, combine, condense, and add new focuses, until now we have identified eight skills that form the core of our approach. We entitle these Lifeskills. Of course, other advocates with other lists have practical formulas for living skillfully—we don't own a monopoly on skillful living. We do have a tried-and-true approach that we believe can help most people better understand themselves and others—and act effectively.

Our shift in emphasis was also stimulated by research showing the health benefits of good relationships. Thus, this book incorporates some new twists that the research of Redford and others has taken in the last few years.

For two decades, Redford's work in the Behavioral Medicine Research Center at Duke University focused mainly on hostility. He and others have found that getting angry, whether the anger is expressed or held in, harms the body. People who exhibit a hostile personality in their twenties are more likely to be dead—from all causes—by their fifties. These health problems appear to stem from frequent and pronounced fight-or-flight responses, as well as risky health behaviors—like smoking, excessive alcohol use, and overeating, habits that angry people are more likely to adopt.

That was the beginning. In the last few years Redford has realized that the same frequent health problems he and his colleagues find among persons with hostile personalities also afflict depressed people. And why do people who are socially isolated, in high-strain jobs, or in lower socioeconomic groups have worse health than most other people? All of these groups practice bad health habits—the individuals are more inclined to overeat, drink too much, and smoke—but that accounts for only part of their additional risk. Determining *why* these groups come to share so many health-damaging physical, psychological, and behavioral characteristics is an important next step toward understanding what is involved. So is determining the underlying biological mechanisms that heighten the risk of heart disease, cancer, and other life-threatening illnesses. Redford will probably spend the rest of his life pursuing potential explanations.

He already has some educated guesses, which he will tell you about in Chapters 3 and 4. And whatever the final explanations, he is confident that—regardless of past stresses and harsh environments, innate personality type, or biological inheritance—understanding yourself and others, as well as changing how you treat other people and how they treat you, can promote health and happiness.

Behavioral change is in the air. The National Heart, Blood, and Lung Institute is sponsoring a multi-site intervention trial for heart attack victims, to see if reducing their depression and social isolation improves their prognosis and survival. At Duke and seven other medical centers, patients are being helped to deal with these problems. One day soon, the results will be in. On the basis of smaller studies already done, all of us who work in the field expect that patients in this study who receive training in skills to help reduce depression and improve relationships will live longer than matched counterparts who do not receive this additional care.

We now offer Lifeskills at Duke University Medical Center to patients experiencing many health problems. The goal is to improve well-being *and* health.

Another byproduct of Redford's expanded research focus is an increasing interest in childhood. As you may already know, children who are treated positively are much better off, in terms of future intelligence, ability to get along with others, and flexibility to deal with whatever comes along. Moreover, exciting new research indicates that the way young children are treated probably influences their future *biological* makeup as well. Studies suggest that animals given sufficient nurturing early in life produce smaller and shorter stress-hormone responses in adulthood. More extensive nurturing further reduces these health-damaging responses. Influenced by these findings, we are devoting more attention to children in our work. In addition, this research, as well as discoveries about what predicts divorce, has led us to add a focus in our Lifeskills workshops on accentuating the positive in dealings with others.

A historian by training, Virginia, remaining on the lookout for cultural influences, is struck by how difficult it now is across the board, compared to earlier times, to get along well with everybody—ourselves as well as our partner, young children, teenage children, and parents, not to mention people more peripheral to our lives. We'll document this state of affairs in Chapter 1 and in the "Current Situation" section of each chapter.

Let us also mention, as an additional influence, *our* own growing realization—we are middle-aged—that we won't live forever. Some cherished friends have developed premature serious illnesses; others have already died. We've begun to ask ourselves, How are we to connect to the bigger picture before it's too late? What purpose do our lives serve? Are we contributing enough? We know we want that intangible "more" from our lives. At the same time, rarely have institutional supports for connecting up to the broader world been so fragile.

Gradually, this mix of influences has coalesced: Feedback from participants in our workshops and readers of *Anger Kills;* observations of what skills worked best during workshops; Redford's new research focus on how hostility, depression, social isolation, poor health habits, and lower social status cluster in the same people and groups, who also experience similar health problems (the result, probably, of similar underlying biological mechanisms of disease); the realization that the time has come for systematic interventions; Virginia's increasing awareness of just how counterproductive to good relationships our current environment has become; and last of all, our growing realization that the time to better our lives is *now.*

Most of us place a high priority on getting along well with our families. When a large survey sample of Americans were asked to choose between $1,000 in cash and Thanksgiving with their families, 79 percent chose the latter! More than did previous generations, Americans today value good relationships with intimates. Yet more than ever before, this goal eludes us.

Most of us want to be part of a caring community, too. Everyone agrees that community life currently needs improving. Achieving that improvement, however, seems elusive. One approach not yet tried on a massive scale was brought home to us one Sunday several years ago, when a responsive reading—attributed to the Taoist philosopher Lao-tzu, but possibly from the sage Mo-tzu—was part of the church service:

> If there is to be peace in the world,
> > There must be peace in the nations.
> If there is to be peace in the nations,
> > There must be peace in the cities.
> If there is to be peace in the cities,
> > There must be peace between neighbors.
> If there is to be peace between neighbors,
> > There must be peace in the home.
> If there is to be peace in the home,
> > There must be peace in the heart.

One way to achieve, both close and far, a caring community— and that is what this book is about—is to change how **each human being,** acting as a single individual, treats others. Consistently applied to intimate *and* distant relationships, a simple set of cognitive and behavior change strategies might alter us, our families—and the world.

When you succeed in learning to act in ways designed to improve relationships, you improve your own mental and *physical* health, as well as that of the other party. Plus, there's always the possibility that your positive interaction may influence that person to treat others in the same way. Imagine: If massive numbers of us lead the way by restructuring how we treat one another, our politicians and institutions will have no choice but to follow or be left behind.

## *How This Book Is Organized*

The biological and historical inheritance of human beings predisposes them to act *both* affiliatively and selfishly. We'll explain this double legacy briefly in Chapter 1.

What is the current state of *your* psyche and social support system? To find out, take the test in Chapter 2.

Why do relationships matter? In Chapter 3, Redford tells you about the research that shows a lack of good relationships is bad for your own physical health. How you treat others—especially young children—affects their health as well (Chapter 4).

In Chapter 5, we introduce the eight Lifeskills: four designed to help you to understand yourself and others, the other four to help you to act effectively.

With these Lifeskills in hand, in each subsequent chapter we focus on one important relationship, following this outline:

- *Vision:* What would getting along well be like?
- *Do You Recognize Aspects of Yourself?* Workshop participants have taught us much. For you as well, they may offer living examples of some behaviors to emulate, others to avoid!
- *Knowledge:* For each particular relationship, we'll give you data about the current situation throughout society, the present wisdom espoused by experts, and research findings on the effect on health and well-being.
- *Crossover:* Improving your relationship with one person or group often has a pervasive effect.
- *Action:* We'll provide specific instructions to help you apply the eight Lifeskills to this relationship.
- *Getting Real:* All of this may seem easy while you're reading about it. However, actually applying Lifeskills in real life requires

creative explorations and hard work. We'll share with you some of the successes—and failures—we and others have experienced.

- *Exercises:* These exercises will guide you in beginning to use your newly acquired Lifeskills.

Such an ambitious agenda may seem overwhelming now, but we believe that as you read about each separate relationship, you will begin to see that getting any one relationship right will help with the others, as all involve some mix of the same set of Lifeskills. And a synergy will set in; once you start getting positive feedback somewhere, you will gain energy for working on other relationships.

To change our community, our world, we must begin by changing *ourselves*—the primary focus of this book. Either each of us changes our treatment of others or positive change doesn't happen in society!

With so many relationships to consider, we may not cover a given topic as deeply as you may require. The world is full of excellent books on how to fix many of the dysfunctional aspects of society; we shall draw freely from some of these useful works. We'll cite additional readings. If that's not enough, you may want to seek help from a counselor, physician qualified to recognize any psychiatric disorder, religious leader, politician—whoever seems appropriate.

Regardless of what further help you may need, this book gets you started. What you learn will help you get along well with others.

We start with the most intimate connections, beginning with the relationship to *yourself,* since high self-esteem helps in all other ties (Chapter 6). You and your *partner* should like and enjoy each other, relishing time spent together (Chapter 7). You and *your children* need to be a source of strength and joy for one another (Chapters 8 and 9). You should value your *parents* and let them know this. You need to encourage them (and other relatives) to respect and appreciate you as well (Chapter 10).

We look beyond your biological family to good relationships with *friends* (Chapter 11). From there, the circle naturally expands outward to *coworkers* (Chapter 12), people in the *community* (Chapter 13); fellow *Americans* (Chapters 14 and 15); and the larger *human family* (Chapter 16).

Getting along with others benefits everybody, adding happiness to your day. The lower death rates observed among heart and cancer patients as well as general populations who have, or were provided with, social support within the family or elsewhere add a second, trickle-down perspective: support from the broader community, your circle of associates, and your family can improve your own health and that of those you care about.

How you act matters, and you *can* act effectively—have that peace in your heart. Mutual respect and commitment will often follow. Beginning with the most intimate connections, *you* can influence others. How far that salutary influence will extend will be up to you.

Let's get started.

# Part I

# Getting Started

MISTER BOFFO © 1995 Joe Martin. Reprinted with permission of UNIVERSAL PRESS SYNDICATE.
All rights reserved.

# 1. The Best of Times, The Worst of Times

What's past is prologue.

*Shakespeare,*
The Tempest, *Act II, Scene i*

Many of us long for the "good old days"—warm, close-knit families, communities that pulled together in times of strife, jobs where loyalty counted. Are we just romanticizing the past, or is life today really different? Knowing where we've come from and where we seem to be heading is important. These are in fact unique times; we simply have to work harder to make relationships succeed. The message here: For the current crises in relationships so many of us are experiencing, we need to stop blaming ourselves or each other and instead get to work acquiring additional Lifeskills needed to live well in our changed world.

## Are All Genes Selfish?

Unfortunately, aggressive and selfish behaviors are, under a number of circumstances, instinctive—bred into generation after generation of our primordial ancestors, who survived to reproduce sometimes because they behaved that way. Throughout evolution, selfish grabbing of food at times increased chances for survival. These "selfishness" genes were passed on. Today, when we decide we want something, we may act as though our very survival were still at stake. Especially among male primates and early humans, the dominant male who could intimidate other males often gained exclusive access to the females—becoming, at the expense of other males attached to the group, the one who reproduced. Such dominance had gene survival value. Today, even when such behavior probably will backfire, we may still want to best others.

But selfishness and aggression are not the only elements of our genetic heritage relevant for relationships. People who are connected to and supported by other people are on average healthier mentally *and* physically—and that means they're more likely to survive. Consider how infants depend on others. Without a parent predisposed to care for them sufficiently, they cannot survive. In turn, if a partner provides for and protects them, the caretaker and infant are inclined to flourish. As a result—on average, over generation after generation—ancient humans with a genetic predisposition toward strong family ties were apt to pass on their genes successfully. We are programmed to care.

When human beings became hunter-gatherers, interdependence expanded. During the last two to four million years, our ancestors for the most part lived in social groups composed of twenty-five to two hundred people. Such an arrangement provided protection and enabled individuals to work together to get food. Given their isolation, group members were bound by blood ties. Belonging to such a group had survival value, indeed exile usually meant nothing less than a death sentence. On the basis of evidence from research conducted by ourselves and others on the benefits of social support, we would guess that human beings probably are hard-wired to need one another.

## Our Cultural Programming May Be Outdated

In *The Evolving Self,* University of Chicago psychologist Mihalyi Csikszentmihalyi argues that the inheritance of modern people extends beyond biology to include the passing on from one generation to the next of cultural information and instructions. Like our genes, our inherited language, religion, scientific theories, lifestyle, and technologies constitute integral parts of who we are and why we act as we do.

However, as with the biological heritage of aggressive and selfish tendencies carried over from the past, our cultural programming is becoming increasingly outdated. The world is changing rapidly, too rapidly. The workplace, the community, our nation, the international community of nations, and the ecological balance of our planet have faltered as we try to sustain them by following old cultural instructions under altered circumstances. To make matters worse and irrespective of our particular political, philosophical, and religious allegiances, we usually feel disturbed when others handle all the changes differently from how we would or do.

For the first time, the majority of people on earth dwell in cities. Tribes are moving to villages, villagers to larger towns, and so on. In highly industrialized societies, many of the most educated already identify with a global culture. How do we learn to care about all these people we're newly associated with? With each change from small tribe to anonymous metropolis and regardless of which larger unit we're shifting into, most of us retain an increasingly outdated, parochial, and therefore ever-weakening set of instructions originally useful in binding us to one smaller, old tribe against all other tribes.

Perhaps this helps to explain why roughly every ten years, rates of depression in some industrial countries have been doubling. Unlike rapidly changing cultures, traditional societies seem protected. The old order Amish, who use no cars, electricity, or alcohol, suffer from depression at less than one-fifth the rate of people in nearby Baltimore. By Western standards, rural villagers in Samoa have extraordinarily low levels of the stress hormone cortisol. The Kaluli of New Guinea do not experience depression.

Whether a particular cultural inheritance is seen as absolute or as one among several reasonable options often depends on whether we retain the perspective of our old tribe at the expense of all other tribes or of the new, larger group we belong to. A cultural heritage that originally functioned to ensure survival of "us" against "them" may reduce our ability to resolve differences with people we must now live with in our increasingly intertwined world. With the end of the cold war between superpowers, local us-them animosities and hatreds (long-suppressed in the shadow of United States–Soviet competition for influence around the world) are reemerging with explosive force—in the former Yugoslavia, Rwanda, and Azerbaijan, to name a few hot spots. And around the globe, people fear terrorist attacks.

Society's problems come not only from those who long for an irretrievable past, when all of us belonged to smaller, cohesive groups. We who switch allegiances to the broader, larger groups tend to be intolerant and nonsupportive of those who do not. People who consider themselves "modern" dislike "traditionalists" who cry in the current wilderness for a return to the old ways. Many of the bitter dissents in the United States involve mutually closed-minded confrontations between such opposing groups—for examples, pro-life versus pro-choice, the liberal left versus the religious right, feminists versus those favoring traditional sex roles. The enmity between such groups shows the clear need for all to have better skills at getting along!

# It's a New World Nowadays

The economic and social advances throughout the developed world during the last century and especially the last half-century have also changed how people relate to one another and what they expect—a change especially pronounced in the United States.

In 1940, only 15 percent of young people in America went to college; by the 1960s, over half did. Through television and the public schools, all of us are exposed to lifestyles and opportunities beyond our parents' grasp. Compared to our grandparents, we have more free time. We have more money. In short, we have options. How can we stay connected to those we've been close to, when we choose to change? And now that such a diverse mixture of people composes our community at large, how can we all get along?

Another big shift marked the postwar period—in an ever-extending circle of relationships and life roles, Americans came to expect a great deal. The Institute for Social Research in Ann Arbor, Michigan, surveyed a sample of almost twenty-five hundred adults in 1957 and another such sample in 1976. In comparing the two groups sampled two decades apart, analysts at the institute stressed that in many ways, both men and women had become more reflective in their thinking about themselves and in their attempts to understand their own lives. Back in 1957, Americans were satisfied to be married and have children; twenty years later, Americans were concerned also about the *quality* of these relationships. Before, men were content with a secure and profitable job, women with fulfillment in their roles as homemakers. By 1976, most Americans—men and women alike—wanted fulfillment in *both* the workplace and the home.

The interpreters of the institute's surveys found men particularly profoundly affected by the changed emphasis. In 1957, the focus for most fathers was on being a good provider. By 1976, they wanted to have a warm, close, "meaningful" relationship with their children, but they felt that such a relationship eluded them. By 1976, the lack of warmth and closeness with their children was what men thought of most often when asked what kinds of problems they had had with their children and whether they ever felt inadequate as parents. All indicators suggest that these expanded desires by men and women for "meaningfulness" at both home and work have only increased in the two decades since the Michigan study.

Individuals now can compare themselves not with other people in their village, but with national models of excellence seen on TV and in magazines. How are they to avoid being overwhelmed by that kind of "supernorm"?

This is the first generation of middle-class families where both partners usually have jobs, yet home responsibilities haven't changed much. The combined double workload weighs especially heavily on those women who still do most of the housework, a situation the women often resent.

Parents face additional challenges, some old, some new: relating in sensitive, practical ways to an ever-developing young person; establishing for their offspring the right mix of freedom and guidelines; finding adequate affordable child care, if both parents work; deciding how much and what kind of television—and other electronic media—to permit; dealing with adolescents subjected to unprecedented pressures to engage in risky behaviors, let alone to prepare for a career and absorb cultural changes. (The influence of peers on teens also is more extensive than ever before.) Add to this mix that in American society adults do not assume much responsibility for other people's children.

The "sandwich generation" also has to deal with aging parents. On average, parents now live many years after their children are grown, with everyone trying to adapt to the circumstances of two sets of adults.

Neighborhoods are either extremely heterogeneous or extremely homogeneous. Your city is probably in the throes of major upheavals—isn't it always? Political deadlocks have become the regional and national norm. All are angry at somebody—some "them" ruining life for the rest of "us," whether by being too selfish or too profligate with public funds, or by exerting wrong opinions on whether governments should regulate behaviors in areas like school prayer and abortion. How can we rebuild the sense of community everyone needs?

At present, we acutely need homes and communities that support us better. From her study of working parents, the sociologist Arlie Hochschild has concluded that homes and communities have become so stressful for many Americans that they are escaping into work. Home has become so much "work" that work seems like "home."

This bewildering mix of new circumstances is affecting people who may have relocated far from family and old friends. While relocation is nothing new—frequent moves to new places have always been the rule in American life—this mobility dramatically reduces our already newly fragile support systems. Between 1985 and 1990, 46.5 percent of Americans moved—9.7 percent to a different county, another 9.4 percent to a different state. Recent figures show less mobility, but as the result of earlier large migrations, many

Americans already are separated from friends and kin. How—and where—are we to get the kind of support from others needed for good mental *and* physical health?

## We Need Help Building Good Relationships

Circumstances have changed. We need supportive relationships more than ever. Have we developed better ways of achieving that? If the participants in our workshops are any indication, we'd have to say no.

Over and over, workshop participants share with us how they're going about building or maintaining relationships, unaware how their behaviors got them in trouble:

*Melanie, from New York, an effervescent mother of a five-year-old daughter:* "There's a character issue here. I need to teach my kid to respect me."
"Do you discipline her?"
"Sometimes. Then I try to make up for the other times I haven't."

*Karen, a rather shy fifty-year-old woman from Florida:* "My husband really makes me mad when he assigns me tasks during one of our presentations without first checking with me."
"Do you let him know how you feel when he does this?"
"No. Our marriage has been pretty rocky recently. I don't want a divorce."

*Paul, a successful entrepreneur from Canada:* "We ended up screaming at each other. But I can't let her walk all over me. I'm not her hired hand, you know."
"Did screaming help?"
"No."

*Danielle, a schoolteacher from North Carolina:* "Ted is impossible. I can't talk to him."
"Do you set aside time for that?"
"No."
"Do you have any strategies for getting a conversation going?"
"No."

*Carolyn, a young lawyer from Colorado:* "My parents *really* hurt my feelings by saying they were coming to see me last weekend and then calling to cancel at the last minute."
"Did you let them know?"

"Well, kind of. I haven't returned any of their phone call messages since."

In each case, the person involved was driving the other person farther away.

## Unique Times Require Unique Solutions

In each of the examples just given, the outcome would have been much better if the participant had practiced the Lifeskills we'll be teaching you—identifying personal thoughts and feelings, next carefully observing the exact circumstances, and then evaluating the situation. After deciding what, if any, actions were called for, each participant could probably have salvaged these situations.

If we are to live well in the unprecedented circumstances of modern life, we need to acquire additional skills. None of the individuals just described were "losers." To the contrary, they were successful in many aspects of their lives and highly interested in improving their relationships. Yet the combination of the unique times they are living in and their presently-outdated set of life skills was overwhelming them.

Now the crux of the argument. Given the demanding modern situation, if we are to succeed in relationships—a state of being necessary for good mental and physical health—we need to substitute acting deliberately for "doing what comes naturally": *to understand ourselves and others; then to act effectively*.

# 2. First, Know Thyself

Oh wad some power the giftie gie us
To see oursels as ithers see us!
It wad frae monie a blunder free us,
    An' foolish notion.

*Robert Burns*
*"To a Louse," st. 8*

At the start of most journeys into new territory, your best first step is to determine exactly where you are at the outset. Consider the questionnaire in this chapter as a compass to help you map where your relationships are right now. You also will see how you rate on the relationship-damaging characteristics of hostility, depression, and stress.

We've based our questionnaire on several standardized questionnaires. To measure relationship quality, we have used the Interpersonal Support Evaluation List developed by Carnegie-Mellon psychologist Sheldon Cohen. We've used questions adapted from the Hostility Questionnaire in our earlier book, *Anger Kills,* to assess hostility. Questions to assess depression are adapted from the CES-D scale developed by the Center for Epidemiological Studies of the National Institute of Mental Health. Stress, on the job and elsewhere—as reflected in demands and in the control one has over how one meets them—is gauged by a set of questions developed by Redford's Duke colleague, Ilene Siegler, based on Robert Karasek's work in Sweden.

Read each question, then circle T for "True" or F for "False." With some questions, both *True* and *False* may seem equally correct for you. This reaction is normal; go ahead and choose the answer *more likely* to be correct. Take as much time as you need, but remember that your first thoughts usually reflect your true feelings. Try to avoid choosing a response that reflects how you think you *should* act or feel. To thine own self be true.

One cautionary note: These questions offer black-and-white scenarios. You may be temperamentally unsuited to making choices that fail to shade subtleties or consider particular circumstances. If you are like this, focus extra energy on keeping the log described in Chapter 5, as this provides a second compass.

Go ahead now and take the test. You can either circle answers here in the book or place the numbers 1 to 114 on a sheet of paper, writing *True* or *False* after each number to indicate your answer. The scoring key is at the end of the questionnaire.

## The Relationships Questionnaire

1. When a teenager drives by my yard with the car stereo blaring acid rock, I can feel my blood pressure starting to rise.
   T     F

2. There are several people that I trust to help solve my problems.
   T     F

3. During the past week, I was bothered on three or more days by things that usually don't bother me.
   T     F

4. If my haircutter were to trim off more hair than I wanted, I'd let him or her know in no uncertain terms.
   T     F

5. If I needed help fixing an appliance or repairing my car, there is someone who could help me.
   T     F

6. When I'm in the express "twelve items only" line at the supermarket, I almost always glance ahead to see if anyone has more than twelve items.
   T     F

7. Most of my friends are more interesting than I am.
   T     F

8. During the past week on three or more days I did not feel like eating; my appetite was poor.
   T     F

9. At work the pace is usually very hectic.
   T     F

10. Most homeless people in large cities are down and out because they lack ambition or self-discipline.
    T     F

11. There is someone who takes pride in my accomplishments.
    T     F

12. At times in the past when I was very angry with someone, I have, on occasion, hit or shoved that person.
    T     F

13. When I feel lonely, there are several people I can talk to.
    T     F

14. During the past week there were three or more days when I felt that I could not shake off the blues even with help from my family or friends.
    T     F

15. When I read in the news about drug-related crime, I wish the government had better educational and drug-detoxification programs, even for pushers.
    T     F

16. There is no one that I feel comfortable talking to about intimate personal problems.
    T     F

17. The AIDS epidemic is largely the result of irresponsible behavior on the part of a small proportion of the population.
    T     F

18. During the past week I felt that I was just as good as other people more than half the time.
    T     F

19. Apart from work, the pace of my life is very hectic.
    T     F

20. When arguing with a friend or relative, I find profanity an effective tool.
    T     F

21. I often meet or talk with family or friends.
    T     F

22. When stuck in a traffic jam, I quickly become irritated and annoyed.
    T     F

23. Most people I know think highly of me.
    T     F

24. When a really important job needs to be done, I prefer to do it myself.
    T     F

25. If I needed a ride to the airport very early in the morning, I would have a hard time finding someone to take me.
    T     F

26. During the past week there were three or more days when I had trouble keeping my mind on what I was doing.
    T     F

27. My work is very demanding.
    T     F

28. I usually prefer to keep my angry feelings to myself.
    T     F

29. I feel as if I'm not always included by my circle of friends.
    T     F

30. If another driver butts ahead of me in traffic, I'll drop back to avoid him or her.
    T     F

31. There really is no one who can give me an objective view of how I'm handling my problems.
    T     F

32. I felt depressed on three or more days during the past week.
    T        F

33. If someone treats me unfairly, I am apt to keep thinking about it for hours.
    T        F

34. There are several different people I enjoy spending time with.
    T        F

35. When the cars ahead of me on an unfamiliar road start to slow down and stop as they approach a curve, I usually assume someone up ahead has had a fender bender or worse.
    T        F

36. I think that my friends feel that I'm not very good at helping them solve their problems.
    T        F

37. During the past week there were three or more days when I felt that everything I did was an effort.
    T        F

38. I'll usually try to correct another person who expresses an ignorant belief.
    T        F

39. I experience being at home or engaging in leisure activities as very demanding.
    T        F

40. It doesn't bother me to be in slow-moving bank or supermarket lines.
    T        F

41. If I were sick and needed a friend, family member, or acquaintance to take me to the doctor, I would have trouble finding someone.
    T        F

42. When someone is being rude or annoying, I can get rough with him or her.
    T        F

43. If I wanted to go on a trip for a day (for example, to the beach or country), I would have a hard time finding someone to go with me.
    T     F

44. During the past week I felt hopeful about the future more than half the time.
    T     F

45. Every time an election year rolls around, I learn anew that politicians cannot be trusted.
    T     F

46. If I needed a place to stay for a week because of an emergency (for example, the water or electricity was out in my apartment or house), I could easily find someone who would put me up.
    T     F

47. Whenever an elevator stops too long on a floor above where I am waiting, I soon start to feel irritated.
    T     F

48. I have no one with whom I can share my most private worries and fears.
    T     F

49. When I am around someone I don't like, I find it hard not to be rude to him or her.
    T     F

50. During the past week there were three or more days when I felt my life has been a failure.
    T     F

51. When I see a very overweight person walking down the street, I wonder why such people are so lacking in self-control.
    T     F

52. If I were sick, there would be almost no one to help me with daily chores.
    T     F

53. When riding as a passenger in the front seat of a car, I try to be alert for obstacles ahead.
    T          F

54. There is someone I can turn to for advice about handling problems with my family.
    T          F

55. During the past week I felt fearful more than half the time.
    T          F

56. When someone criticizes something I have done, it makes me feel annoyed.
    T          F

57. I am as good at doing things as most other people are.
    T          F

58. When involved in an argument, I can feel my heart pounding and I breathe harder.
    T          F

59. If I decided one afternoon that I would like to go to a movie that evening, I could easily find someone to go with me.
    T          F

60. There were three or more nights during the past week when my sleep was restless.
    T          F

61. I have a lot of privacy at work.
    T          F

62. When a friend or coworker disagrees with me, I am apt to get into an argument with him or her.
    T          F

63. When I need suggestions on how to deal with a personal problem, I know someone I can turn to.
    T          F

64. When someone else is speaking very slowly during a conversation, I am apt to finish his or her sentences.
    T          F

65. If I needed an emergency loan of one hundred dollars, there is someone (friend, relative, or acquaintance) I could get it from.

    T    F

66. It's fear of being caught that keeps most people from sneaking into a movie theater without paying.

    T    F

67. During the past week I was happy more than half the time.

    T    F

68. Hearing news of another terrorist attack makes me feel like lashing out.

    T    F

69. In general, people do not have much confidence in me.

    T    F

70. When talking with my significant other, I often find my thoughts racing ahead to what I plan to say next.

    T    F

71. Most people I know do not enjoy the same things that I do.

    T    F

72. At times in the past when I was really angry, I threw things or slammed a door.

    T    F

73. There is someone I could turn to for advice about making career plans or changing my job.

    T    F

74. During the past week there were three or more days when I talked less than usual.

    T    F

75. At home or during leisure activities off the job, I have a lot of privacy.

    T    F

76. The little annoyances of everyday life often seem to get under my skin.

    T    F

77. I don't often get invited to do things with others.

    T        F

78. When I disapprove of a friend's behavior, I usually let him or her know about it.

    T        F

79. Most of my friends are more successful at making changes in their lives than I am.

    T        F

80. During the past week I felt lonely more than half the time.

    T        F

81. I have very little control over how I spend my time at work.

    T        F

82. When checking in at an airline ticket counter, I generally leave the seat assignment to the agent.

    T        F

83. If I had to go out of town for a few weeks, it would be difficult to find someone who would look after my house or apartment (the plants, pets, garden, etc.).

    T        F

84. I feel grouchy some of the time during nearly every day of the week.

    T        F

85. There is really no one I can trust to give me good financial advice.

    T        F

86. During the past week there were three or more days when people were unfriendly.

    T        F

87. If someone bumps into me in a store, I am apt to feel irritated at the person's clumsiness.

    T        F

88. If I wanted to have lunch with someone, I could easily find a person to join me.
    T     F

89. When my significant other is preparing a meal, I keep an eye on things to make sure nothing burns or cooks too long.
    T     F

90. I am more satisfied with my life than most people are with theirs.
    T     F

91. I enjoyed life more than half the time during the past week.
    T     F

92. At home and during leisure activities, I don't have much control over how I spend my time.
    T     F

93. If a friend calls at the last minute, pleading he or she is "too tired to go out tonight," and I am stuck with a pair of twenty-dollar tickets, I will tell my friend how inconsiderate he or she is.
    T     F

94. If I were stranded ten miles from home, there is someone I could call who would come to get me.
    T     F

95. When I recall something that angered me in the past, I feel angry all over again.
    T     F

96. No one I know would throw a birthday party for me.
    T     F

97. Many of the people I see walking around shopping malls are just wasting time.
    T     F

98. It would be difficult to find someone who would lend me their car for a few hours.
    T     F

99. During the past week I had crying spells during three or more days.
    T        F

100. When someone is hogging the conversation at a party, I make it a point to put him or her down.
    T        F

101. If a family crisis arose, it would be difficult to find someone who could give me good advice about how to handle it.
    T        F

102. When I have to work with incompetent people, it ticks me off to have to put up with them.
    T        F

103. I am closer to my friends than most other people are to theirs.
    T        F

104. During the past week I felt sad more than half the time.
    T        F

105. I have very little latitude in making decisions at work.
    T        F

106. When my spouse (boyfriend/girlfriend) is going to get me a birthday present, I usually prefer to pick it out myself.
    T        F

107. There is at least one person I know whose advice I really trust.
    T        F

108. When I hold a poor opinion of someone, I will probably let him or her know about it.
    T        F

109. If I needed some help in moving to a new house or apartment, I would have a hard time finding someone to help me.
    T        F

110. During the past week there were three or more days when I felt that people disliked me.
    T        F

111. In most arguments, I am the angrier one.
     T　　F

112. I have had a hard time keeping pace with my friends.
     T　　F

113. During the past week I could not "get going" on three or
     more days.
     T　　F

114. At home or in my leisure activities, I have very little latitude in
     making decisions.
     T　　F

The most direct indicator of the quality and quantity of your relationships is your score on the forty social support questions. Your
total social support score is made up of four distinct sorts of support:

- *Emotional support*—the degree to which you have someone to
  help in dealing with emotional problems.
- *Belonging support*—the degree to which you have a network of
  family and friends to do things with.
- *Tangible support*—the degree to which you have someone to help
  in meeting material needs, like a ride to the airport.
- *Self-esteem*—the degree to which your relationships boost self-worth.

To evaluate emotional support, give one point for each of these
answers:

| | |
|---|---|
| 2–T | 63–T |
| 16–F | 73–T |
| 31–F | 85–F |
| 48–F | 101–F |
| 54–T | 107–T |

To measure belonging support from networks of family and
friends, give one point for each of these answers:

| | |
|---|---|
| 13–T | 59–T |
| 21–T | 71–F |
| 29–F | 77–F |
| 34–T | 88–T |
| 43–F | 96–F |

To score tangible support, give one point for each of these answers:

| | |
|---|---|
| 5–T | 65–T |
| 25–F | 83–F |
| 41–F | 94–T |
| 46–T | 98–F |
| 52–F | 109–F |

To tally self-esteem, give one point for each of these answers:

| | |
|---|---|
| 7–F | 69–F |
| 11–T | 79–F |
| 23–T | 90–T |
| 36–F | 103–T |
| 57–T | 112–F |

Add up components for your total social support score:

Emotional support        _____

Belonging support        _____

Tangible support          _____

Self-esteem                 _____

                                     _____

Total social support     _____

The *higher* your social support score, the better your relationships. If your total score is *less* than 28 out of a possible 40, bettering the quality and quantity of your relationships probably will improve your health and well-being. To locate any problem area, look over your scores on the components. If all are 7 or less, you need to work on all aspects of your relationships. On the other hand, if one component is clearly lower than the others, that component is presumably the one you need to focus on. How to improve the quality and quantity of your relationships—from the closest to the most distant—is what the rest of this book is about.

The low energy and sense of hopelessness characteristic of depression can impair relationships. To score your level of depression, give yourself one point for each of these answers:

| | |
|---|---|
| 3–T | 60–T |
| 8–T | 67–F |
| 14–T | 74–T |
| 18–F | 80–T |
| 26–T | 86–T |
| 32–T | 91–F |
| 37–T | 99–T |
| 44–F | 104–T |
| 50–T | 110–T |
| 55–T | 113–T |

If your depression score is 5 or *higher,* your level of depression is probably detracting from your relationships. Again, the skills you will learn about in the rest of this book will help you overcome the drag that depression can impose on your ability to build and maintain good relationships. By using these skills to improve relationships, you may diminish the depression as well.

Hostility consists of cynicism, which leads you to mistrust the motives of others; frequent anger in everyday interactions with others; and aggression directed toward others. These characteristics obviously can impair relationships.

To score your level of cynicism, give yourself one point each for these answers:

| | |
|---|---|
| 6–T | 53–T |
| 10–T | 66–T |
| 17–T | 70–T |
| 24–T | 82–F |
| 35–T | 89–T |
| 45–T | 97–T |
| 51–T | 106–T |

To profile anger, give yourself one point for each of these answers:

| | |
|---|---|
| 1–T | 68–T |
| 15–F | 76–T |
| 22–T | 84–T |
| 33–T | 87–T |
| 40–F | 95–T |
| 47–T | 102–T |
| 56–T | 111–T |
| 58–T | |

To tally your level of aggression, give yourself one point each for these answers:

| | |
|------|--------|
| 4–T | 62–T |
| 12–T | 64–T |
| 20–T | 72–T |
| 28–F | 78–T |
| 30–F | 93–T |
| 38–T | 100–T |
| 42–T | 108–T |
| 49–T | |

Now you can add up your total hostility score:

| | |
|-------------------|--------|
| Cynicism | _____ |
| Anger | _____ |
| Aggression | _____ |
| | _____ |
| Total hostility | _____ |

If your total hostility score is *higher* than 16, your level of hostility is probably impairing relationships. Your cynical attitude, angry feelings, or aggressive behavior may need work. The skills you will learn in the rest of this book will help you control your hostility.

Finally, stress on the job and off can leave you without the emotional or physical resources to build and maintain good relationships. To score your level of stress at work, give one point for each of these answers:

| |
|-------|
| 9–T |
| 27–T |
| 61–F |
| 81–T |
| 105–T |

To measure your level of stress at home and during leisure, give yourself one point for each of these answers:

19–T
39–T
75–F
92–T
114–T

A score of 3 or *more* on work or home and leisure stress suggests that stress in these areas may be impairing your relationships.

If you scored in the *low* range—less than 28—on social support, it's probable you'll find you scored *high* on depression, hostility, and/or stress, as research we will review later indicates that these tend to cluster in the same individuals. And if your income level and/or educational attainment are low, it's more likely you will score low on social support and high on the other psychosocial risk factors.

If you scored high in any of the categories profiled, you may have health problems, too.

# 3. Relationships Matter! The Scientific Evidence for Effects on Our Health

> When you can measure what you are speaking about, and express it in numbers, you know something about it.
>
> *William Thomson, Lord Kelvin*

Relationships matter.

Redford, along with many, many other scientists, has been intensely involved in mind-body research throughout his career. After nearly three decades, he is reporting to you with confidence the verdict of modern science: Poor relationships with fellow humans can damage your own physical health. The news isn't all bad, however. At least for patients with heart disease and cancer, interventions that lead to improved relationships can also improve your health.

Let us say at the outset that not all illnesses result from poor relationships. Many factors—genetic makeup, environmental pollutants, and lady luck among them—influence health. Do all you can to stay healthy, but don't blame yourself if you become sick.

A NOTE TO THE READER: *We recognize that some readers are not interested in the detailed scientific evidence. "You're the expert," they say. "Just tell me the bottom line, and I'll take your word for it." If you are of similar mind, you might want to skip right now to the story "The Prince and the Pauper (Updated and with Apologies to Mark Twain)" that begins Chapter 4. Then, if you like, you can come back and skim the more detailed scientific story in this chapter and Chapter 4.*

*On the other hand, if you prefer to review the evidence yourself, read on, as Redford chronicles two decades of mind-body research.*

For several decades, I and other mind-body researchers have been trying to pinpoint those psychosocial risk factors that damage health.

For the most part, we have focused on one feature at a time, with some scientists trying to show that personal characteristics such as hostile personality or depression harm health, while others concentrated on damaging social environments—like lower income, poor social ties, or jobs that impose high strain on the worker.

From the perspective of my long research career, I can now see some patterns in the mind-body research findings:

- The psychosocial factors now known to damage health—lack of social support, hostility, depression, high-strain jobs, low socioeconomic status—do not occur in isolation, but tend to cluster in the same individuals and groups, where their health-damaging effects are compounded. *All of these psychosocial risk factors adversely affect, both directly and indirectly, the quality and quantity of our relationships.*
- Research has identified both biological and behavioral accompaniments that are likely to mediate the health-damaging effects.
- This clustering of psychosocial risk factors and associated health-damaging biobehavioral characteristics could stem from the tendencies of both genetic and environmental factors to reduce brain levels of the neurotransmitter serotonin.
- Encouraging recent research indicates that patients with heart disease or cancer live longer when they receive psychosocial treatments aimed at reducing the health-damaging impact of these psychosocial risk factors. *All of these health-enhancing psychosocial treatments favorably affect, both directly and indirectly, the quality and quantity of the patients' relationships.*

## *Psychosocial Risk Factors and Health: Epidemiological Evidence*

Epidemiologists study groups of people to discern any associations between various characteristics (termed *risk factors*) and the incidence of developing (or dying from) various diseases. Thus, epidemiologists in the renowned Framingham Heart Study found that people who had high blood pressure, were smokers, or had high blood cholesterol levels when first observed were more likely to suffer or die from a heart attack when followed over the next several years. Thanks to their painstaking, meticulous research, smoking, high blood pressure, and high blood cholesterol levels are now recognized as *physical* risk factors for coronary heart disease. Similarly, mind-body researchers have used the epidemiological approach to document the increased risk of health problems among persons with various psychosocial characteristics. I'll discuss each of these characteristics below.

## Lack of Social Support

Can support from others improve your health? To determine this, researchers have measured any of several variables:

- a sense of being accepted by others
- the support believed to be available, if needed
- the support actually received
- the recipients' perceptions of that support and their satisfaction with it

Some studies measure material help, like whether participants could ask someone for a ride to the doctor's office, and other studies look at the less tangible support that comes from feeling valued. We shall use the general term *social support* to refer to all of these definitions.

Almost all of the studies, no matter what method of measurement is used, concluded that social support affects physical health. A twenty-nine-year study of nearly seven thousand healthy persons living in Alameda County, California, found that those who reported fewer community social ties such as club memberships or church attendance were more likely to die from coronary heart disease, cancer, and other major illnesses. This increased risk of dying could not be explained by higher levels of the physical risk factors. Thus, something else about those who are less well-connected with their fellow humans is responsible for their higher death rates.

Social isolation also affects the prognosis of patients who already have coronary heart disease. In one study of heart attack victims, the cardiologist Robert Case and his colleagues at Columbia University found that those who lived alone were twice as likely to die or have another heart attack within two years following their first heart attack. In a follow-up study of patients with coronary disease at Duke, we found that fully half of those who were very isolated— unmarried patients saying they had no one they felt they could confide in—were dead within five years, while during the same time span only 17 percent of those with either a spouse or confidant (or both) died. In both studies, these higher death rates among socially isolated heart patients could not be explained by any differences in the severity of the underlying heart disease.

## Hostility

In addition to actual social ties, even the way people *think* about others can take a toll on their bodies. Duke psychologist John Barefoot surveyed doctors and lawyers who had filled out a psychological test in medical or law school in the 1950s. As opposed to their more trusting counterparts, those who at age twenty-five reported high levels of mistrust—seeing others as mean, selfish, and out for themselves—were five to seven times more likely to be dead by age fifty. While only 2 percent of those with low hostility scores in medical school died during the ensuing twenty-five years, nearly 14 percent of those with high hostility scores had died by age fifty.

Numerous other studies, both in the United States and abroad, have confirmed the health-damaging impact of hostility. On average, persons with a cynical mistrust of others, more frequent angry feelings toward others in everyday life, and more frequent open expression of this anger through aggressive treatment of others die sooner.

Being hostile can keep us distanced from others. Evidence suggests that from young adulthood hostile people are isolated. Their marriages can be rancorous. The authoritarian style hostile people display at work makes them less likely to be successful top bosses. And their ever-present distrust estranges them from broad groups of fellow human beings. In terms of personal relationships as well as health, hostile people are at risk.

## Depression

Depression can harm us too. Clinical depression is a serious medical disorder in which feelings of sadness, hopelessness, and exhaustion, as well as bodily alterations (change in sleep patterns, lack of sexual desire, decreased appetite), are profound enough to impair normal daily functioning. In less extreme forms, this can be no more than a chronic tendency toward the "blues" and the "blahs," but not to the degree that would warrant a diagnosis of major depression. Studies of healthy persons in both the United States and Denmark show that persons with even this slighter tendency to feel sad and blue are more likely to suffer a heart attack or to die from any cause during the years after they take a psychological test that measures these depressive tendencies.

The impact of depression is even more ominous among patients who already have had a heart attack. Psychologist Nancy Frasure-Smith and her colleagues at McGill University in Montreal found that only 3 percent of patients who were not depressed following a heart attack died within six months of their attack. In marked contrast, over five times as many depressed patients (16 percent) died during the same period. My colleague John Barefoot also has found higher death rates over a much longer follow-up period—sixteen years—among heart patients at Duke with a high score on a depression scale. Since both Frasure-Smith and Barefoot controlled for the severity of underlying heart disease, the higher death rates cannot stem from more serious heart damage among the depressed.

Withdrawal from social interactions constitutes one of the surest signs of depression, in addition to the changes in mood and biological function already noted. People who are depressed simply lack the energy to maintain ties with other people. It is possible, indeed, that lack of social ties can even predispose a person to becoming depressed. It follows that depressed persons really need social support.

## High-Strain Jobs

Most of us spend a considerable portion of our lives at work. Industrial psychologist Robert Karasek and his colleagues have shown that, for many of us, work is a source of health-damaging stress. Particularly damaging—in terms of increased rates of heart attack, high blood pressure, and other serious illness—are jobs that place high demands on workers to produce some product or service, while at the same time providing them with little control over how those demands are met. Such jobs, termed *high-strain,* include assembly line work and other situations where the worker has little or no latitude in setting work pace.

In contrast to depression, where one's own lack of emotional or physical energy causes relationships to suffer, in high-strain jobs, a social environment isolating workers from one another impoverishes relationships. In a study of women workers at a large corporation, my colleagues and I found that those who reported high strain (high demands and low control) were also more likely to score low on a social support scale and high on a depression scale. It's not possible to say what's chicken and what's egg here, but in any case, people in high-strain jobs are more likely to be socially isolated. Other researchers find that improved social relationships help workers cope better with stress on the job.

## Low Socioeconomic Status

Whether low socioeconomic status (SES) is indexed by income, educational attainment, occupational status, or some combination of these, persons at the low end of the SES ladder are far more likely to develop (and die from) a broad range of life-threatening health problems, including coronary heart disease, cancer, infections, and accidents. As with depression and social isolation, which identify not only persons more likely to develop coronary heart disease in the first place but also those more likely to die sooner after a heart attack, studies at both Duke and Cornell university medical centers found that low SES heart patients are about twice as likely as more affluent patients to die, when followed up for five years after a heart attack.

The reasons for the higher rate of health problems among low SES groups are only partly understood. For example, lower-grade government civil servants in London have more health problems than those with higher rank. Since all had comparable medical care through the British National Health Service, reduced access to good medical care cannot explain the findings. Other research conducted among the British civil service, however, does indicate that no more than one-third of the excess deaths among low SES groups can be laid at the doorstep of increased physical-risk factors—smoking, high blood pressure, high cholesterol levels. Clearly, physical risk factors are not the whole story behind the health-damaging effects of low SES. And, *why* do poorer groups have poorer health habits? Is this the result of ignorance and/or lack of personal discipline, or are other factors at work?

## Risk Factors Cluster, Causing Extra Harm

If an individual has one risk factor, he or she is more likely to have others as well. For example, my colleagues and I found in a recent study of working women that those who described their jobs as high in strain—high demands, low control—also scored higher on measures of hostility, depression, *and* social isolation. People in low socioeconomic groups are, in general, at special risk, since they have been repeatedly found to be more hostile, socially isolated, depressed, and likely to hold high-strain jobs. My Duke colleague John Barefoot found that people with low incomes have higher levels of depression and hostility and that this impact of low income is larger among African Americans than European Americans.

Now for the really bad news. As with physical risk factors, when it comes to the health-damaging impact of psychosocial risk factors, the sum of one and one is more than two. In his study of Alameda County residents, psychological epidemiologist George Kaplan found that the combination of low SES, increased depression, *and* social isolation was associated with a far higher death rate than would be expected from the simple addition of the death rate increases associated with each psychosocial risk factor alone. This synergistic effect is neatly shown in the figure entitled "Impact of Depression, Social Isolation, and Income on Relative Risk of Dying." If the death rate for the non–isolated, non-depressed, high-income group is used as the reference, then adding only the two psychosocial risk factors—depression and social isolation raised the death rate 2.3 times. In persons with all three psychosocial risk factors, however, the death rate is *over four times higher*. Kaplan found a similar impact from the combination of high levels of cynical hostility and social isolation in low SES residents of Kuopio, Finland. In a study of elderly residents in Glostrup, Denmark, my Duke colleague John Barefoot found a similar synergism of hostility, depression, and low SES in boosting death rates.

## Impact of Depression, Social Isolation, and Income on Relative Risk of Dying

*Alameda County Study*

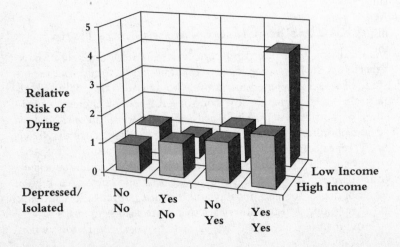

Let's summarize:

- Mind-body research has identified five psychosocial risk factors—hostility, depression, social isolation, high job strain, and low SES—clearly harmful across a broad spectrum of life-threatening health problems.
- These psychosocial risk factors tend to cluster in the same individuals and groups, compounding health-damaging effects.
- Each of these psychosocial risk factors affects, either directly or indirectly, the quality and quantity of one's relationships with other people—the worse your levels of psychosocial risk factors, the worse the state of your relationships.

Put another way, the research on psychosocial risk factors teaches us that the worse your relationships are, the worse your health is likely to be.

*Relationships matter.* That's the bad news—and the good news. Research with heart and cancer patients offers encouraging evidence that providing social support and teaching skills that can improve the quality and quantity of relationships enhances both the quantity and quality of life as well. I'll review this at the conclusion of the chapter—first, some relevant, exciting frontiers of biological research.

Why do relationships matter so much for our physical health? Just how do these psychosocial risk factors that affect our relationships actually bring about the development of major illnesses, like coronary heart disease and cancer? While final answers must await further research (that caveat cautious scientists love to use when launching into speculative waters), there are several promising leads. As with the psychosocial risk factors themselves, biological mechanisms also tend to cluster in the same individuals and groups, and they are in many instances triggered by negative interactions between us and those around us.

## Our Bodies Under Stress

Over millions of years, living organisms evolved bodily responses that increased their chances of surviving in dangerous situations, where failure to succeed in a fight-or-flight situation could be fatal. When our prehistoric ancestors confronted a hungry saber-toothed tiger, a complex and exquisitely orchestrated set of bodily responses was set in motion—all designed to increase their chances of surviving the next few minutes. It usually was only a matter of seconds to minutes before the issue was decided. They escaped, vanquished the attacker, or were killed. In terms of your hard-wired bodily responses, when you conclude you are in an emergency situation, you respond the same way your ancestors did.

Let's begin at the beginning, when the hypothalamus—the emergency command center deep in our brain—gets the signal "Danger ahead":

- Your sympathetic nervous system causes your heart to beat harder and faster, increasing the amount of blood being pumped around your body from an average of 5 quarts per minute to over 18 quarts per minute.
- The sympathetic nervous system carefully allocates this increased blood flow to where it's needed—away from the kidneys, intestines, and skin. (If you're about to be slashed open, you need to conserve precious bodily fluids and avoid becoming a meal, rather than digesting the last one you ate!) That extra blood is shunted instead straight to your muscles—the organ system you must have working at full tilt in order to succeed in the fight-or-flight situation.
- Under normal, that is, non-life-threatening, conditions, your parasympathetic nervous system kicks in, to counter the actions of the sympathetic nervous system on your body. Thus, when the sympathetic nerves to your heart cause it to beat more rapidly, the parasympathetic nerves start to fire off and block the heart-speeding sympathetic effects. When a real threat to life and limb exists (or is *perceived to exist*) your fight-or-flight response is turned on, and the parasympathetic calming system is turned off, to permit the sympathetic system to keep you fired up longer.
- The stress hormones adrenaline and cortisol are poured into the bloodstream from the adrenal glands. In addition to initiating and maintaining heart and blood-vessel responses, these hormones perform other important functions. They cause your body's fat depots to break down molecules into small, quickly usable packets, which are dumped into the bloodstream to provide a source of high energy that keeps muscles going during those critical few minutes.
- These stress hormones also make blood stickier and quicker to clot—not a bad idea if someone is likely to get slashed by tooth or claw and doesn't want to bleed to death on the spot.
- The hormones also suppress functioning of the immune system. We don't fully understand all the reasons for this yet, but one

idea is that when they're slashed, bodily tissues and proteins not normally in contact with the immune-system cells circulating in the blood could stimulate these cells to make antibodies to your own body, possibly leading to autoimmune diseases later on. So a temporary shutdown of the immune system might be a good idea too.

There are undoubtedly many more bodily changes that occur, all serving the same purpose—to give you that extra edge critical to surviving just a few minutes longer in an emergency situation and recovering in the aftermath with a minimum of harm to your possibly injured body. When the emergency *was* a real saber-toothed tiger, this was well and good, and your ancestor either escaped, prevailed in the fight—or was dinner.

## The Stress Response in Modern Life

While the research is still somewhat incomplete, current evidence seems to indicate the mechanisms just described have carried over to modern life. Today, what turns on a fight-or-flight response is all too often a situation where relationships, whether with intimates or strangers, have gone sour. Instead of saber-toothed tigers or fights to the death with a rival out to steal one's mate, in today's world, fight-or-flight responses are turned on when hostile personalities are angered by the real or imagined misconduct of others, ranging from a spouse and children to unseen persons in far-off corners of the world. And if your social ties are impoverished—whether because job strain leaves you drained, depression saps energy and initiative, your hostility drives others away, or your social environment actually lacks the necessary resources—you're left without the buffer of social support that you may especially need. Here is some evidence that suggests this.

My Duke colleague Edward Suarez has been one of the pioneers in documenting the biological consequences of hostility. In his research, Ed first measured hostility levels and then deliberately got his subjects angry over some conflict, either occurring in the here and now or recalled from the past. As their anger rose, subjects who measured high in hostility showed larger increases than their non-hostile counterparts in every component of the fight-or-flight response measured: blood pressure, heart rate, muscle blood flow, and adrenaline and cortisol levels in the blood.

These excessive fight-or-flight responses among hostile persons are not confined to contrived laboratory experiments. During daily life as well, the amounts of both adrenaline and cortisol excreted in the urine of hostile persons surge higher during the day.

Other experiments demonstrate that when important relationships are in trouble, our bodies suffer. One example: Over many years University of Washington psychologist John Gottman has been studying married couples in his "love lab." He has found that in simply recalling a recent argument, partners in distressed marriages have blood pressure surges upward almost as high as during the actual disagreement. University of Utah psychologist Timothy Smith has found that the higher the hostility level, the larger the blood pressure surge when married couples discuss a topic about which they disagree.

In a parallel to the findings of increased reactivity in the sympathetic nervous system of hostile persons, several studies have found weaker parasympathetic calming effects—hostile individuals may have worn themselves out in the more frequent and intense fight-or-flight reactions to everyday life situations in which negative views of others led to anger.

The same health-damaging biological characteristics found among hostile persons also are present in depressed persons. Thus, increased sympathetic function (evidenced by increased noradrenaline levels), decreased parasympathetic function, and increased cortisol levels have all been observed when depressed persons are compared to non-depressed control groups.

Though less extensive in scope, research on biological accompaniments of the other psychosocial risk factors reveals similar changes. Persons who report low social support excrete more adrenaline in their urine during a typical day than persons reporting high levels of social support. This could result from direct effects of social isolation in boosting stress levels, but it could also reflect an absence of the protective, stress-buffering effects of social support. The latter possibility is favored by results from several studies showing that the presence of a supportive friend actually reduces heart rate and blood pressure surges in persons subjected to stress during laboratory experiments.

Blood pressure levels during the day are higher among persons working in high-strain jobs than in persons whose jobs impose fewer demands and/or permit more control. Persons in high-strain jobs also have enlarged hearts, probably as a result of staying in a chronic state of fight-or-flight activation. Working women with young children living at home—a high demand, low control situation par excellence—excrete more of the stress hormone cortisol in their urine during a twenty-four-hour period than coworkers without children at home.

Few researchers thus far have looked directly at the biological accompaniments of the fifth psychosocial risk factor, low SES. Considering the effects of the other psychosocial risk factors on biological markers of the fight-or-flight response, it is probable that this research will reveal that persons of low income and/or low educational attainment show similar biological changes, perhaps in response to the well-documented higher levels of violence and alienation in the neighborhoods of low SES groups.

*Interpersonal relationships* are critical in moderating the biological mechanisms just described. It is anger resulting from conflict-laden interchanges with others that drives up blood pressure and adrenaline levels in hostile persons. It is a lack of the stress-buffering benefits of supportive relationships that appears responsible for geared-up stress response in socially isolated persons. Among depressed persons and those in high-strain jobs, an absence of the protective effects of social support is probably responsible for at least some of the increased health-damaging stress reaction.

Individuals with psychosocial risk factors also practice poor health habits. Large-scale studies involving more than five thousand persons, one led by my Duke colleague Ilene Siegler, have found that hostile persons smoke more, drink more, eat more (600 more calories per day in hostile compared to non-hostile persons), have a higher body mass index (weight to height), and have a higher cholesterol/HDL ratio (a combination of blood fat components that strongly predicts increased heart attack risk). Depression is associated with increased smoking and alcohol consumption, as well as with appetite changes (both increased eating and decreased), and higher blood lipid levels. And remember the point made earlier about the mediators of health problems among low SES groups: Approximately one-third of their excess health problems stems from their tendency to engage in risky health behaviors—smoking, increased alcohol use, and eating and exercise habits that contribute to obesity, increased blood lipid levels, and higher blood pressure levels.

In summary, psychosocial risk factors are associated with a wide range of potentially health-damaging characteristics:

- increased adrenaline and cortisol levels
- a weaker parasympathetic nervous system
- increased blood pressure

- increased smoking
- a bad blood lipid profile
- increased alcohol use

## How Do Psychosocial Risk Factors Contribute to Disease?

To understand fully how all of this works together to contribute to life-threatening illnesses, more research will be necessary. This research must take advantage of the revolution in molecular biology. By this, I mean that scientists need to understand how the biological and physical risk-factor accompaniments of psychosocial risk factors affect disease-causing processes at the cellular and molecular levels. Then, researchers are more likely to succeed in developing effective prevention approaches that will correct malfunctioning underlying biological mechanisms.

This research is only now just getting under way. At Duke, Ed Suarez and I have been collaborating with Saul Schanberg and Cynthia Kuhn from the Department of Pharmacology, with contributions from the Department of Pathology by Jim Lewis and the late Dolph Adams. We hope to use the tools of cellular and molecular biology to understand—at the most fundamental cellular and molecular level—how psychosocial risk factors contribute to the development of major life-threatening illnesses like coronary heart disease and cancer. We already have some interesting, but very preliminary observations—they must be confirmed in larger studies before we can be confident they are real.

The high adrenaline levels in hostile persons appear to cause a reduction in the number of receptors for adrenaline on lymphocytes—key cells of the body's immune system that circulate in the blood. Monocytes are another class of cells circulating in the blood that may play a key role in the development of both arteriosclerosis and cancer. This role appears to be mediated by the turning off or on of genes that regulate monocyte functions critical for the development of arteriosclerosis or for the killing of tumor cells that form in the body. Our preliminary findings indicate that persons with high hostility or high depression scores have circulating monocytes with some of the same genes turned off that we find turned off by oxidized-LDL in our more basic studies with mouse monocytes. Oxidized-LDL is an altered form of the "bad" cholesterol, LDL, and is seen as a potent stimulus for the development of arteriosclerotic blockages in the coronary arteries that feed the heart. When these arteries become completely blocked, a heart attack results. Thus, our preliminary findings point to a mechanism at the cellular and molecular level—similar changes in monocyte gene expression caused by a known pathogen, oxidized-LDL—whereby hostility and depression could increase the risk of coronary heart disease.

This work, as well as that of other scientists around the world, offers a promising beginning to the task of identifying cellular and molecular mechanisms. In the same breath, let me again hasten to add this statement: More research will be needed before we can be confident these early findings are on the right track.

## The Role of the Brain

A growing understanding of how the brain might be involved is another area where I believe we have made a promising beginning in our quest to understand and eventually prevent the health-damaging effects of psychosocial factors.

These psychosocial, biological, and behavioral characteristics tend to cluster in the same individuals and groups:

- hostility, depression, and social isolation
- an overactive sympathetic-nervous-system-mediated fight-or-flight response
- an underactive parasympathetic-nervous-system-mediated calming response
- poorly regulated eating behavior
- increased alcohol consumption
- increased smoking and reduced ability to quit

How can researchers explain the clustering of such a broad and seemingly unrelated gaggle of characteristics?

Scientists attach a high value to *parsimony:* economy in explanations of natural phenomena. Experience teaches us that the simpler and more economical a theory, the more often (not always!) it is true. As I became increasingly aware in recent years that hostility, the main object of my research, was often accompanied by the broad and seemingly unconnected array of other risk factors, I yearned for parsimony. Might not a simple, economical, even stingy hypothesis explain this clustering?

I have had the good fortune since the mid-1970s to be a member of a biological psychiatry research organization—the American College of Neuropsychopharmacology (ACNP)—that meets annually for participants to present new and exciting basic research. The primary focus is how the brain and its functions contribute to various psychiatric disorders. Attending ACNP annual meetings over the years, I began to be struck—about the same time I was noting the clustering of psychosocial and biobehavioral risk factors—by the bewildering array of characteristics that appear to be associated with reduced function of the neurotransmitter *serotonin* in the brain.

Neurotransmitters are chemical compounds that help nerves "talk" to one another. Thus, after being stimulated, a nerve ending will "spit" out a neurotransmitter packet into the space between it and another nerve. The neurotransmitter latches onto receptors on the second nerve that recognize only it and very similar chemicals, causing that receptor to "switch on." This sets in motion a chain of other chemical events inside the second nerve that cause it to do things, like lower our threshold to act impulsively, or cause our adrenal gland to secrete adrenaline into our bloodstream.

Scientists have known for a long time that low brain serotonin function is associated with depression. (Depression is also associated with reduced function of another neurotransmitter, norepinephrine.) Moreover, people—most of these studies involved men—with a history of aggressive, violent behavior problems, often associated with excessive alcohol use, also have low brain serotonin function.

The best measure we have of brain serotonin is the amount of a breakdown product—5-hydroxyindolacetic acid, or 5-HIAA for short—in the cerebrospinal fluid that bathes the brain. Getting some cerebrospinal fluid to use in measuring 5-HIAA requires a spinal tap. This approach has been used in several studies, including the one measuring low brain serotonin among men with a history of alcoholism and violence.

Other approaches involve giving a drug that temporarily either raises or lowers the level of serotonin in the brain in order to see what happens to both behavioral and physiological functions. Thus, fenfluramine, a drug that releases serotonin in the brain, causes secretion of the hormone prolactin by the pituitary gland. The less serotonin there is in the brain to be released, the smaller the increase in blood prolactin levels.

Psychiatrist Emil Coccaro and colleagues used this latter approach to show that persons with high scores on various aggression scales have reduced brain serotonin function—as indexed by a smaller prolactin increase following fenfluramine treatment. Bowman-Gray researcher Jay Kaplan and his colleagues also found that monkeys rated as more aggressive in their natural habitat had lower brain serotonin function (that is, smaller prolactin responses to fenfluramine) than less-aggressive counterparts. National Institutes of Health researcher Dee Higley and colleagues found that the more aggressive monkeys also had lower levels of 5-HIAA in their cerebrospinal fluid.

If low serotonin causes increased aggression and hostility, then raising brain serotonin function should have the opposite effect. In one study, monkeys given the serotonin-enhancing drug Prozac showed a decrease in aggression toward other monkeys. Interestingly, they also showed an increase in "affiliative" behaviors— approaches toward other monkeys, time spent grooming other monkeys, and time spent in close proximity to other monkeys. So these monkey studies suggest that in addition to reduced hostility and aggression, brain serotonin enhancement is also associated with positive, affiliative behaviors that would boost social support.

Such effects are not limited to monkeys. In a study of patients with borderline personality disorder—a condition associated with frequent angry interchanges with friends and relatives, as well as poor interpersonal relationships—Harvard psychiatrist Carl Salzman and his colleagues found that the clearest benefit among the patients receiving Prozac (compared to those on sugar pills) was a decrease in anger that led to improved relationships with family and friends.

Drugs that enhance brain serotonin function help reduce craving for cigarettes among smokers trying to quit. These same drugs reduce appetite and thereby the weight gain that so often plagues those trying to quit smoking. Other research shows that reduced brain serotonin stimulates appetite and eating in rats; drugs that increase brain serotonin function are now being used to help overweight humans lose and keep off weight.

Thus far, evidence links low brain serotonin function to hostility and aggression in monkeys and humans, increased alcohol use in humans, depression in humans, increased eating in humans, decreased social support in monkeys and humans, and increased smoking in humans. All that remains to be shown is the altered sympathetic-parasympathetic balance that also clusters in hostile and depressed persons, and there is evidence that this pattern, too, can be the result of low brain serotonin. Harvard physiologist Richard Verrier has shown in studies of cats that raising brain serotonin levels by giving tryptophan, the amino acid from which serotonin is made, is associated with a decrease in the firing rate of the sympathetic nerves going to the heart, as well as increased resistance to the development of fatal stress-induced heartbeat irregularities. Other research shows that stimulation of the same serotonin receptors in the brain that leads to decreased activity of the sympathetic nervous system also causes an *increase* in parasympathetic nervous system activity.

The brain research just reviewed makes a compelling, albeit circumstantial case. That is, evidence suggests that low brain serotonin function is capable of causing each of the health-damaging psychosocial, biological, and behavioral risk factors that tend to cluster in the same persons and groups. Favoring the most parsimonious explanation of this clustering, I have seized on these capabilities of low brain serotonin to formulate the theory that low brain serotonin function is one—almost certainly *not* the only—cause of a clustering of hostility, depression, social isolation, increased sympathetic function, decreased parasympathetic function, increased eating, increased alcohol use, and increased smoking in the same individuals and groups.

It remains to be seen whether my parsimonious serotonin hypothesis for the clustering of psychosocial, biological, and behavioral risk factors will prove true. Many colleagues whose wisdom I respect tell me it is *too* simple and fails to take into account the many complexities—for example, the role of other neurotransmitters or the multitude of different serotonin receptors, with their often different effects on behavior and physiology—that are surely at work in modulating such a complex and diverse array of human behavior and physiology.

To them I say, "You may be right, but this hypothesis is testable, and that is the ultimate standard upon which it will prove true and useful or flawed and worthless." The research to test it is just now beginning, and it will take the hard work of many researchers over many years before we have final answers.

## Improving Relationships Improves Health

Having learned that psychosocial factors damage health by increasing the risk of developing a wide variety of major illnesses, including heart disease and cancer, mind-body researchers are now expanding their focus to interventions aimed at ameliorating the impact of psychosocial risk factors. Interventions that directly provide heart and cancer patients with social support and/or teach them skills to manage their negative emotions and improve their relationships are already showing the most important benefits possible: longer survival and reduced recurrence of the disease.

For example, psychologist Nancy Frasure-Smith and her colleagues at McGill assigned patients, upon discharge from the hospital following a heart attack, to one of two groups. Everybody received regular cardiological care, but the intervention group got a monthly telephone call during the first year. When the caller detected a problem, a nurse would come in to help the patient deal with it. By the end of the first year of follow-up, the patients in the social support enhancement group showed a 50 percent reduction in death rates, relative to the usual-care group. In other words, by providing the patients with at least one good, helping relationship, Frasure-Smith and her colleagues achieved an improvement in prognosis that would be hailed—and prescribed—by the entire cardiology establishment, if it had been achieved by giving some new pill.

A similar 50 percent reduction in the rate of recurrent heart attacks and deaths was achieved by San Francisco cardiologist Meyer Friedman and his colleagues in a study of one thousand heart attack survivors. This intervention provided patients with direct social support, in the form of weekly group meetings. During these meetings, patients also learned skills to control their anger and improve time management, as well as to reduce stress—all useful in helping them build relationships outside the group. As with the Frasure-Smith study, patients randomly assigned to the "active" (group meeting) treatment condition showed a 50 percent reduction in recurrence rates over a three-year follow-up period, compared to the patients getting the usual care.

Instead of reduced recurrence rates as the endpoint, another San Francisco physician, Dean Ornish, enrolled patients with severe coronary arteriosclerosis in an ambitious study designed to test the effects of a comprehensive intervention. This program included dietary changes to reduce cholesterol, exercise to improve fitness, support group meetings to improve relationships, and yoga training to build resistance to stress. As reported in the prestigious British medical journal *Lancet,* those patients randomized to the active treatment (intervention) group showed significant reduction in the size of arteriosclerotic plaques clogging the coronary arteries supplying their hearts, while the usual-care group showed a slight worsening of their arteriosclerosis. While it was not possible for Dr. Ornish to be sure whether any one aspect of his comprehensive treatment program was most helpful, he tells us that he believes that the social support (leading, we might expect, to improved relationships) was a key ingredient.

While the results of these interventions appear encouraging, our confidence in the results of these studies must be tempered by the small number of subjects. Dr. Ornish's initial study included fewer than fifty patients, and Dr. Frasure-Smith's fewer than three hundred. Even Dr. Friedman's sample of one thousand patients is small, compared to the typical large-scale drug studies. The landmark study evaluating beta-blocker therapy, for example, included more than twenty thousand patients. It will be necessary to undertake studies with much larger patient samples before we can be sure the 50 percent reductions in recurrence rates among patients given psychosocial treatments are valid.

Showing how far mind-body research has come in the past few years, the National Heart, Lung, and Blood Institute has recently begun just such a large-scale, multicenter trial of a psychosocial intervention, which will eventually enroll over three thousand heart patients who are depressed and/or socially isolated. The goal: showing that training in skills to overcome depression and build better relationships leads to a better prognosis.

The preliminary evidence from studies of psychosocial interventions with cancer patients is equally encouraging. Stanford psychiatrist David Spiegel and his colleagues randomly assigned women with metastatic breast cancer to either usual care or a weekly support group that included training in a range of skills designed to help them achieve better relationships and manage stress. Compared to the women in the usual-care group, those in the support groups survived twice as long—thirty-six months on average versus eighteen months—with this ultimately fatal form of cancer.

In another study, UCLA psychiatrist Fawzy Fawzy and his colleagues discovered that patients with malignant melanoma who participated in only six 90-minute sessions of a similar support-group intervention had half the recurrence and death rates of patients who got usual care over a six-year follow-up period.

As with the results with heart patients, whenever a new cancer chemotherapy drug is shown to produce results like those in Spiegel's and Fawzy's studies, it is hailed by cancer specialists as a major breakthrough in the war on cancer. Just as we need larger studies for heart patients, it will be essential to undertake much larger scale studies of psychosocial interventions in cancer patients, so that we can be more confident of the true size of the potential beneficial effects.

What is the active ingredient in these interventions? Put another way, why and how do they lead to improved prognosis? While a final answer is not yet available, several studies suggest that improved social support may play a role. University of Pittsburgh psychologist Thomas Kamarck has shown that subjects have smaller blood pressure surges under stress if they are stressed in the presence of a supportive friend. And Southern Methodist University psychologist

James Pennebaker has found that persons provided with an opportunity to talk about past traumatic events with a supportive listener enjoyed similar reductions in damaging cardiovascular activity, as well as improved immune function.

Taking a different tack, Syracuse University psychologist Craig Ewart and his colleagues have trained married couples to improve communication skills. After such training, the participants experience smaller blood pressure surges when discussing conflicts than prior to communication skills training.

And finally, I and my colleagues at Duke have shown that when married working women with children living in the home—the group with the highest stress, you may recall—are provided with support-group-based training in skills designed to help them build better relationships and manage stress, they show a marked improvement in their levels of social support, compared to women who got either no treatment or an educational-lecture series on stress that provides no training in relationship or stress-management skills.

Scientists don't have much indication yet whether these sorts of interventions, which improve prognosis in heart and cancer patients, can also prevent the development of these dread diseases in the first place. Given what we are learning about the benefits of reducing physical risk factors—it appears that giving up smoking and lowering cholesterol reduce the risk of both the first *and* recurrent heart attacks—there is reason to be encouraged that the same interventions that help improve prognosis in heart disease and cancer will also help reduce or delay risk of developing those diseases.

～

This review has made the case that one reason to build better relationships with our fellow humans is that by so doing we lay the foundation for a life both happier *and* healthier:

- Social isolation, hostility, depression, and high-strain jobs all increase the risk of disease and death, especially when several of these factors are present at once, as often happens in lower socioeconomic groups. Of special interest here is that all of these problems intimately affect and are affected by relationships.
- Plausible biological mechanisms exist—ranging from health behaviors, like smoking and eating, to the molecular level of monocyte/macrophage gene expression—that may account for these health-damaging effects.
- Reduced brain levels (or function) of the neurotransmitter serotonin may be responsible for both the psychosocial risk factors

and the accompanying behavioral and biological characteristics that damage health—a hypothesis we will explore further in the next chapter.

- Clinical trials, in heart and cancer patients, of psychosocial interventions that provide social support, as well as training in skills needed to build better relationships, have led to improved prognoses.

There is another, more altruistic reason for us to want to build better relationships: In addition to affecting our *own* health, we can affect *others'* health as well.

To see how this might come about, read on.

# 4. Relationships Matter! The Scientific Evidence for Effects on *Others'* Health

... the magnitude of children's accomplishments depends less on the material and educational advantages available in the home and more on the amount of experience children accumulate with parenting that provides language diversity, affirmative feedback, symbolic emphasis, gentle guidance, and responsiveness.

> *Betty Hart and Todd Risley,*
> Meaningful Differences in the
> Everyday Experience of Young
> American Children

... a prevention agenda for children is needed in which building character is as important as building competence, where developing trust is as important as developing skills with technology, and where learning to communicate is as important as acquiring information.

> *Rune J. Simeonsson,*
> Risk, Resilience, and Prevention:
> Promoting the Well-Being of
> All Children

Train up a child in the way he should go and when he is old he will not depart from it.

> *Proverbs, 22:6.*

That relationships matter for your own mental and physical health provides one motivation for building better relationships.

Another potential motivation is the influence you can exert. By treating others—especially the very young—with respect, commitment, and compassion, you can help them lead happier, healthier lives as well.

This benefit sometimes multiplies, as skills that build good relationships are like an infectious disease: whenever you "expose" another person to being treated appropriately and effectively, he or she is more likely to behave similarly toward still others and in turn to "infect" them. Unlike diseases such as AIDS, influenza, and tuberculosis, this "epidemic" of good relationships will not diminish the quality and quantity of anyone's life. Instead, it only enhances them. Here is a story that shows what we mean.

## The Prince and the Pauper (Updated and with Apologies to Mark Twain)

In a modern American city on a crisp autumn day in the third quarter of the twentieth century, a boy was born to a poor family by the name of Smith. Though his parents wanted to love the unexpected new arrival, they were ill-equipped to care for him. On that same day another American child was born to a family named Jones, equally poor, but who were much better able to provide their new son with a caring environment.

Neither Edward Jones nor Tom Smith had chosen the situation he was born into. Nor had the boys chosen the genes that programmed their bodily functions—the genetic inheritance of each boy was totally determined by the particular mixing of genetic material that resulted when one of his father's sperm fertilized one of his mother's eggs. Through one of those tricks that nature can play, the genes Edward and Tom got from their parents contained instructions that were remarkably similar. These two sets of genes programmed both boys to develop the same dark eyes and hair, the same medium stature, an amazing similarity of facial appearance, and even the same foot size. By outward considerations, they might as well have been twins.

Edward and Tom were quite similar on the inside too—even down to the level of the molecular apparatus that determines the functions of cells throughout their bodies, from brains to toenails. Thus, both were born with brain cells that, if nothing interfered, would support the development of identical intelligence: an I.Q. test at age twenty would give the same number—a bit above average—for each. Also relevant to our story is that they inherited similar sets of machinery for making the enzymes necessary to convert the amino acid tryptophan into the neurotransmitter serotonin—one of those chemicals that nerve cells throughout the body use to communicate with one another. Given identical environments, these two boys would grow up to be men of similar countenance, ability, and temperament. But the environments into which they were born were not alike at all, at least not in some of the ways that matter most.

## Edward's Early Life

Edward's mother and father were poor, with other children besides him to supply with food, clothing, and shelter. Edward's father worked on an assembly line in a factory on the city's edge; his mother, as a clerk in a large office building downtown. Within weeks after his birth, Edward's mother returned to work, since she could not afford more than one month of maternity leave. During those first weeks together, she picked him up and cuddled him every chance she got. Edward had barely to whimper from hunger or at the discomfort of a wet diaper, and he was swept up into his mother's arms with loving strokes on his back and bottom, as well as cooing words in his ear that told him what a wonderful, handsome little man he was.

*Each time this happened—it could have been the loving touch, the caring tone of the tender words, or both—a specific and important sequence of molecular events was triggered inside Edward's brain. In a part of his brain called the hippocampus, the serotonin-making apparatus cranked up, and the serotonin started to accumulate in nerve cells there. These cells squirted this extra serotonin into the spaces around them, where it stimulated a specific type of receptor on other hippocampal cells. When this receptor was turned on, like a light switch, it set in motion a train of events that began with the formation of two chemical messengers—cyclic-AMP and PKA—inside the cells. These two chemicals then traveled from the cell's surface, where the receptors for serotonin and other neurotransmitters are, to the genes located in the nucleus deep in the interior of each hippocampal cell. There, the cyclic-AMP and PKA flipped another switch, telling the gene that makes the receptor for the stress hormone cortisol to crank up and start making cortisol receptors. As these receptors were made, under instructions from the gene that had been switched on by the cyclic-AMP and PKA, they migrated to the surface of the hippocampal cells.*

*Once embedded within the membrane surrounding Edward's hippocampal cells, these extra cortisol receptors took on an important function. Whenever Edward was stressed in any way, the hypothalamic emergency center deep in his brain sounded the alarm and fired up the baby version of a fight-or-flight response. His sympathetic nervous system would crank up, with adrenaline pouring from the adrenal gland into the bloodstream, making his heart beat faster and harder. His parasympathetic nervous system shut down temporarily, so that Edward's heart continued to pump more blood longer. His adrenal gland also poured the stress hormone cortisol into the bloodstream, where it caused the adrenaline effects to last longer, mobilizing fat for energy, and even shutting down Edward's immune system. This cortisol did something else, however—with important consequences.*

*The cortisol traveled to Edward's hippocampus, where it switched on all those extra cortisol receptors that have been made each time Edward's mother showered him with "TLC." Once switched on, they caused the hippocampal cells to signal Edward's hypothalamus to "turn off" the fight-or-flight response currently raging. This "negative feedback loop," whereby the cortisol surge during a fight-or-flight response tells the hippocampus to tell the hypothalamus to turn off the response, is the body's way of telling Edward's brain: "Okay, the emergency's over, so cool it for now." Of course, if whatever had fired up Edward's fight-or-flight response continued—let's say a colicky pain in his tummy—then his hypothalamus would keep the response going, overriding any "stand-down" signals that might come in from his hippocampus, and Edward would continue to squall. The net result of all this? Because of those extra cortisol receptors on the surface of his hippocampal brain cells, Edward's brain shuts down his fight-or-flight response more quickly, after it's turned on by some distressing situation, once the distressing circumstance goes away.*

When Edward's mother goes back to work, she's no longer around during the day to give him all that good brain serotonin-boosting TLC. Luckily for Edward, his grandparents live just a few blocks away, and mornings on her way to work, his mom drops Edward off there, before leaving his older brother and sister at the child care center and kindergarten. His grandmother showers him with the same kind of loving touch and sounds his mother has been using—until three o'clock, that is, when his father, whose shift at the plant began at 6:30 that morning, bursts into the house, shouting, "Where's my little man!" As his father picks him up and thrusts him into the air, Edward literally wiggles with delight at this reunion with the man whom he has learned he also can count on for loving sounds and touch, albeit a tad more vigorous than the versions he expects from his mother and grandmother.

*Every time little Edward gets this sort of caring attention—even his brother and sister throw in their share—his hippocampal cells manufacture*

*even more serotonin, that, in turn, causes even more cyclic-AMP and PKA
to be generated to stimulate the making of still more cortisol receptors. The
result: When something bad happens, his fight-or-flight response kicks in,
but unless the bad situation continues, all those extra cortisol receptors in
his hippocampus cause the fight-or-flight response to shut off rather quickly.
Furthermore, the extra serotonin is not confined to his hippocampus, but
builds up as well in other areas of his brain, where it does other good things.
In that part of his brain just behind his forehead, known as the frontal
cortex, the extra serotonin enhances Edward's ability to control impulses to
lash out whenever he feels the least bit frustrated. In his hypothalamus low
down in his brain, the serotonin directly decreases the outflow of his sympathetic nervous system and boosts the action of his parasympathetic "calming"
response.*

*Edward benefits in other ways from the caring family that surrounds him.
All those comforting contacts spur the development of a more active endorphin
system to tickle comfort and pleasure centers in his brain. At the same time
that this caring environment is producing those good biochemical changes in
his brain, it is also teaching him that he can count on his world and the
people in it to be safe and nurturing—a lesson that will make him less
cynical and more trusting.*

When Edward is two years old, he goes to the same child care
center each day as the other Jones children before him. It's run by
the church the Joneses belong to, and is ably staffed not only by
committed and caring volunteers but also by two women with
degrees in early child development. They make sure that the kids are
not warehoused in front of the TV, but play games requiring active
involvement. The kids in this child care center get plenty of attention and stimulation both from the plentiful staff and each other.
When older, Edward enjoys playing with the others. He has many
friends and is always one of the first chosen to be on a side in team
games like red rover. He is rarely drawn into fights.

At home, he talks often and displays lots of curiosity. His parents
hardly ever scold him with harsh words—"Stop that *right now!*"—
when his explorations propel him close to trouble. Instead, they distract him, "Oh, Edward! Look at this dump truck over here, waiting
for you to drive it to help Daddy at the factory!" If you could spend
a few days as a fly on the wall in the Jones household, you would be
able to count five such positive, affirming sorts of utterances by
Edward's parents to him for each negative, prohibiting comment.
Like that "home on the range," at the Joneses "seldom is heard a
discouraging word."

Edward's caring *early* environment made the greatest difference, by stimulating his brain to make serotonin. Later, caring acted like a booster dose, to maintain his serotonin system at a high level of function. Those extra cortisol receptors on his hippocampal cells are still there and *will remain for the rest of his life*. He'll always be able to terminate quickly fight-or-flight responses, once any real emergency is over.

This effective early care also will have long-lasting benefits for his habits. Like many modern teens, he experiments with cigarettes and beer, but his well-developed brain serotonin system makes him less needful of these calming drugs. He likes good food, but his high brain serotonin level keeps his appetite in check so that he maintains a healthy body weight, even later on when many tend toward a middle-age spread. He doesn't even drink much coffee.

Good early treatment also boosts Edward's intelligence above the level programmed by his genes alone. In school Edward does well in his studies, always staying in the top quarter of his class. Those grades are good enough to get him into State College, where he majors in computer science.

Edward's sociability also reflects the early treatment he received. His robust brain serotonin system protects him from depression, even when, at age thirty-six, his technical job at E-Comp, a major electronics firm, falls prey to down-sizing. Rather than giving up and moping for months, he sends around his résumé. Within the year, he has a new position at a start-up educational software company, with an income higher than before.

People like Edward, and he likes most people he meets. Trusts them, too, rather than feeling he always has to be on guard against their meanness and misbehavior. Occasionally someone will take advantage of Edward's good nature and cause him some anguish. When this happens, his fight-or-flight response will kick in, but thanks to his extra hippocampal cortisol receptors and robust brain serotonin system, he quickly calms back down. Rather than seething endlessly and carrying a grudge, Edward can tell when someone's not worth the effort and makes it a point to avoid that person in the future.

As yet another benefit of his early upbringing, Edward possesses high partnership and parenting skills. He fell in love with Sally while attending State, and they married two days after graduation. Theirs has been a happy union. Each has loved and cared for the other; their marriage has been a constant source of pleasure and strength for them both. They've had their rough spots, but they've always both been able to hang in there and work it out. (When Sally wanted to apply for a job teaching history in the local school system,

Edward wanted her to stay home and take care of the kids. They coped with this, as well as many other crises, large and small.) On average, daily, they have five positive, caring interchanges for every negative, abrasive one. When one of them is cross, the other usually doesn't take the bait. Their kids are both bright and good-natured—following in their parents' footsteps.

## Tom's Early Life

You will recall that Tom Smith came into this world with genetic equipment similar to that of Edward Jones. Sadly for Tom, his family was far less equipped to provide the unexpected new arrival with a caring environment.

Tom's parents both worked—he in a factory on the city's edge, she as a clerk in a high-rise downtown. His mom felt overwhelmed by the added burden of having to care for Tom in addition to his older brother and sister. When they came home from the hospital—after only two days—Tom's mother was so depressed that she felt barely able to give him his bottle, let alone any extra TLC. When he cried, she stuck a bottle in his mouth. His diapers got changed when she felt like it, which was not often. Tom's father had a drinking problem, so he wasn't much support to Tom either.

*Given the low level of TLC Tom received, there was little to stimulate his brain serotonin systems. As a result, there was no stimulation of his hippocampal cells to make extra cyclic-AMP and PKA, so that his hippocampal cells did not make any extra cortisol receptors. Without these to speed the switch-off of his fight-or-flight responses, when Tom became distressed, he cried and fussed longer.*

Tom's fussing made him even more of a burden to his mom, who withdrew even more. She was almost glad to get back to work, a scant two weeks after Tom's birth—at least she didn't have to listen to a squalling baby all day, in addition to all night!

Every morning after getting his older brother off to kindergarten, his mom would take Tom and his three-year-old sister to the apartment of a woman in their building, who took care—all by herself—of four other toddlers as well. As the only infant, Tom was pretty much left to himself in a crib, while the overworked woman—she was unable to get a job that brought in as much money as the baby-sitting—plopped the other kids in front of the TV all day and plied them with junk food—whatever it took to keep them from squabbling. When his dad picked Tom up each day after his shift ended, he was brusque and in a hurry to get back to their apartment, where he would put Tom in a playpen in front of the TV, while he tossed back the first of several beers.

*Tom's serotonin systems, in his hippocampus and elsewhere, received little stimulation under these conditions. Indeed, the lack of positive caring and the outright neglect and deprivation of loving touch and sounds actually resulted in the failure of Tom's serotonin-making machinery to develop as fully as it was programmed to do by his genes.*

With this atrophied serotonin system making him less able to control his impulses, as he grew into a toddler Tom often got into trouble, both with his parents at home and with the other kids in the warehouse environment of the woman who continued to mind—*care for* is not applicable here—him and several other kids, until he was old enough for school. In kindergarten he fared no better. He was too distractible and impulsive to pay much attention to the teacher or the activity of the moment. Instead, he would wander off and pick on the other kids—not infrequently getting into brawls. Not popular, Tom was usually almost the last chosen to be on a team.

Just as positive, caring attention can spur growth of the brain serotonin systems, so also can negative, rejecting treatment cause atrophy. This is what happened to Tom. As he grew older, he became even more alienated—learning to be wary and on guard. His mom and the old man never physically abused him, but the neglect and deprivation of loving parental TLC was nearly as bad in many ways. If you were a fly on the wall of the Smith household, you would hear at least as many negative, prohibiting utterances from his parents as positive, affirming communications—different from the five-to-one ratio of affirmations to negations in the Jones household.

Tom's low brain serotonin affected his body. When he first tried cigarettes, he really liked the way they made him feel. Somehow the nicotine made up for the low serotonin levels in his brain and helped him calm down and cope better with the stresses that he encountered all too often at home, at school, and in the streets. He would sneak his dad's beers and spend money earned in after-school jobs on beer for bingeing with pals on the weekend. Eating helped too: although he was not really fat, by the time he was sixteen, he had a paunch.

Not surprisingly, in school Tom's performance was mediocre. He counted himself lucky to maintain a B- average. In the technical institute in the city, he did learn a trade, repairing and maintaining electronic equipment.

Tom never outgrew the anger and hostility normal for all teenagers. Even as a "twenty- and thirty-something," he always found others basically mean, out only for themselves. Consequently, he flared up at any slight—however large or small, real or imagined.

*Each time this happened, his adrenaline and cortisol levels surged, his blood pressure shot up, and fat poured into his blood; his cholesterol level rose a few points with each passing year. All this combined with his smoking habit and proclivity for large fatty meals to increase the levels of oxidized LDL in his blood. This excess oxidized LDL suppressed certain critical functions of his monocytes, causing them to cluster around areas lining the inner surface of his heart's coronary arteries already damaged by the blood pressure surges he had when angered. Those monocytes turned into stationary macrophages, soaking up all that extra fat circulating in his blood, gradually growing into larger and larger arteriosclerotic plaques narrowing his coronary arteries. These narrowed areas in his coronary arteries reduced their capacity to deliver oxygen-carrying blood to his heart muscle, but not to a dangerous degree. Not yet.*

Tom didn't have many friends—no one, in fact, who was the kind of real friend you call up, even when you have nothing to say. He did eventually find someone he thought he could relate to. In his first job in equipment maintenance at E-Comp, he met Amy, a clerk in the payroll office, about his age—a pretty blonde, pert, with a bouncy sense of humor. Amy loved to go out dancing. Even though he hated crowds, Tom was so smitten that he went along, just to be with her. Though reluctant at first, Amy eventually succumbed to Tom's protestations that he could not stand life without her.

Even on the honeymoon, however, things began to sour. First of all, now that they were safely married, Tom didn't feel he had to take Amy dancing to the orchestra at the mountain resort hotel. He preferred instead to stay in the room—to watch baseball on TV while he tossed back a few beers, just as his dad had done. Their marriage almost ended right there, when on their third night Amy threatened to find someone else to dance with. After a major row, Tom sullenly accompanied Amy to the resort's nightclub—but danced only once, preferring to camp at the table and glare at all the "jerks out on the floor, making fools of themselves."

At work Tom was talented at troubleshooting the bugs that computers were prey to. He found few hardware problems he couldn't solve. Amy continued to work in payroll. Over the years, they maintained a wary truce. Tom never did learn to enjoy going out with Amy, but when the kids came along, both became too busy with work and managing the kids ever to have the energy for a social life.

Just as his caring family had taught Edward Jones to be less hostile, less depressed, more engaged with others—and had altered his brain in ways that supported the development of these health- and happiness-enhancing traits—so had the lack of these caring features in Tom Smith's family accomplished the opposite result. At birth both had had the same genetic potential, but the circumstances of their lives, especially during those crucial early years, differed in ways that resulted in two quite different human beings by the time they met—about a year prior to that downsizing at E-Comp, when Edward lost his job.

Anyone who saw Tom and Edward side by side would assume from their outward appearances that they were twin brothers. But all who knew them well would quickly tell you just how fundamentally different they were on the inside.

## Tom's Meeting with Edward, and Afterwards

Trying to debug a spreadsheet program on the new version of a computer that E-Comp wanted to introduce to the market within the next six months, Edward had been working hard all morning. At one point in his travails, he was convinced the hardwired math coprocessor must not be working properly. He could probably have pulled the cover off and taken a look himself, but this updated computer had a new interior layout, and Edward felt he should call in the hardware technician to help him.

"So what have you done to it now?" Tom snapped as he stomped into Edward's office, his brow furrowed and his chest and jaw muscles tensely held. "I understand you have a software glitch," he added, with ever so slight a sneer. To himself Tom was thinking, "Why can't these software nerds ever do anything for themselves!"

At first Edward was startled by how much he and Tom resembled each other. But Tom's expression let him know he should get right down to business. "Look here," Edward said, "I've been struggling with this monster all morning. I know the math coprocessor's probably not the problem, but I can't find anything wrong with the software so far. Since this is that new model, with its modified interior architecture, I thought it might save time to get somebody from technical support to take a look." To himself: "What's bugging this guy? You'd think I'd dropped it on the floor and called him to sweep it up!"

"Get out of my way," Tom said gruffly.

Off came the cover. Tom moved quickly, checking the resistance and current levels, across first the motherboard that contained the brains of the machine and then the math coprocessor. "I'll be damned!" he swore. "The coprocessor's dead. It looks like you were right." (The expression on his face seemed to add the words "for once in your life.") "I'll be back in a few minutes with a new one to slip in."

With the new math coprocessor installed and the spreadsheet working fine, Edward said to Tom, "Hey, this is great! I could have spent another day spinning my wheels, and now the problem's solved." Edward paused and then added, "Look, I don't know what was bugging you earlier, but I really appreciate your help on this. It would have taken me all morning just to *find* the coprocessor!"

"Ah, that's okay," Tom answered. "I've been assigned too many things to do, as usual. And most of the time it does turn out to be some screwup that's you guys' fault."

"Strung out or not, I was impressed with how quickly you found and fixed my problem. If it's okay with you, when I need help in the future I'd like to call on you." Edward smiled, holding out his hand to Tom, "Oh yeah, and my name's Ed Jones."

Tom took Edward's hand, and grinning back, said, "Sure, anytime you need bailing out. Tom Smith, here."

Edward and Tom didn't become fast friends after that—Tom wasn't fast friends with anyone, not even himself. But they did maintain a decently good relationship, largely thanks to Edward's ongoing bantering comments—"Bailed out any software nerds today?"—tossed Tom's way as they passed in the halls or cafeteria.

Tom even remarked to Amy that evening, "I finally met a software jock who's a halfway-decent human being!"

Unfortunately, Tom was not so lucky in other relationships. With Amy, it was more or less a sullen armed truce. They lived in the same house, but they didn't really live together. With the kids now in school, they led parallel lives. They didn't fight much anymore, but the ratio of positive-to-negative interactions always teetered below the five-to-one that keeps a marriage strong and viable.

Tom fell victim to the same downsizing that cost Edward his job. Unlike Edward, Tom didn't handle the blow well. His anger surged because he was certain his supervisor—with whom he had had a poor relationship at best—had singled him out for the ax on purpose. He also became quite depressed and spent even more time in front of the TV, beer in hand. His temper was more on edge, flaring with even the slightest provocation. Amy and the kids tried less and less to reach out to Tom. His withdrawal continued.

Eventually, in the electronics shop at the university medical center, he did find another position—not as good as the one at E-Comp but better than nothing. Becoming even more exasperated when she saw the new job did little to improve Tom's disposition, Amy tried to talk him into going with her to a marriage counselor.

"No damn shrink's gonna mess with my head!" was Tom's only answer.

Amy and the kids were getting exhausted from the effort required to keep from setting Tom off. She asked him to move out. He did, taking a one-bedroom apartment closer to his new job. Tom drank even more beer nightly, made fatty junk food an even larger proportion of his diet, and upped his smoking to a pack and a half each day. With the jerks he had to contend with at work, he became even angrier. His isolation was such that he had no one he could talk to, conversations which might have helped calm him down.

*Tom's adrenaline and cortisol levels stayed high. Blood pressure surges scraped away ever-larger patches of the lining of his coronary arteries. The monocytes, clustering at those nicks, turned into macrophages, soaking up the cholesterol that had climbed to such high levels in his blood. The arterio-sclerotic plaques grew, and his coronary arteries got narrower and narrower at the points where those plaques were growing.*

Tom didn't see much of Amy or the kids. The divorce came through. They all worried about him, but he rebuffed overtures.

One morning at work a few years later, after a particularly infuriating altercation with a secretary, Tom's adrenaline surge caused his platelets to get so sticky that they formed a blood clot, completely plugging up one of his already narrowed coronary arteries. The massive heart attack stopped Tom's heart, and he slumped to the floor in front of the half-opened computer, as the secretary screamed in fear. Luckily, a surgeon in the adjoining office was able to perform CPR until the code-5 emergency team took over, got his heart started, and transferred him to the coronary care unit.

Tom did survive but became even more depressed and isolated. Not many people came to see him, and he didn't make any effort to get out or be with other people.

Four months, two weeks, and three days after his first heart attack, Tom Smith, aged forty-three, died alone, sitting in front of his TV.

⌒

Edward Jones lived on to a ripe, happy old age. It was well into the twenty-first century before he died in his sleep in his eighty-eighth year, just a few weeks after he and Sally had celebrated their sixty-seventh anniversary. What an occasion! As usual, many family members came: all three of their children and their spouses; five of the eight grandchildren; and three of six great-grandchildren. Those who couldn't make it sent letters. Especially touching to Edward and Sally was that year's addition to their treasured quilt. For their sixtieth anniversary, every family member had prepared a square, commemorating some special memory. Now each anniversary, a new square was added. This year's addition pictured a stethoscope in honor of the graduation from medical school of a granddaughter.

⌒

It's long after that day in the second quarter of the twentieth century when two little boys were born with such similar genetic endowments. Despite biological similarities at the start, one lived a short, relatively miserable life, the other a long and happy life. The contrasting ways each was treated, in early childhood and afterwards, made all the difference.

## The Facts Behind the Story

Though we fabricated the story of Tom Smith and Edward Jones, for the most part, with some allowances for literary license, it's based on facts now emerging from research on the impact of early-life experiences upon subsequent bio-psycho-social development. Those readers who feel they've read enough and need no more convincing of the importance—for their health—of how we treat others should feel free to skip the last section of this chapter. For those from Missouri, who prefer to know the facts behind the story, read on.

Everyone knows that extreme conditions associated with outright physical abuse profoundly damage a child. Over 80 percent of all violent offenders in United States prisons, for example, were abuse victims themselves in early childhood. But it doesn't take such extreme, obvious mistreatment to rob children. Short of overt physical abuse, lesser degrees of neglect and deprivation also damage; the earlier neglect and deprivation occurs, the worse and more long-lasting the harm, important research demonstrates.

## Deprivation of Maternal Care

During World War II, many children, often mere babes, were orphaned by the Blitz in London. These infants were placed in facilities where their physical needs were met, but by a staff too stretched to provide emotional, social, and spiritual support. The infants would be housed—many to a room—in small cribs. A care-taker would see that each was adequately fed and diapered, but that was about all she could manage—no cuddling, cooing, stroking. No other human contact, apart from giving the bottle and changing the diapers. Officials soon noticed that these babies were not growing— literally not gaining weight at anywhere near the normal rate, despite finishing their bottles at each feeding. When first placed in the nursery, the young children had fussed and cried in protest, but after a while, they became withdrawn and placid. Many died, simply wasting away, before they could be placed in foster homes.

At the University of Wisconsin, psychologist Harry Harlow found that young rhesus monkeys reacted the same way when totally deprived of all contact with the mother or other monkeys. When separated from the mother, at birth or soon after, and housed completely alone, they protested vigorously at first—crying and calling for the mother. Soon, however, huddling in a corner of their cage, they listlessly withdrew. Just as with the London Blitz orphans, these totally deprived monkeys consumed adequate amounts of food but didn't grow. Returned to the mother soon enough, they recov-ered after a time and proceeded to develop normally. If totally deprived of maternal care long enough, like the most unfortunate of the London Blitz babies, they wasted away and died.

Over the years since Harlow's early research with total maternal deprivation, researchers have studied lesser degrees of deprivation in animals and shown lesser, but still serious, degrees of harmful impact. In research conducted at the National Institutes of Health, Dee Higley, Steve Suomi, and colleagues have shown, quite con-vincingly, that genetic influences among rhesus monkeys play a major role in determining the level of functioning of the brain neuro-transmitter serotonin—and consequent behavioral differences. Also, however, they found that the social environment contributes importantly to the development of both brain serotonin systems and behavior. Separated from their mothers at birth and peer-reared in small groups of similar-aged monkeys, rhesus monkeys do not show nearly as severe emotional and bodily consequences as the totally deprived monkeys in Harlow's experiments. Apart from a tendency to cling more, rhesus monkeys who are peer-reared from birth to six months of age appear superficially to develop more or less normally. When returned to the monkey colony at six months of age, however, they show a number of behavioral abnormalities: more aggression and less sociability than mother-reared monkeys; a preference for spending most of the time apart from the other monkeys; and if given the choice, a tendency to consume more alcohol than mother-reared monkeys.

Compared to mother-reared monkeys, the peer-reared also show slightly (but statistically significant) lower levels of 5-HIAA in their cerebrospinal fluid at six months of age, indicating a decrease in brain serotonin level. Over the years, after the peer-reared monkeys return to the colony, their aggressive behaviors and reduced affiliative behaviors result in their being more or less rejected by the rest of the group. In contrast, the mother-reared monkeys show the normal desire for, and ability to get close contact with, other monkeys. By five years of age, the peer-reared monkeys show a far greater decrease in brain serotonin levels compared to mother-reared monkeys than at six months of age. This larger brain serotonin deficit is probably the result of the continuing rejection their poor social skills and aggressive tendencies elicit.

Can you see parallels between Tom Smith's early life and that of the peer-reared monkeys in the NIH research?

Another line of research, conducted by psychologists Martin Reite and Maria Boccia at the University of Colorado, offers some encouragement that maternal deprivation need not always cause bad outcomes. In their studies of two other monkey strains—bonnet and pigtail macaques—these researchers found that when the mother is removed from the colony, a bonnet macaque infant will show great distress and, if the mother is not returned fairly soon, become depressed, much like what happens in the early stages of the behavioral reaction in Harlow's totally deprived monkeys. The picture in pigtail macaques is quite different: there is moderate distress at first, but it soon subsides and the infant rarely becomes depressed to the same degree as the bonnet macaque infant separated from its mother.

Reite and Boccia surmise that the reason for the less-distressed reaction in the pigtail macaques is that the other females in the colony quickly "adopt" and comfort the "orphan." In a colony of bonnet macaques, on the other hand, other females ignore the abandoned infant. When the researchers disturbed the feeding situation in the pigtail macaque colony—making food available only at irregular intervals, so that the females are continually distracted by the need to forage—the abandoned infant was no longer adopted and comforted. Under such conditions, pigtail macaque infants developed the same distress and depression as separated bonnet macaques. The greater distress among the bonnet macaques is simply, therefore, the result of there being no attachment figures available. Rather than being an indication of some "biological vulnerability" to stress, their reaction to maternal deprivation results from their lack of a relationship with another adult monkey. The tendency of pigtail macaque females to substitute for the absent mother with the distressed infant seems to be what makes the separation less harmful.

Can you begin to see the similarities between Edward Jones' grandmother's care of him and that of the adopted pigtail macaque infants in the Colorado research? Also note that in the more varied human situation, it is not just the mother but also the father, grandmother, and others who provided the nurturing that helped Edward develop in more positive ways. Let's now describe some research that shows how the TLC showered on Edward may have changed his brain and set him on a stronger life course.

## An Increase in Maternal Care

In an elegant research program conducted at McGill University, neuroscientist Michael Meaney has been studying what now turns out to be a manipulation in newborn rat pups that *increases* the amount of maternal TLC they receive. When rat pups are separated from their mother for a period of only twenty minutes once a day during the first seven days of life—the effects I'm about to describe weaken, the later separation begins—they undergo some interesting and long-lasting changes in their reactions to stress. When tested at six months of age (adulthood for rats), they show a smaller and more quickly terminated surge in blood levels of corticosterone (the rat version of the human adrenal stress hormone cortisol) in response to the stress of being immobilized in a small tube than rats that had not been separated. The separated rats are also less fearful than nonseparated rats.

Meaney and his coworkers have now shown that, rather than less maternal care as one might expect, the separated rat pups actually get *more* total daily licking, nursing, and general rat TLC than nonseparated pups. It seems that the mother rat has been worried about her missing pups, and when they are returned to her in the home cage, the prodigal pups are warmly welcomed! What we have, then, in Meaney's maternal separation experiments is actually an example of an experimental manipulation that results in *more TLC* during days one through seven of life, which has long-lasting effects that make the adult rat more resistant to stress—in terms of both less-fearful behavior and smaller and more rapidly terminated stress hormone responses.

Being a meticulous, innovative scientist, Meaney did not stop there. He was interested in learning *how* the early separation from the mother (and consequent increased maternal TLC) actually caused the smaller, more rapidly terminated adrenal stress hormone responses in the adult rat. A major mechanism whereby adrenal stress hormone responses are terminated following a fight-or-flight response is by stimulation of receptors for cortisol (or corticosterone) in the hippocampal formation of the brain. When stimulated, these receptors cause the hippocampal cells to become activated and send down to the hypothalamus nerve impulses that turn off the stress response. Based on this knowledge, Meaney measured the number of such cortisol (corticosterone) receptors in the hippocampus of adult rats that—during days one through seven of life—had been separated or not. As predicted, separated rats had *more* receptors in their hippocampus than nonseparated rats. This told Meaney how the extra maternal care made the rats more resistant to the biological effects of stress as adults—by increasing the number of stress hormone receptors in their hippocampus, thereby producing a more rapidly and strongly activated negative feedback loop for the adrenal stress hormone.

These were exciting findings, but Meaney still wasn't satisfied. He wanted to know exactly how—right down to the specific molecules involved—the early separation that increased maternal care caused the increase in hippocampal stress hormone receptors. In further experiments, he has been able to show that the level of serotonin in the hippocampus (and also the frontal cortex of the brain, a part of the brain that is involved in impulse control among other functions) rises in separated pups compared to nonseparated pups. This increased serotonin stimulates a particular serotonin receptor: the $5HT_2$ receptor on hippocampal cells. When stimulated, the $5HT_2$ receptor causes an increase in the levels of two second messengers— cyclic-AMP and PKA—inside the hippocampal cells. These second messengers, in turn, stimulate the DNA in the gene in the cell nucleus that makes the adrenal stress hormone receptor, thereby causing the cell to make more receptors, which migrate to the cell's surface to be incorporated into the cell membrane. When stimulated by stress-induced corticosterone surges later in life, this larger number of corticosterone receptors causes a larger and more rapid activation of the hippocampal cells' inhibitory signals down to the hypothalamus, thereby accounting for the greater resistance to stress in adult rats that early in life got more maternal care secondary to brief separation periods. (If the separation goes on too long—for several hours each day—instead of rising, the serotonin levels fall, like those in the peer-reared rhesus monkeys described earlier.)

From Meaney's research several conclusions emerge:

- Brief separations early in life result in more maternal TLC in rat pups.
- More TLC causes an increase in hippocampal serotonin levels.
- The extra serotonin stimulates $5HT_2$ receptors on hippocampal cells to generate more cyclic-AMP and PKA inside the cells.
- This extra cyclic-AMP and PKA turn on the gene that makes receptors for the adrenal stress hormone corticosterone (cortisol in humans).
- These extra hormone receptors migrate to the hippocampal cells' surface, where they persist into adulthood.
- When the adult rat is stressed, its fight-or-flight response is smaller and more rapidly terminated because the larger number of hippocampal stress hormone receptors cause a larger and more rapid inhibitory signal to be sent from the hippocampus to the hypothalamic emergency response center.

Meaney's work provides a fine example of documentation—using the tools of modern molecular neurobiological science—for the importance of lots of TLC early in life: TLC activates long-lasting molecular mechanisms that enhance the organism's resistance to stress.

## Studies Involving Humans

Can you begin to see how all the extra TLC that Edward Jones got from his caring family changed his brain in ways that helped him live a long, happy, healthy life?

"But," you may be saying to yourself at this point, "animal research is okay, as far as it goes, but what about *humans*? How do you know the same things happen in us?"

To this concern, our first response is to remind you that much—most—of what we know about the molecular workings of the brain and body comes from research in animals. The basic mechanisms whereby neurotransmitters are formed and have their action, for example, are pretty much the same in rats as in humans. And our cousin the monkey is even more biologically and neurobiologically like us. Proceeding even closer, 98 percent of human genes and those of our closest primate relative, the chimpanzee, are identical!

Our second response is that there is already mounting evidence that the same processes are also active in humans. Psychologists Betty Hart and Todd Risley have conducted an ongoing study of communication patterns between parents and child. The families studied were drawn from varying socioeconomic levels, ranging from those on welfare, to working class families, to professional (doctors, lawyers, college professors) families. Standardized observations began when the children were less than a year old and continued until the children were three. Hart and Risley found, as a function of SES, striking and stable differences in communication patterns. By age three, the average child of parents on welfare has heard fewer than 100,000 positive, encouraging, affirming utterances from his or her parents. In contrast, at the same age the average child of professional parents has heard over 500,000 positive utterances.

This relative deprivation from positive parental attention, Hart and Risley also found, has profound and long-lasting effects upon the child's subsequent development. As the amount of positive communication increases, during the period from birth to age three, so also does the child's subsequently measured I.Q. and school accomplishments, sociability, and adaptability to change and opportunities. This impact of parental communication patterns is independent of parental I.Q. and SES. Hart and Risley have not yet reported on other aspects of behavioral development in the children they studied, nor have they speculated on, or obtained any data pertaining to, brain serotonin levels that could be related to the earlier parental communication levels.

What I have learned about the impact of adversity on brain serotonin leads me to propose that children who heard fewer positive communications from their parents might also experience a consequent reduction in brain serotonin levels, with all such a reduction would imply. Several lines of evidence provide indirect support for this proposition.

First, as we noted in the preceding chapter, lower SES groups have been found to have many of the bio-psycho-social characteristics that low brain serotonin is capable of producing: increased hostility, depression, and social isolation, as well as increased smoking and alcohol use. Ongoing research is likely to document other potential consequences—for example, increased sympathetic nervous system function and larger cortisol responses to stress—in low SES groups. One reason for the clustering of these psychosocial and behavioral risk factors in low SES groups could be that effects of the early deprivation to which they are subjected—as documented

above by Hart and Risley's findings—lead to reduced brain serotonin function, an effect strongly supported by the extensive animal
research also reviewed above.

Further indirect evidence for the actual occurrence of just such a
sequence is provided by Danish studies, which found that children
subjected to parental neglect or poor quality of housing (an index of
low SES) are more likely to be obese in young adulthood. Low
brain serotonin function is known to result in increased food intake.
The Danish results could be explained by effects of parental neglect
and poor housing (and all that comes with this) in childhood,
leading to reduced brain serotonin function and consequent
increased eating and weight gain by young adulthood.

Studies by University of Pittsburgh psychologist Karen Matthews
show that more negative and fewer positive interactions between
parents and their twelve-year-old sons predicted increased hostile
attitudes and behaviors when the boys were retested three years
later. These effects of a higher negative-to-positive ratio in parent-
child interactions on later hostility in the child could be solely the
result of the boys' learning that the world is a hostile place and
acting accordingly. It could also, however, partly be that negative
interactions lead to a reduction in brain serotonin levels, which also
contributes to the development of hostility.

One study provides direct evidence of the effects of low brain
serotonin function on the development of subsequent behavioral
problems in human children. At the National Institutes of Health,
spinal taps were performed on children deemed at high risk for later
behavioral problems, and levels of the serotonin marker 5-HIAA
were determined. On follow-up studies, the children with lower
5-HIAA were more likely to get into trouble because of aggressive
and impulsive behavior problems. This study did not address the
question of *why* some children had lower brain serotonin function,
so both genes and environment (neglect or deprivation) could be
causes. In any event, this study draws a clear line linking a child's
brain serotonin function and his or her later likelihood of aggressive
behavior.

## A Summary and Some Final Thoughts

Good relationships benefit our own health and happiness, as well as
that of others—especially children in our care. The dark side of the
coin is that when we have poor, uncaring relationships, our health
and happiness suffer. Whether because of a hostile personality that

drives people away, a depressive tendency that causes us to withdraw, or for some other reasons, if we have chronically poor and uncaring relationships, dire consequences ensue that can be measured in terms of early disease and death.

There are several take-home messages we want to leave with you. If your relationships cause you problems—because you have a hostile personality, a tendency to depression, or just feel socially isolated for any other reason—you should not despair. Research has shown that patients with heart disease and cancer live longer when they are provided with direct social support, as well as training in skills that help them build better relationships and otherwise cope better with stress. This gives us confidence that similar interventions to help healthy people counter the forces that impair relationships will improve their health and happiness as well. That's one of the reasons we wrote this book—to provide information that will enable you to build better relationships and thereby increase your own chances for health and happiness.

That's not our only motive, however. As outlined in this chapter, not only our own health and happiness are imperiled when we have poor relationships. When we treat others poorly, especially children during the critical early years of life, their brains and bodies can change in ways that exert long-lasting effects on *their* health and happiness.

We hope that you will want to consider the effect you have on others, that you will want to treat them as you would like them to treat you. By developing and using the skills presented in this book, you will be not only helping yourself but increasing the chances that others—both those you know and those you don't—live happier, healthier lives.

As we said at the outset, relationships matter.

# Part II

# Groundwork

CALVIN AND HOBBES © Watterson. Dist. by UNIVERSAL PRESS SYNDICATE. Reprinted with permission. All rights reserved.

# 5. Lifeskills

Whatever you do, or dream you can do, begin it. Boldness has genius, power, and magic in it.

*Goethe*

Let everyone be quick to listen, slow to speak, slow to anger.

*James 1:19*

This is your initial introduction to Lifeskills. In each subsequent chapter, we'll show you how to apply these Lifeskills to one category of relationships. By the time you finish the book, you will have had a chance to practice each skill on a number of occasions, in a wide variety of situations. You will be on your way to being able to act effectively without having to work so hard at it.

We'll offer you ways to practice these techniques in each chapter. However, you will need to adapt these behaviors further to each particular situation. Our lives and individual circumstances are too nuanced to be captured completely with formulas. Still, Lifeskills are an efficient set of tools to get you started on an effective track. First, make the suggested new behaviors habitual; then fine-tune.

Some lucky people seem naturally predisposed toward behaving in ways that lead to the good life; perhaps their genes programmed them to have unusually high levels of the neurotransmitter serotonin in the brain. Others, equally lucky, received excellent training in capable living during childhood; they had competent role models *and* maybe high levels of serotonin as a result of early good treatment. Fortunately, those of us who lack these skills—and that's most people—can acquire them. This book provides you with initial exposure. It's up to you to continue *purposeful* application for the rest of your life.

Learning Lifeskills may seem daunting at first. Any task becomes easier, however, if broken down into simpler, more easily mastered parts. In learning to play tennis, you don't start out by going onto the court to play a full-blown match. You must first learn how to serve the ball, return it, hit a forehand, hit a backhand, and so forth. Only after you have become at least somewhat proficient in each component skill—by practice, practice, practice—are you ready to begin combining them. Here, then, are the eight components that contribute to better understanding and action.

To understand yourself and others:

1) *Identify your thoughts and feelings.* Observe what you are thinking and be aware of when you are angry, afraid, happy, loving, surprised, disgusted, or sad, or are experiencing another, perhaps complex emotion.
2) *Evaluate negative thoughts, negative feelings, and options.* Is the situation important? Are your thoughts and feelings appropriate? Can you modify the situation? When you balance the needs of yourself and others, is taking action worth it?
3) *Communicate better.* Listen carefully when another is talking; speak up to share your feelings and thoughts.
4) *Empathize with and understand others' behavior.* In a caring manner, look at a situation from the perspective of the other person.

Once the stage is set, four additional basic skills help you act effectively:

5) *Solve problems*—on those occasions when it's a *situation,* rather than another person, that's the source of distress.
6) *Practice assertion*—to get another person to behave as you wish or to practice self-protection.
7) *Practice acceptance*—if you decide the needs of others are more important.
8) *Emphasize the positive*—keeping a high ratio of affirmations to negations in each relationship.

## Understanding Yourself

When you fail adequately to gauge your own true thoughts and feelings, you may act against your best interests. You may also bewilder others, for a mist in the pulpit is a fog in the pews!

## Identify Your Thoughts and Feelings

In the song of life, thoughts are the words and feelings the music. Both are important parts of your reaction to any situation.

## Thoughts

*Thoughts* are the words you can "hear" yourself saying silently some-where inside your head, the radio program that's always playing something. When you look at a beautiful sunset over a lake, if you tune in to your thoughts, you might hear your mind's voice saying, "What a beautiful sunset!" Or when a car cuts in front of you so sharply that you have to slam on the brakes, "Just who does he think he is?" Thoughts are often accompanied, followed, or even pre-ceded by *feelings*—joy at the sunset or anger at the other driver.

## Feelings

When researchers interrupt people at random and ask them if they're feeling any level of emotion at the moment, most report they're experiencing some mild emotion, which they can identify as pleasant or unpleasant. You too probably are experiencing some feeling most of the time, whether you are aware of this or not.

Being conscious of feelings is a necessary, sometimes hard, early step in acquiring Lifeskills. Sometimes you may hide from yourself emotions you don't approve of: frustration, pique, anger, fear, jeal-ousy, lust, covetousness, insecurity, pride, exhaustion, boredom. On other occasions, it may be another person who questions the legiti-macy of your feelings. Poppycock! Don't listen—you are the world's expert in what you are feeling! No one, not even you, ever has the right to tell you what you are feeling isn't real. Nor is it useful for someone to say that you "shouldn't be feeling that." Feel-ings just *are*.

Having—and acknowledging to yourself—feelings does not always mean you will act on them, nor even that you will decide to report them.

Being aware of your feelings is a prerequisite for applying other Lifeskills. Unless you are aware of having a particular feeling, you cannot proceed to decide whether you want to try to savor that feeling, just accept it, diminish it, or use it as a signal to take action. You also are going to learn how to speak up competently—this requires you to be specific and often to share your feelings. Self-protection also requires you to be aware of negative feelings. Some-times you will then want to say no to a request; on other occasions instead of attacking whoever is causing the problem, you will elicit the person's help in getting over the negative feelings his or her behavior is occasioning.

Timing affects personal relations; "now" is often better than "later." When someone mistreats you, you're usually wise to nip it in the bud, at the time it's happening. In contrast, it's usually counterproductive to save up a string of grievances and then attack the other person broadside with your long litany about how you have been mistreated on a number of occasions. The response is usually either a defensive counterattack or an emotional withdrawal from listening to what you are saying. With positive feelings, letting the other person know right then that he or she is making you feel loving or happy reinforces the behavior you are enjoying.

The more specific the diagnosis, the more specific the attempts at remedy. Even when you are not fully in touch with negative feelings—anger, fear, disgust, sadness—you probably still experience a vague sense that something is wrong and will attempt to "get right." Often, overeating, overdrinking, addiction to TV, reading nonstop, smoking, or overexercising are attempts to feel better when you feel bad and "need a boost." Far better is first to determine *exactly* what you are feeling, next to evaluate your options, and then to apply the best remedy possible for that specific circumstance. These behaviors work much better than general self-medications and certainly have fewer negative side effects!

What you are thinking and feeling affects your body, a topic already explored in Chapters 3 and 4.

To get you started in identifying your thoughts and feelings, try our version of an "up close and personal" exercise, developed by behavioral medicine colleagues at the University of Miami.

1. Think of a person with whom you have a very good relationship and whom you love (or care deeply about). Close your eyes, to picture that person, seated beside you. Notice the face. What color are the eyes? the hair? Can you see the nose and mouth? Notice what the person is wearing. What kind of facial expression is most typical? Think about the sound of the voice. How does the person smell?

   Now think about how you usually feel when you are with this person.

   Be aware of your body. Are you aware of physical sensations? Pay close attention to your chest. Your abdomen. Your throat. Your forehead. Describe what your body feels like.

   What emotions are you feeling?

   Do you have any thoughts?

   When you are ready to do so, let the image of that person fade. Then get up and walk around for a few minutes.

2. Sit down somewhere else. Think of someone you have difficulty with. Close your eyes, to picture that person. Imagine that person seated a little closer to you than you would like. Notice

the face. What color are the eyes? the hair? Can you see the nose and mouth? Notice what the person is wearing. What facial expression can you observe? How does the person's voice sound? How does the person smell?

Now think about how you usually feel when you are with this person.

Be aware of your body. Are you experiencing physical sensations? Pay close attention to your chest. Your abdomen. Your throat. Your forehead. Describe what your body feels like.

What emotions are you feeling?

Do you have any thoughts?

When you are ready to do so, let the image of that person fade. Then get up and walk around for a few minutes.

For many, this can be a powerful exercise. Thoughts and feelings matter. And your body is aware of them.

### Record-Keeping of Thoughts and Feelings

We encourage you to keep a log that sets an initial scene, records what you are thinking and feeling, then records how you and others subsequently acted. This trains you to be observant—and eventually more aware—of what really is going on in your life.

Once you've mastered log-keeping, your earlier entries will become an excellent resource. By reviewing them, you can evaluate what triggers your positive and negative feelings, look for patterns in how you subsequently act, and evaluate those actions.

You can differentiate between behaviors that lead to successful outcomes and those that lead to unsuccessful outcomes. You then continue what you are doing right. Once you identify your problem behaviors, you can try substitutions, again evaluating their effects.

Review of your log will indicate patterns in your relationship with an individual or a group. What happens initially when you come in contact with certain people? What are the patterns of subsequent reactions from both of you? Are some relationships especially satisfying? Can you identify individuals or groups with whom you continue to have a deeply troubled or indifferent relationship, despite applying Lifeskills? (This will signal that greater investment on your part—or even professional help—is needed. If even these extra steps fail, you may be faced with the reality that this relationship cannot be improved—though this will never be true if you are dealing with a child or with broad groups of humanity.)

Log-keeping works best for intimate relationships, less well in impersonal situations. Nonetheless, you can still get a sense of how

well overall you are communicating with others and whether you
and they are supporting each other.

## Technique

We suggest purchasing a small notebook that fits easily into your
pocket. Averaging several entries a day, write up happenings in your
life, what you are thinking and feeling at that time, and any actions
taken.

Deciding what to write up in your log requires you first to decide
what perspective you want to adopt. You may choose to concentrate on one important relationship, like with your partner or child.
Alternatively, you may prefer to sample various relationships. You
can focus on the big moments, when you are experiencing strong
positive or negative feelings, or you may prefer to focus on typical
times. Remember that you can always adopt one approach initially
and then change to another, as needs shift or you become aware of
new problems.

We suggest initially adopting this simple format. As new rounds
of thoughts, feelings, and actions occur, keep recording.

> *Scene:* Describe the specific situation, with enough details that
> you will be able to recall the occasion. Stick to *objective facts,*
> not your opinion about what is going on.
>
> *Thoughts:* Record whatever thoughts you have.
>
> *Feelings:* Angry? Afraid? Disgusted? Sad? Happy? Surprised?
> Contemptuous? Interested? Ashamed? Excited? You may expe-
> rience an emotion other than these and several feelings simulta-
> neously, like being angry and afraid at the same time. And each
> emotion comes in a wide range of gradations. Does being angry
> signify rage, irritation, or just pique?
>
> *Actions:* What you are thinking and feeling may result
> in some new action on your part. Keep recording your pos-
> sibly changing thoughts and feelings as long as the situation
> continues.
>
> *Consequences:* What happened following your action?

Let's illustrate with entries of a composite character called
Susan—wife, mother, daughter, and real estate broker. These examples avoid the cryptic phrases and shorthand you will probably want
to employ. (Here we'll spell out incidents in some detail, to give the
flavor of what went on. Your purpose will be to create a permanent
record that enables you to recall what happened, not to write a perfect essay.)

### First Entry

*Scene:* The alarm has just gone off, and Tom and I are still in bed. Meredith and Bob [her eight- and ten-year-old offspring] need someone to fix breakfast. We have to confirm that Meredith has a ride home from the game. Tom asks if I would get the kids off, since he stayed up late last night, working on his report.

*Thoughts:* I want to stay in bed too.

*Feelings:* Sleepy, *grouchy,* and *resentful.*

*Actions:* I agree and ask him if he would fix spaghetti for dinner tonight.

*Thoughts:* That's only fair—he'd better say yes!

*Feelings: Involved. Hopeful* he will say yes and *fearful* he will say no.

*Consequences:* He agrees. Says he doesn't want to have spaghetti but will pick up ingredients he prefers on the way home. I am off the hook. It's fair he cooks what he wishes. I feel *conciliatory. Pleased* I have some leeway with my last appointment. *Kindly disposed* toward Tom. *Proud* of being able to ask for a return favor.

### Second Entry

*Scene:* I have fixed oatmeal. Five minutes until the bus comes. Bob complains that the cereal is lumpy and looks in the refrigerator for something better.

*Thoughts:* Ingrate!

*Feelings: Angry.*

*Actions:* I call him an ingrate and tell him he is very lucky to have parents who fix breakfast for him.

*Consequences:* Bob gives me a disgruntled look. I continue to stew, but bite my lip. I feel *angry* and *resentful.*

### Third Entry

*Scene:* Thursday meeting. Melvin [boss] and all the others [other real estate brokers in the company] are there. Melvin is telling us who will cover which weekend in April. He assigns me one of the weekends during the kids' spring break.

*Thoughts:* I asked him last month not to assign me that weekend. Did he forget? Is this some sort of test to see how loyal I am?

*Feelings: Angry* that he did this, for whatever reason; *worried* about whether I will jeopardize my chances for a promotion if I protest.

*Actions:* Remind Melvin that I had requested not to work that weekend or the previous one. Tell him that I am disappointed he didn't remember since I want to do my fair share of the work. Request that he reassign me to another time.

*Consequences:* None at the moment. If this is a test, I've given him a test back. Melvin says he'll have "to see." What does he mean by that? Could be anything or nothing. I think this will tell me a lot about how highly Melvin regards me, and on the other hand, how I feel about here as a place to work.

## Twelfth Entry

Note that this entry has several rounds of thoughts and feelings, as Susan thinks the matter through.

*Scene:* Listening to the news, driving home. Senator X of the Foreign Relations Committee is describing what he sees as the problems with the proposed trade agreement.

*Thoughts:* I like that agreement. Senator X may kill its chances of being passed.

*Feelings:* Unbelievably *pissed*.

*Actions:* None.

*Thoughts:* I hate Senator X. I hate politics. This country is in a mess.

*Feelings:* Even more *ticked off*.

*Thoughts:* What is the opponents' perspective? I bet they are concerned about American jobs and the resulting decline of the world's greatest democracy. It's understandable that a person who reasons that way would be against the treaty. But how about jobs for people living outside the United States? And isolation in the end will result in American goods becoming noncompetitive outside our borders. I've heard some argue that jobs here will increase overall. These are stronger arguments. I need to fight for this trade agreement, but not in a way that puts down the opponents. Given my limited free time, what little actions could I take? I could write my representative, but she never listens. Hmmm— I could write a letter to the newspaper.

*Actions:* Resolve to write a short letter this evening to the newspaper.

*Feelings:* Upset at first; then a little bit *empowered*.

*Consequences:* I feel better having thought this matter through. The letter may make some difference. Its effect will be hard to judge.

Once you have kept your log for a few days, you will want to examine entries systematically:

- Are your actions usually appropriate to what you are thinking and feeling?
- Is one or several relationships eliciting thoughts and feelings more troublesome than the rest are?
- Are your actions usually improving those relationships or making them worse?
- Are the people close to you acting in ways that support you?
- Do your actions lead people close to you to feel supported themselves?
- In distant relationships, do other people provide you with as much help as you need?
- Are you in turn providing such support?

Keeping a log only requires that you record what happens in your life. From this simple first step, you can quickly progress to becoming an insightful observer of patterns in your relationships. From there, you are on your way to becoming your own wise counselor.

## Evaluate Negative Thoughts, Negative Feelings, and Options: The I AM WORTH IT! Road Map

You need to evaluate your negative thoughts and feelings so you can decide what actions to take. Here is a road map for doing that.

First, observe *exactly* what circumstances occasioned those thoughts and feelings. Stick to objective facts you can see and hear—information that might hold up in a court of law, not assumptions about the motives of the other person, or surmises you can't prove. If in doubt about how to describe—first to yourself, sometimes eventually to others—the objective facts in any situation, pretend that Detective Sergeant Joe Friday of *Dragnet* has said, "Just the facts, please!" Somebody loudly calling you a jerk is an objective fact. Someone looking at you with an expression you think means she thinks you are a jerk is your interpretation of her expression and would not hold up in a court of law.

After formulating in your own mind the objectives facts—you might even want to write out this description to see if it holds up upon reading—you are ready to evaluate a negative thought or feeling by asking yourself four questions.

**I**   *Is this matter IMPORTANT to me?*

If you answer no, you are wasting your time even thinking any further about this situation. Drop the matter completely, without bothering to ask the last three questions. A number of participants in our hostility control workshops have told us that often they can get rid of anger by simply telling themselves, "This is not that important." On the other hand, this statement may not suffice, so at the end of this section we'll offer additional "erasure" strategies.

If your answer is "Yes, this is important to me," proceed to the second question.

**A**   *Are my thoughts and feelings APPROPRIATE, given the facts?*

This can be tricky. Try to consider only exact, objective circumstances. Sometimes your knowledge of the facts will be too scanty to substantiate a confident yes. In a marketing meeting, the updated projections of sales have just torpedoed your ideas for a new advertising campaign, and one of your coworkers is sitting across the table, with an expression that you suspect reflects secret pleasure. But you really can't be sure that his faint smile means he is out to get you. Maybe he's thinking about heading for the beach just as soon as this boring meeting ends.

Suppose instead of silently smiling, the coworker had blurted out, "It doesn't matter. Your scheme wasn't going to work anyway!" Then the objective facts to be described to Sergeant Friday are altered. Your coworker has labeled your idea unworkable, and it is appropriate to feel anger or some other negative emotion when attacked this way.

As with the first question, if your answer to this second question is no, reconsider your first negative reaction. You may decide your initial thought or feeling was inappropriate, in which case you may be able to let it go. We'll detail later strategies to use in the not-uncommon eventuality where you still feel upset.

Here's another consideration. Your first thought or emotion probably won't be your only one, once you have time to think about the matter: "I may not be angry when I think about it, but I *am* disappointed that my advertising plans won't get approved." You can then subject any newly discovered negative feeling to the same questions.

Having come this far, you next decide—by asking two additional questions—whether you want to act on your thoughts and feelings, including whether you plan to report them.

**M**   *Is the situation* MODIFIABLE?

Consideration of the objective circumstances may lead you to conclude that nothing you can realistically do will fix this unpleasant situation. Life is full of such occasions:

- The TV news shows pickets carrying signs supporting a position you oppose.
- Your spouse needs you at home to help prepare for dinner guests, but you're stuck in traffic.
- The rain starts just after you've arrived at the beach for a much-needed day off.

Of course if your unhappiness is caused by another person, you'll need to listen to the other party and try to put yourself in his or her shoes; otherwise, you may be overlooking solutions the other person can help you to see.

**WORTH IT**   *When I balance the needs of myself and others, is taking action* WORTH IT?

Your goal is truly good relationships, which will mean considering the feelings, thoughts, and needs of both yourself and others. Balancing the two requires a lifelong juggling act. Aim for the right balance.

Again, until you have communicated with the other parties, you may not be fully enough aware of their perspective to answer this question well.

You've probably noticed a letter or words at the start of each of the four questions you will always want to ask in evaluating your feelings: *I*mportant? *A*ppropriate? *M*odifiable? *WORTH IT*? Together, these letters and words spell out an important message:

I AM WORTH IT!

Whenever you become aware of a negative thought or feeling, just remind yourself, I AM WORTH IT! and the four questions will pop up on your mental screen, ready for use.

If *any* of your four answers is no, you need to accept the status quo. Here are some aids to help you quell negative feelings and thoughts.

1. *Reason with yourself.* The process of answering the evaluative questions will lead to "self-statements" that often do the trick. "Hey, it's not really important!" "I can't be sure it's really some jerk holding the elevator just so he can finish flirting with the

pretty receptionist on the thirty-second floor." "Only nature can stop this rain that's ruining my weekend!" Sometimes reasoning with yourself will suffice—at other times this process may defuse your feelings, but they are still there, albeit in milder form.

2. *Tell yourself "Stop!"* Silently yell at yourself to stop concentrating on the disturbing situation. Sometimes this action will be enough to derail your train of thought. On other occasions, it will at least calm you down a little bit.

3. *Distract yourself.* Pick up a tabloid to read in that slow-moving "express" checkout line at the supermarket. Plan your next vacation when stuck in that traffic jam. File your nails while waiting for that seemingly never-changing traffic light to turn green. Mentally refurbish a room in your home while waiting for someone. As your supervisor rants on about the same irrelevant topic she's mentioned in exactly the same words ten times before, imagine her dressed as Glenda, Good Witch of the West. Go out and run a mile; besides getting your mind off the aggravating situation, the exercise benefits your heart! Right now, before you need them, try to come up with your own list of favorite distractions. Children? Grandchildren? Pets? The NCAA basketball tournament? You name it!

4. *Meditate.* It is good for everyone to be able to focus attention at will. The basic technique is simple.
   a. Pay attention to your breathing.
   b. On the in breath—or the out, it doesn't really matter—say a word or phrase that helps you relax. Try "Ommm," "Calm down," or "The Lord is my shepherd."
   c. When your mind wanders—which will happen—simply observe that and come back to concentrating on breathing and saying the word or phrase.

If you find yourself needing this "heavy gun" each day, practice meditation for ten to twenty minutes, so that you become skilled. Regular meditation—being in the moment, with equanimity—enables you to center yourself quickly and quiet your mind and body. It's a way "on the spot" to get out from under a situation engendering negative thoughts and feelings.

On the other hand, if you answer all four questions with a "Yes, I AM WORTH IT!" you need to act.

If you decide action is called for, you next need to decide what the problem involves—just a situation or a particular person? If it's just a situation, you will want to resolve the issue. If another person

# *Road Map*

## I AM WORTH IT!
## Evaluating Negative Thoughts, Negative Feelings, and Options

The Situation   What are the objective facts? Stick to evidence that would hold up in a court of law.

IMPORTANT?   Is this matter important to me?

↓
Yes
↓

APPROPRIATE?   Is what I am feeling and/or thinking appropriate to the facts of the situation?

↓
Yes
↓

MODIFIABLE?   Is this situation modifiable in ——————→ **NO** ways that will reduce my negative feelings and/or thoughts?

↓
Yes

WORTH IT?   When I balance the needs of myself and others, is taking action worth it?

↓
Yes
↓

*Action Skills*
Problem solving
Assertion
Acceptance

*Deflection Skills*
Reason with yourself
Tell yourself "Stop!"
Distract yourself
Meditate

is the problem, you will need to decide between assertion and acceptance.

# Understanding Others and Being Understood by Them

## Communicate Better

So far, we have focused mainly on you. Now it's time to bring the other party in. Many of the problems between you and others— your partner, teenage children, relatives, neighbors, people you know and can't stand, and your political enemies—begin with miscommunications: either too little information or misinformation.

Let's begin with listening to one another share thoughts and especially feelings, as this simple action creates a solid foundation for a relationship.

### Listen

*Keep Quiet!* As a start, keep your mouth shut—just keep quiet while the other person is speaking. Your mind will probably start to wander. That's okay. Just gently bring your attention back to the speaker, as often as necessary, until he or she appears to have finished. Don't interrupt. If you do only this, you will be a better listener than most people.

*Use Positive Body Language* Competent listening advances beyond just keeping quiet. Psychologist John Barefoot, a colleague at Duke, has focused his research on measuring hostility—concluding from numerous interviews conducted over a number of years that the tone of the speaker's voice is a better indicator of hostility than either the content or the intensity of his or her speech.

John looks for evasions that keep the other person at a distance and show contempt. "Maybe," "You can't really say," or "That may be" sometimes can be spoken in ways that invalidate what was said before, without explicitly challenging the other person. Body language speaks volumes. Hostile persons may cross their arms, avoid eye contact, or curl the upper lip to the side, while slightly wrinkling the nose. John also watches out for indirect challenges, which can be as subtle as answering in a tone of voice that implies the question is stupid. "Of course!" roughly can translate as "That was a dumb question, if ever I heard one!" In the midst

WHEN A PERSON PAUSES IN MID-SENTENCE TO CHOOSE A WORD, THAT'S THE BEST TIME TO JUMP IN AND CHANGE THE SUBJECT!

IT'S LIKE AN INTERCEPTION IN FOOTBALL! YOU GRAB THE OTHER GUY'S IDEA AND RUN THE OPPOSITE WAY WITH IT!

THE MORE SENTENCES YOU COMPLETE, THE HIGHER YOUR SCORE! THE IDEA IS TO BLOCK THE OTHER GUY'S THOUGHTS AND EXPRESS YOUR OWN! THAT'S HOW YOU WIN!

CONVERSATIONS AREN'T CONTESTS!

OK, A POINT FOR YOU, BUT I'M STILL AHEAD.

CALVIN AND HOBBES © Watterson. Dist. by UNIVERSAL PRESS SYNDICATE. Reprinted with permission. All rights reserved.

of considering these relatively subtle cues, don't forget that direct challenges—"You're wrong" or "I don't think so"—are also a great way not to listen!

Instead of allowing your body message to alienate, use it to convey caring. Begin by keeping still. Focus your eyes on the speaker's eyes, glancing away occasionally so that your gaze does not feel invasive. (Direct looking increases intimacy.) You can still appear bored if your expression is glazed, so make looking an active process. Unknit your brow. Relax your jaw. Uncross your arms. Lean slightly forward. Even though you are being silent, it's okay to nod your head occasionally or murmur "uh huh" to let the speaker know you are interested and involved in what's being said. Small movements of the head at the neck also can indicate attentiveness. Being aware of these details may feel awkward at first but becomes less so with practice, especially as you find yourself becoming interested. To get a better idea of how good listeners behave, pay close

**The Galsteins were experiencing some serious communication problems.**

CLOSE TO HOME © 1996 John McPherson/Dist. by UNIVERSAL PRESS SYNDICATE.
Reprinted with permission. All rights reserved.

attention to expert interviewers on television—like Barbara Walters, Oprah Winfrey, Charlie Gibson, Jane Pauley, Joan Lunden, Katie Couric, Larry King, and Mike Wallace. Chances are you'll observe that they appear interested in what the interviewee is saying.

As you become practiced, you'll exceed the assumed posture—you will be *really* paying close attention.

*Reflect Back What You Heard* Once the other person finishes, reflect back *only* what you heard. Concentrate on the literal ("I hear you saying that you're doing most of the housework") or the emotional ("You sound fed up") content of what is said.

Do *not* give advice, add information, judge, or grill. And above all, do not bring the focus of attention back to yourself! What kind of message do you think you are giving a person who has just told you about his daughter's acceptance into college if the first words out of your lips when he finishes are "That's nice. Robert just got into Stanford and Columbia!"

Here's a simple trick that will almost always force you to reflect back what the other person has been saying and not say anything that will detract from that. After he or she has finished (grateful, we guarantee you, for having been allowed to finish without interruption), just say **"What I hear you saying is . . ."** and then make sure that whatever you say is based *only* on what you have heard, whether you simply play back or you add slight inferences (*not* interpretations) about the speaker's feelings. Don't feel you need to repeat the speaker's words verbatim—this could sound odd to both of you—but use words that clearly capture the sense of what you heard.

> Eight-year-old Johnny comes in, slamming the back door and grousing, "Soccer is stupid; I want to throw away my cleats!"
>
> An untutored listener might say "Oh, come on now, it can't be *that* bad!" or even worse "How many times do I have to tell you not to slam that door!"
>
> A good listener, on the other hand, would say "Soccer is stupid, huh?" or, at a more emotional level, "Sounds like you are down on soccer!"

It works with kids, and it works with grown-ups too. If your usual style is to cut to the chase with incisive counter-comments instead of repeating what the other person has said, you may feel awkward at first with simple repetition. But persevere—you'll probably be impressed by how effective your comments will be. Here's a review of listening:

- Keep silent until the other person is finished.
- Use body language that conveys your interest in what is being said.
- When the speaker finishes, reflect back what you heard.

Of course, all of this emphasizes behavior. Indeed, you listen best with the heart as well, always keeping an open mind. **You are not truly listening unless you are prepared to be changed by what you hear.**

That's all there is to it. Good listening is an important communication skill you need if you want to build better relationships. You

## *Listening*

1.  Keep quiet until the other person finishes speaking.
2.  Use body language that conveys your interest in the other person.
3.  When the other person finishes speaking, reflect back the emotional and/or literal content of what you heard—do *not* add information, judge, grill, or offer advice.
4.  Be prepared to be changed by what you hear.

also need to be able to speak clearly, so that you inform others of your own thoughts and feelings.

*Speak with Clarity and Compassion* Attentive listening is best balanced with equal-time speaking; that's how talk becomes conversation, not monologue. (Exception: With children, you need to listen most of the time.) While most of our workshop participants have greater difficulty listening, perhaps a third—usually those taking the workshop because they have to live or work with a disagreeable person—have greater trouble talking to others. When asked during a communication exercise to talk to one other person for seven minutes, they run out of things to say and fall silent. They offer us varying explanations.

"Joyce wouldn't be interested in hearing about that."

"Everybody probably feels about the same way I do."

"There's nothing out of the ordinary here. . . . I don't have any thoughts on the matter, really."

"After the first three minutes, I couldn't think of anything to talk about."

Once workshop participants begin to recognize their hesitancy to speak, they realize that this in itself constitutes a problem. How can they have a good relationship with someone else if they send out so few signals about what they are like and what they need and want?

At this point, participants realize that part of their problem is that they don't care enough for themselves. They eventually grasp that they see their own needs as trifling, their opinions unimportant. They exist to help others, but not vice versa. They think they can gain self-worth *only* by being attentive to others. Clearly, they need higher self-esteem. This is a lifelong task for many of us, and a topic we address directly in Chapter 6.

Meanwhile, here are guidelines for better speaking.

*Just Do It* If you are shy and often silent, an important early step to better relationships is to begin speaking out. Initiate and maintain conversations with interest and even enthusiasm. Introduce yourself to the other person at your table in the cafeteria at lunch. Listen to what he has to say, and if you get a chance, tell him a little about yourself too. Go up to someone you don't know during coffee hour after the church service. When he starts a conversation, listen intently, reflecting back what you heard; then tell him something of special interest to you on a related topic. If children come to the coffee hour, ask one of them if she has a favorite sport. At a family dinner, ask a relative what he's been up to lately, then tell him what you've been doing recently. If you are shy, *assume* the other person will be interested. (If you aren't shy, but usually are rather talkative, focus on the listening strategy instead of this one!)

*Make "I" Statements* Try, as frequently as suitable, to use **"I" statements**. These enable you both to share yourself and allow others to disagree.

> "I dislike fried chicken."
> (Instead of "Fried chicken tastes lousy!")

> "I'm disappointed supper isn't ready."
> (Instead of "It's terrible that supper isn't ready.")

> "I like red roses best."
> (Instead of "Red roses are the most beautiful flowers in the world.")

> "I'm cold."
> (Instead of "This room is too cold.")

> "I don't like buttered popcorn."
> (Instead of "You ruined the popcorn.")

> "I feel so stressed when the living room is messy."
> (Instead of "You never do your fair share keeping this place picked up.")

The second of these paired statements (in parentheses) puts the other person on the spot, to either agree or disagree. In contrast, the first statement is apt to elicit caring concern or at least make the listener feel there's room for his or her own opinion.

*Report Your Feelings* The best way to let another person truly know you is to tell him or her what you are feeling: hostile, friendly, sad, happy, scared, courageous, whatever. Also share doubts and dreams. How can you possibly become connected to others if they don't to some degree know you?

Of course, once you've learned to identify and evaluate your feelings, sharing yourself becomes easier.

> "I feel lonely."
> (Instead of "You aren't giving me enough attention.")

> "I feel disappointed that the peanut butter is gone, when I was so looking forward to a good sandwich."
> (Instead of "*You* finished the peanut butter, without any reminder added to the grocery list!")

*Speak out of Your Personal Experiences* Doing this will keep you from sounding vague or authoritative. This gets easier, once it becomes customary.

> "I opened the door to our study. Papers covered the desktop and half of the floor besides. I felt so frustrated, tired, and annoyed."
> (Instead of "You are incredibly messy. Can't you ever do your share of the work?")

> "I had trouble finishing Samuel Pepys' journal."
> (Instead of "Only a twerp would read all of Samuel Pepys' journal.")

*Be Specific*
> "As you sit there, with the moonlight hitting your face, I think you look beautiful."
> (Instead of "You are wonderful.")

> "You promised to empty the garbage by this morning; the bin is still full."
> (Instead of "You never empty the garbage.")

*Send Appropriate Nonverbal Messages* When you speak, synchronize your spoken words and the **nonverbal message,** so both reflect what

PEANUTS reprinted by permission of United Feature Syndicate, Inc.

you want to communicate. If inconsistencies exist, the nonverbal message usually dominates.

Intonations, general forcefulness—even which word gets emphasized—affect meaning. Try accenting in turn each word in this sentence:

"I did not say you stole my money."

**Balance is the key.**

Some of us listen well. Others speak with flair. When one skill is highly developed at the expense of the other, you can participate in monologues, but not conversations. Balance is the key to relationships of *mutual* respect and caring.

## Empathize to Understand Others' Behavior

To be empathetic, you must be aware of and sensitive to the other person's perspective.

Empathy may be a natural behavior that evolved early in human development, possibly growing out of the need for rapid and accurate evaluation of the motivations of others. Newborn babies will make cries of distress in responses to the cries of other infants, though this may be because of their limited ability to differentiate between themselves and others. Children a year and older are upset by the distress of others and will try to help. They respond more fully as they mature.

In his excellent book, *Sound Mind, Sound Body,* Stanford University psychologist Ken Pelletier reports on the scientific respect empathy got at the 1993 annual meeting of the American Association for the Advancement of Science. In a session focused on what it

## Speaking Up

1. Just do it.
2. Make "I" statements.
3. Report your feelings.
4. Speak out of your personal experience.
5. Be specific.
6. Send appropriate nonverbal messages.

means to be human, Harvard Medical School neurobiologist Terrence W. Deacon said empathy may hold a key. He theorizes that the human brain has evolved in a way that allows humans uniquely to "represent to ourselves what goes on in other people's minds." To Deacon, empathy forms the essence of human, moral reasoning. While this remains a controversial stance, it does illustrate that some "hard scientists" are beginning to take empathy seriously.

Mirja Kalliopuska, a University of Helsinki psychologist who examined over four thousand young people between the ages of fourteen and twenty, found that young people who were more empathetic were also more assertive, less narcissistic, less self-focused, and more sensitive. They smoked less and used less alcohol than the least empathetic. Further, Dr. Kalliopuska has successfully trained children, teachers, nurses, doctors, and retired persons to be more empathetic.

Many acrimonious arguments, blowups at children, and antipathies toward disliked groups can be transformed by practicing empathy. The ability to put yourself temporarily in the other person's shoes can be hard. Most of our workshop participants don't empathize well at first. They do learn eventually. Once they practice this skill habitually, they build bridges of understanding.

Here are the key ingredients of empathy:

- Begin by learning what the other person or group is thinking and feeling. Often what we guess will relax, stimulate, or threaten the other person doesn't—the person's dreams and fears are different than we imagined.
- Be aware of how that person perceives himself or herself, what role he or she plays in the world, from that person's own perspective. Most people and groups see themselves as basically good and also right. How do they arrive at that conclusion?

• Be emotionally receptive to appreciating where the person is coming from (the most difficult step, of course!).

To empathize well with those close to you, start by listening and reflecting back what you have heard. Just the process of doing this, especially repeating aloud what was said, will make you receptive to appreciating the other person.

If you're trying to empathize with a group you may not have direct contact with, you might try speaking about their thoughts and feelings as though you were a member of that group. Assume people in that group like themselves and are committed to making the world a better place. Try to put yourself inside such a person's head, and use all the speaking skills you've just read about to convey that person's position from his or her perspective. Use "I" statements, share what you imagine the person's feelings are, and speak out of what you imagine are his or her personal experiences. For example, if you are pro-life on the abortion issue, assume the position of a sincere pro-choicer. Write down or just speak aloud the reasons why you hold that position. If you are pro-choice, practice this empathy exercise from the perspective of pro-life.

Being empathetic, even toward a group you vehemently oppose, does not mean you have to embrace their point of view, or even let them continue to espouse their position without trying to change them. That would be accepting their position. Rather, by being able temporarily to see the world from their perspective, you will understand them better. Even if you continue to oppose their view, this exercise may lead to a more respectful relationship.

If all opposing groups currently warring against each other around the world—a couple contemplating separation, a disgruntled teen and his parents, Bosnians and Serbs, Irish Catholics and Protestants, Palestinians and Israelis, Hutus and Tutsis—did this empathy exercise, they would be taking a step toward peace. (They would need to sit down with each other and practice good listening and speaking skills, to prepare for that empathy exercise, of course!)

Whether those whose views we dislike are close to home or on the other side of the world, being empathetic can help reduce conflict intensity:

> "Yes, I want to go to the beach this weekend. But I can see if I were as tired as Joe and found sand and heat disagreeable, I might not be so enthusiastic."

With a young child, development charts that indicate age-appropriate childhood behaviors often must substitute for listening: "I hate the sight of Jimmy screaming and kicking the air. But I need to put him in time-out quickly instead of blowing up. I know that his behavior is normal for a two-year-old. If I stay cool, he'll outgrow acting this way, all by himself."

"Those pickets are misguided. But they aren't jerks. From their perspective, they think they are engaging in a very moral act."

"Iraqi parents who lost sons in that attack must feel overwhelmed with sorrow."

## Acting Effectively

You have determined the objective facts of your situation, and whether another person is involved. You have identified and evaluated what you are thinking and feeling. You have made sure that you and the other party understand each other. Thoroughly oriented to the situation at hand and therefore aware of what is needed—you're ready to act!

## Problem Solving

Sometimes you experience negative thoughts or feelings caused not by some other person but arising out of troublesome life circumstances: a serious illness freights you with depression, anxiety, and fear; too much work overwhelms you; a canceled flight strands you in Fargo, North Dakota, for the night. To deal with your negative state of mind, you need to learn problem solving, which we've broken down into five stages.

### Define the Problem

You have already learned about the tools you need. By keeping your log and using the road map, you know how to identify and evaluate the objective aspects of a situation that is causing distress. When you apply the I AM WORTH IT questions and come up with four yeses, you know that action is called for. If these steps do not point to your relationship with another person or group as the source of the distress, then you know that problem solving is the next order of business. You have already pinpointed the source(s): depression after a heart attack; being overwhelmed by the responsibilities added to your job when your company downsized last year; being stuck in Fargo. The process of evaluating your feelings will help answer several further questions.

- What do you need to do in order to cope with the problem situation?
- What negative thoughts and feelings do you need to control?
- What do you want to accomplish in this situation?

## Generate Alternatives

Brainstorm with yourself to develop a list of at least three or four coping options. Start with general approaches. Move to specifics later. An active behavioral strategy, like starting an exercise program and a low-fat diet after a heart attack, usually works better than passive approaches, such as telling yourself, "I'm just not going to think about my heart today!"

## Make a Decision

Identify the best coping alternative.

- Begin by *eliminating* seriously flawed possibilities. "There is no comparable job. Also, I can't afford to walk away from all the benefits I've accrued."
- Make a list of the positive and negative *consequences* for yourself and others of the remaining alternatives.
- *Select* the one alternative apt to have the best payoff.
- Brainstorm specific ways of *carrying out* the strategy selected. This sometimes identifies an even better solution.

## Implement the Decision

Carry out the actual behavioral changes called for by your decision-making process. Work out the specific action steps involved and set up a timetable for carrying them out.

"I'll research local rehab programs by January 15 and choose one by January 20. I'll see the program nutritionist about a diet before the end of that month. I'll pencil into my schedule exercising there three afternoons a week—beginning by February 15 at the latest!"

"I'll ask for a raise by June 1. If I get at least $50 a month, I will hire a lawn maintenance company. I'll use the free time to volunteer to be assistant soccer coach."

"I think that Al Charneco was from Fargo. I'll see if he still lives here. Maybe he and I could get together this evening."

### Evaluate the Outcome

If the outcome proves satisfactory, declare victory and terminate the problem-solving process. If it is unsatisfactory, consider going back through the problem-solving process, trying to re-identify alternatives.

## Practice Assertion and Acceptance

Many problems involve another person. Suppose that you have identified your negative thoughts and feelings, and answered yes to the first three evaluative questions. On such occasions, your answer to the fourth question—whether the situation is worth action— becomes critical. You can practice assertion. Or just accept the situation or other party as is.

### Consider Assertion

Assertion means caring for yourself. You ask for what you want and need—or you say no to the requests of others, when to say yes would keep you from what you want or need.

In a small study comparing extremes, highly assertive individuals reported fewer health problems than individuals low in assertiveness. They also more often believed that their behavior—not environmental factors—determines what happens to them.

Good relationships *require* balance between giving and getting. Only when relationships are positive does being connected to others benefit health. A number of studies suggest that getting along badly with someone—or even being involved in a relationship that doesn't allow for personal autonomy and growth—damages rather than enhances health.

Families can also become overinvolved with each other— worrisome, overprotective, intrusive, or excessively indulgent or self-sacrificing. Not surprisingly, family therapists caution that this is harmful to mental and physical health.

Researchers also advocate a fair balance in relationships between giving and getting. One-sided connections that place a stressful number of demands without offering a reciprocating amount of support actually harm health. Studies suggest that women are more inclined than men to get into such situations.

The take-home message from all these studies is clear: Being connected to another is healthful—but only if the relationship is positive, has suitable boundaries, and is balanced between giving and getting.

As you read this book, you will be examining relationships for balance, in addition to determining how well you get along. You may conclude that some relationships don't measure up. Instead of just giving up right then and there, try assertion. You may be pleasantly surprised at how much improvement results.

Assertion values your feelings and needs, but in ways designed to get you what you want, rather than to put down the other person. Assertion is *not* the same as "letting it all hang out" when you are angry; we are not talking about venting unbridled emotions, but rather about acting respectfully and competently.

*How to Ask for What You Want* At its most basic level, assertion involves simply requesting that another person engage in a specific behavior. Stick to the present moment; avoid vague requests.

> Instead of "Please do your fair share of the work," try "Please take Linda to her seven o'clock dance rehearsal at the gym."

Sometimes, but not always, you will want to spell out exactly what the situation is. (Do not bring up past grievances, however!)

> "I carpooled Linda to her seven o'clock dance rehearsal at the gym the last two times. Would you please do it tonight?"

Reporting your feelings almost always supports your specific requests to get others to change their behavior. You switch your attention from the behavior of another to asking the other person to help you get over your own bad feelings. As we pointed out when discussing speaking, use "I" statements, never "you," so you express your own anger, sadness, fear, whatever, without blaming the other person. Learn to identify precisely what you're feeling and say exactly that. "I feel irritated" is not the same as "I feel angry." And remember, "I feel that" (as in, "I feel that you're at fault") is an argument, not an emotion. Don't use it! Stick to the specific situation at hand.

Here's how such a sequence might go:

> "Suzy needs to go to her seven o'clock dance rehearsal at the gym. I have driven her there the last two times." **[Statement of exact situation.]**

> "I am feeling grouchy and resentful at the thought of taking her again." **[Sharing feelings with "I" statements.]** "I don't want to feel that way about my family."

*"What I'm proposing is this. No."*

© The New Yorker Collection 1996 Richard Cline from cartoonbank.com. All Rights Reserved.

"Would you please take a turn tonight?" **[Specific request.]**

Occasionally, if you have repeatedly failed with the techniques described above, you may need to add *consequences*—limited ones, as the goal is not to get into a battle of wills, with no room for anyone to back down gracefully.

"If I have to drive Suzy again, I won't have time to fix the apple strudel I had planned on making tonight."

*How to Say No* The other part of assertion is **refusing**—if you *routinely* overextend yourself on behalf of others and then end up feeling exhausted and resentful. You will need to decide if you are one of those people either afraid of rejection or simply more sensitive to the needs of others than to your own. Such people consequently end up on numerous committees, always entertaining the rest of the family, etc. In short, they usually do what the other person wants, while neglecting their personal needs. If you qualify, learn to say no, without a moment's delay.

How you say no is important. Sometimes it's best to begin with a restatement:

"You want me to chair the Social Activities Committee next year."

Empathize, if that seems fitting:

"I know how important getting a chair of that committee is to you."

You might next want to share a statement of feeling. Omit this step if these feelings are hostile, ranging from mild pique to raging anger ("Give me a break! 'I work—you play' has gotten old"). Do consider sharing feelings you are experiencing as too much ("I feel tired already!"). Do *not* share feelings with persistent people apt to argue that your feelings are the problem.

Always include an explicit no. Should you prefer to leave it at that, you are never under any obligation to justify your simple no. And whatever tack you take, avoid long-winded explanations, excuses, or apologetic behavior.

"Sorry, but no. I do not want to chair the Social Activities Committee next year."

### Consider Acceptance

You can develop a capacity to recognize and respect the beliefs and practices of others, even when they're not like your own. It is possible for you to accept others—or situations—as they are. You have made an "active" decision *not* to act.

Acceptance sometimes works magic. No longer self-righteous—convinced that we are better than the other person—we escape the apartheid of good. And sometimes the other person reciprocates. For improving relationships in the workplace, schools, neighborhoods, communities, national debates, and international conflicts, acceptance is the "star strategy."

Researchers often measure hostility using the Hostility subscale of the long- and widely used Minnesota Multiphasic Personality Inventory (MMPI). Our Duke group, in one project that further broke down this subscale, identified "rigidity of moral standards" as one of three major categories of the Hostility subscale of the MMPI. In other words, persons with high hostility scores—who, research shows, are at high risk of early death—are likely to be intolerant of others unlike themselves. It follows that practicing acceptance can be good for health, as well as relationships.

Acceptance, however, is never right toward a person or group whose continued espousal of goals could result in major harm.

## Assertion to Get What You Want

1. Describe the specific behavior that caused your negative feelings.
2. Describe your feelings.
3. Request the specific change of behavior you need.
4. Optional, if the first three don't work: State the consequences.

## Assertion to Protect Yourself

Just say no. (Simple, isn't it!)

You can be empathetic—hence understand them better—but this does not lead automatically to acceptance. Thus, while it can be understandable how some people neglected and abused in childhood may be, as adults, prone to violence, this does not mean you don't do all in your power to stop them from causing harm.

On the other hand, when your octogenarian Aunt Sue complains yet again about your three-year-old's atrocious table manners, you could decide that this situation is important, that your anger is appropriate (after all, three-year-olds aren't *supposed* to have impeccable table manners!), and that you probably can get her to stop criticizing. But when you really think about it, you may decide that it's simply not WORTH IT—in terms of your aunt's hurt feelings, and the fact that your three-year-old couldn't care less.

### Emphasize the Positive

This last skill can make the difference between an adequate versus a *great* life; between the feelings of "work" and being "in the groove," between skiing downhill and slogging uphill. **Most of your interactions should be positive.** In fact, to get quite specific, you want to aim for *five times* as many positive as negative interchanges.

Using volunteer subjects, unobtrusive mikes, and TV cameras set up in an apartment "laboratory," University of Washington psychologist John Gottman and colleagues have patiently observed and categorized the interchanges between newly married couples, counting the positive and negative. What predicts whether the couple will stay married is not how many contacts a couple has, but the ratio of positive to negative. **Five-to-one** turns out to be the necessary proportions. If there are five positive interactions for each negative one, the marriage stands an excellent chance of lasting. Marital dissatisfaction, separation, and ultimately divorce become increasingly probable as the ratio falls below this critical level. In fact, once the five-to-one ratio begins to erode, it may precipitously drop to one-to-one, with disastrous consequences.

For successful development in children, this same ratio appears essential. As you recall from Chapter 4, psychologists Betty Hart and Todd Risley observed parent-child interactions at home over several years. They found that children who are the most intelligent, self-confident, and flexible when retested at ages six to eight had experienced five times more positive than negative interchanges with their parents by age three. Children who scored low on these desirable assets had experienced about the same number of positive as negative interchanges with their parents. Even when the researchers controlled for the effect of parents' intelligence and social class, these benefits of five times more positive than negative interchanges between parents and children still held true.

It is equally important to be positive with oneself. Researchers report that the ratio of positive to negative emotions a person experiences over time stays about the same and also remains stable, whether the person is alone or with others, at work or at play. The ratio itself is what is most important, because **having mainly positive feelings throughout the day**—rather than intensity of emotions—**correlates with happiness. In contrast, income, physical attractiveness, social skills, and good health don't correlate all that closely with happiness**!

While less systematically than in these longitudinal observations, we have observed, in our experiences with workshop participants, that people who treat everyone well most of the time usually are happy and have relationships that on both sides are committed and respectful. Part temperament, part nurture—a habit of looking for positive ground can be acquired. This is not to say that you should deny troublesome truths, but try to keep at least a five-to-one ratio of positive-to-negative interchanges. Avoid seeing anybody—from your teen to foreigners—as enemies. When tempted to use a put-down with anybody, especially your partner—*don't!* Five, you will soon discover, is a lot larger number than one, so in each chapter we'll give you specific suggestions of ways to affirm the other party.

Our workshop participants often at first define a positive interchange as any flowery compliment. Not surprisingly, they feel unnatural and manipulative in doing that. Soon they realize the need for judgment, so that the positive statement feels right.

They also recognize that they can affirm others by nonverbal means. Here are some affirmations you can try, if they feel right to you:

- paying complete attention
- maintaining eye contact and positive body language when the other is speaking
- reflecting back what the person just told you
- agreeing with a justified complaint, especially if it's against you ("You're right, I could have been more careful.")
- apologizing when wrong
- providing a pat on the shoulder (Be sensitive whether the other person would be comfortable receiving that.)
- giving a hug (Be sensitive whether the other person would be comfortable receiving that.)
- smiling
- proffering the front section of the newspaper
- offering half your apple, orange, candy bar, or other treat
- laughing together (Focus on making fun of yourself or the situation overwhelming you—she or he who laughs, lasts.)

For the past few summers, at a week-long church retreat at a college in Virginia, we have led a workshop on acquiring Lifeskills. Attendees live in the sometimes noisy dorms. One participant last summer told us that by applying the technique of being positive in her dorm, she countered this drawback, with good results.

Instead of barging down to chew out the teenagers who were partying in a room down the hall until the wee hours each night, she went down to their room early—during the night after the workshop session covering the five-to-one ratio—and told them, "You know, I am truly amazed at the stamina you young folks have! I just can't see how you do it—staying up and partying with such gusto till all hours! You must be made of strong stuff!"

After telling them this, she simply left. That night, the party sounds ceased by 11 P.M., and our workshop participant got the first sound night's sleep since arriving. She asked the teens the next day what had happened last night.

"Oh, we decided it might be fun to move the party to a new room," they replied.

❧

# *Lifeskills*
## *Understanding Yourself*

1. Identify your thoughts and feelings.
2. Evaluate negative thoughts, negative feelings, and options:
   The I AM WORTH IT! road map
   • Is this matter *important* to me?
   • Are my thoughts and feelings *appropriate*, given the facts?
   • Is the situation *modifiable*?
   • Is taking action *worth it*?
   Any no means you try to get over your negative thoughts and feelings.
   Four yeses means you need to solve the problem yourself or to practice assertion.

## *Understanding Others and Being Understood by Them*

1. Communicate better.
   • *Listen* attentively and reflect back what you've heard.
   • *Speak* in specific, personal terms to report feelings and thoughts.
2. Empathize to understand others' behavior.

## *Acting Effectively*

1. Problem Solving: When evaluating a situation leads to four yeses and does not involve another person, clarify the problem, brainstorm, and evaluate potential solutions.
2. Assertion: When evaluating a situation leads to four yeses, and involves another person, assert yourself to get what you want or to keep from being taken advantage of.
3. Acceptance: If assertion seems not worth it, accept the status quo.
4. Emphasize the positive.

Applying Lifeskills gets easier with practice. When you begin, you may find yourself acting before identifying and evaluating feelings. You may forget either to listen or to speak out to report your perspective. Or you may get stuck, trying to decide between acceptance and assertion. In many situations, you can halt whatever is proceeding by announcing you need "time out." ("You know, I want to think some more before I respond to that. Let me get back to you." Or "I hear that you're really upset with me. Let me digest what we just talked about and discuss it more later.") Come back to the situation after you become aware of your feelings, weigh your options, and decide on a deliberate course of action.

Let's get to work, one relationship at a time!

# 6. Begin with a Good Relationship with Yourself

Whoever dies with the most toys wins.

*bumper sticker*

Be a light unto yourself.

*Siddhartha Gautama,*
*founder of Buddhism*

This life, therefore,
is not perfection
but growth in perfection,
not health but healing,
not being but becoming,
not rest but exercise.

We are not what we shall be
but we are growing toward it,
the process is not yet finished
but it is going on,
this is not the end
but it is the road.

*Martin Luther*

To be effective in other relationships, first be respectful of and committed to the most important person in your life—yourself!

## Vision

While not oblivious to past or future, you stay mostly in the now. This moment truly interests you, and you look, listen, smell, think, feel intensely.

Sometimes you grant yourself some slack. You take time to slow down, to think. You say no, and don't feel guilty. You change your mind. Occasionally you do less than you could. You accept most of your mistakes and those of others, without harshly dwelling.

When you need help, you ask for it. Equally often, you provide support. This results in the right mix of giving and getting.

You expect other people to like you; they usually do. You like yourself as well.

## *Do You Recognize Aspects of Yourself?*

Susan was fifty-five years old when she enrolled in one of our workshops at a church camp. She had divorced many years earlier, and her two children were grown; but her mother took up much of her free time. Susan didn't visit often enough, her mother informed her. This made Susan feel guilty, though she already felt burdened by her public school nursing job and the long trips to visit her mother twice a week, including every Saturday, for the day. Once she arrived, her mother always gave her a long list of tasks, accompanied by the usual litany of complaints.

In early conversations that first year, Susan would tell us how guilty she felt. She described her mother's health, which sounded reasonably good. "Do you have any needs of your own which aren't being met?" we asked. "No," Susan answered shyly, her expression that of a timid rabbit. She slouched and responded only when directly questioned. During communication exercises, she listened wonderfully, but had difficulty when her turn to speak came round. Nonetheless, she reported liking being listened to attentively.

Gradually during that week, with the help of outside coaching and our workshop exercises, Susan came to realize that she was very sensitive to the needs of her mother, but completely oblivious to her own. She was tired, she discovered. She wasn't, she came to realize, having much fun.

As Susan told us later, once she left camp, life began to get better—the change was gradual, subtle, with much backsliding. Still, she began to experience self-value. Sometimes she said no. She still went to see her mother regularly; but she wasn't internalizing criticisms, and she tried to avoid feeling guilty. For a while during each visit, she would take time out to call upon a friend.

Next year, Susan again came to church camp for the week, enrolling in a new Lifeskills workshop we were giving to try out ideas for the present book. We also ate some meals with her, where we got a chance to talk. We both sensed a new Susan. Her brown eyes sparkled now and then. She sometimes smiled. She validated our impressions, telling us life was much, much better—largely because she was paying a lot of attention to developing and taking care of herself. And each evening during that week, Susan attended the nightly dance. Sometimes she would sit at one of the tables, tapping her fingers to the beat of the music, happily chatting with whoever sat nearby. She danced some too. Watching her happily twirl around the dance floor was a joy to see.

<hr />

Arnold's lack of self-esteem manifested itself differently from Susan's. No one could ignore Arnold; he never shut up. He held a very important job—was indispensable, as he let all persons within earshot know. Until we changed the ground rules, every time we asked workshop participants for comments, Arnold spoke first, making comments on other people's comments too. He was not always careful to wait his turn when he wanted to get in or out of a room, and when he was late, he did not enter noiselessly.

Look at Arnold, so you can feel sorry for him. Arnold was enrolled in our Hostility Control Workshop because all of his relationships had gone sour and he was very angry about that. Did Arnold gain any insights during the workshop? Maybe a few, but the last time we saw him, he was still loudly proceeding, full speed ahead.

# Knowledge

## The Current Situation

Being a socially competitive species, human beings naturally compare themselves with others. When people lived in villages or ethnic neighborhoods, most members of those communities could excel at something. But today, we are exposed to idealized images of rich, famous, gorgeous, articulate, brilliant people on TV, in advertisements, movies, and magazines. Our own wives and husbands, fathers and mothers, sons and daughters can pale by comparison. So we are dissatisfied with them and even more dissatisfied with ourselves.

How we deal with dissatisfaction constitutes a further problem. In an article in *American Psychologist,* Philip Cushman argues that the two professions currently most interested in healing us are psycho-

**Another first date is ruined by
an embarrassing commercial.**

CLOSE TO HOME © 1996 John McPherson. Dist. by UNIVERSAL PRESS SYNDICATE.
Reprinted with permission. All rights reserved.

therapy and advertising. The cosmetics industry, the diet business,
the electronic entertainment industry, preventative medical care, the
New Age movement, and the self-improvement industry (containing mainstream psychology, pop psychology, and pop religion)
are there to help individual growth, enjoyment, and fulfillment.

And how do we pay for all of this "self-improvement and enjoyment"? Through the creation and use of universal, easy credit. We
seem entrapped in a vicious cycle of borrowing and spending, to
keep our empty selves filled and the economy fueled.

## Present Wisdom

Low self-esteem can cause people to behave ineffectively. Over the
twelve hours spent together in one of our Lifeskills workshops, participants get to know each other quite well, for so brief an acquaintance.
One time this happens is when we share negative entries from our logs.

Often an individual will report he or she has lashed out, usually over some petty matter. The rest then help the person review the incident. What we often discover together is that he or she felt somehow vaguely threatened and reacted aggressively in self-protection.

*Mary, a computer analyst:* "We were stopping by the grocery store on our way home after a trip. Our three-year-old was tearing around the grocery store, pushing our cart. I got extremely upset and lashed out at my husband that he needed to control her. We argued heatedly over whether Margaret should be pushing the cart or in it."

"What had Margaret been doing before this time?"

"Riding."

"For how long?"

"Several hours."

"Was she running into other customers?"

"No."

"Was this part of any long-term conflicts you and your husband are having?"

"No. It doesn't seem like such a big deal now. I don't know why I was so upset. Hmmm— I guess I worried that people would think I couldn't control my kid."

On other occasions, a workshop participant will take too little action, because of low self-esteem.

*Andy, a retiree from Maryland:* "When my daughter called me so late at night, I felt really annoyed and hurt that she would be so inconsiderate."

"Did you let her know how you felt?"

"No . . . I do want to have a good relationship with her, you know."

"Why would telling her this be bad for your relationship?"

[Silence.]

We have seen so many participants in so many workshops reveal their basic concerns of being seen in a bad light or, worse, becoming unlovable, that we are increasingly convinced that self-acceptance and high self-esteem are key to good relations with others—whether one is a tiger or timid pussycat.

Similar conclusions were earlier reached by Meyer Friedman, co-originator of the Type A concept of time urgency and hostility as risk factors in heart disease and pioneer in intervention studies designed to reduce Type A behavior. After years of observing his Type A patients trying to change, Dr. Friedman has come to see the sense of time urgency and free-floating hostility as the *overt* components of Type A. *Covert* components are either insecurity, inadequate self-esteem, or both.

During one of their early weekly sessions, each participant in Dr. Friedman's Recurrent Coronary Prevention Project is asked whether he had *sufficient* love and affection from *both* parents. Participants whose parents were divorced, after which the child lived essentially with only one parent, are told to answer no. Usually the percentage of noes is 70 percent or higher. Dr. Friedman and his associates have also developed a written test to measure insecurity, with similar results.

High self-esteem is essential for energetic participation in group actions as well. During the first half of this century, Mohandas Gandhi and his followers launched a campaign to free India from British rule. In their attempts to galvanize the masses, they focused on building up the self-esteem of malnourished and unemployed Indians, in addition to emancipating them from British rule. Millions of Indians began to weave cloth in their homes. This liberated them from total passivity and the resulting lack of self-regard, as well as providing them with useful cloth. Previously completely powerless, these people fostered that minimum level of self-respect indispensable for meaningful participation in nonviolent campaigns. For those Indians playing a larger role in the movement, emphasis shifted to developing enough self-esteem that no attack from opponents was ever perceived as humiliating, because their sense of independence came from within and could not be threatened by others' actions. Gandhi's campaign was successful and has been widely emulated.

Several systematic surveys of large groups of people suggest the surprising fact that health and age don't affect happiness much. Though people with greater income are happier in general, when income in a country goes up, happiness doesn't rise. In fact, characteristics such as health each match up only about 10 percent of the time with a person's level of happiness. In contrast, *satisfaction with self matches up almost 30 percent of the time, suggesting that people with high self-esteem are more likely to be satisfied with their lives.*

## Effects on Health and Well-being

To the extent that self-esteem influences personal habits, it affects health. Causes of death usually are reported in terms of a disease, such as cancer. In a twist on this, two epidemiologists published an article in the *Journal of the American Medical Association* itemizing deaths in the United States in terms of the behaviors responsible for what they called, by definition, premature deaths. Their breakdown of estimated deaths follows:

| | |
|---|---|
| Tobacco | 400,000 |
| Diet and activity patterns | 300,000 |
| Alcohol | 100,000 |
| Microbial agents | 90,000 |
| Toxic agents | 60,000 |
| Firearms | 35,000 |
| Sexual behavior | 30,000 |
| Motor vehicles | 25,000 |
| Illicit use of drugs | 20,000 |

They concluded that taken together, these behavioral choices account for about half of all deaths in the United States.

Self-esteem, obviously, also affects mental health. In a 1993 study, self-esteem matched up about 28 percent of the time with a person's life-satisfaction scores in eight Western countries. (Across thirty-one Western and non-Western countries, however, the amount of crossover depended on the degree of individualism versus collectivism in the country.)

The Recurrent Coronary Prevention Project, mentioned in the last section, did result in improved self-esteem *and* improved health outcomes.

Our experience leading workshops has taught us that persons with low self-esteem sometimes can be oblivious to many of their own feelings (especially negative ones) while being very sensitive to others. The 1996 meeting of the American Psychosomatic Society held one fascinating session on the possible effects on health of such repression. The experts pointed out that a person at times may be aware of an experience without being conscious of that awareness. When the eye is injured, humans may retain a "blind spot," able to avoid objects they have no conscious cognizance of seeing. Some people, especially children, can "smell" odors they are unaware of knowing about.

Maybe "emotional blind spots" also can register on the brain, if not on consciousness. These experts—two psychophysiologists, a psychoanalyst, and a clinician—presented evidence that people who repress thoughts and emotions, like anger at an immediate situation at hand, still can have extensive immediate bodily responses—

sweating, patterns of brain activity, endocrine activity. Repressors who fail to face a severe long-term stress—such as the death of a child—may also have long-term unhealthy bodily responses, these experts argued provocatively. If these scientists are correct, getting in touch with your feelings—followed by evaluation, then practical action—is good for *physical* and mental health.

In Antwerp, Belgium, cardiac patients took psychological tests upon entry into a rehabilitation program. When followed up after six to ten years, patients with a tendency to suppress substantial emotional distress were much more likely to have died of all causes, including heart disease. This relationship held, even when the severity of the earlier cardiac disease was taken into account. Social isolation and depression likewise related to mortality, but suppression of emotional distress predicted increased risk of death, independent of these factors.

Most successful intervention programs are designed to bolster self-esteem and often include assertiveness training. The studies of David Spiegel with breast cancer patients, of Fawzy Fawzy with patients with metastatic melanomas, and of Dean Ornish with heart patients—interventions you were introduced to in Chapter 3—all include this. Redford hazards a guess that one of the ways this increased self-esteem may help is to enable patients to increase their awareness of distressing emotions, which they can then deal with more directly.

## Crossover

Problems of low self-esteem carry over. In a study of university students, researchers report that persons genuinely self-accepting and high in self-actualization also seem to be more open to the experience of romantic love. They are subsequently less emotionally dependent on their partner and may be involved in love as a fulfilling personal experience rather than as an intense interdependency with another person.

One conclusion from the overall research picture presented in the state-of-the-science handbook on parenting sponsored by the National Institutes of Health is that a parent's level of self-esteem affects the quality of parenting he or she can provide.

In a 1979 study of satisfied and dissatisfied middle-class parents in two Milwaukee suburbs, mothers depressed and deeply dissatisfied with their lot in life were prone to be dissatisfied with parenting. In contrast, satisfied mothers had more self-confidence, more psychological ease, and usually more calm forbearance of the relatively minor irritations of life with children. Satisfied fathers were inclined to report good communication with all their children and probably were more financially secure. (We would guess that gender differences have lessened and that psychological well-being relates to good family relationships even more strongly today.)

Several studies indicate that many people will do almost anything to preserve and affirm their concept of the kind of person they think they really are, even when they see themselves as a dud. To maintain their self-image—what feels safe and "tried and true"—people lacking sufficient self-esteem sometimes behave in self-destructive ways. If they think of themselves as "losers," someone telling them that they are a "winner" may just bewilder and upset them.

> "Joe thinks that I am intelligent and sociable, while Tom knows that I am not. I'll never be able to live up to Joe's expectations—sooner or later he is going to ask more of me than I ever will be able to deliver. Better to spend time with Tom—I can be my real self with him."

In light of this research, can you begin to perceive that a positive relationship with yourself is an essential ingredient in connecting up with affirming people?

Fortunately—especially among people with some uncertainty about the kind of person they really are—this crossover works the other way as well: Being treated well by others can boost self-esteem. And as you extend yourself on behalf of others, many will respond positively; some will reciprocate. This appreciation will reinforce your own sense of self-worth. Even when others don't return your caring, you will know in your heart of hearts that you are worthy of self-respect.

If you can view yourself from the broadest perspectives, you may realize at a deep emotional and intellectual level just how wonderful you are.

By being born, you have won an ultimate sweepstakes. If your mother is typical, her ovary contained a total of about 100,000 germ cells. Of these, about 4,000 were released as eggs over her lifetime. Your father in his twenties, thirties, or forties could produce 200 to 300 *million* sperm a day. When he was over fifty years of age, he might produce 50 to 150 million sperm a day. About 180 to 300 *million* sperm were released with each ejaculate. The odds against your parents creating unique you—distinct from all of the other possible children your parents could have had—are numbers beyond human imagination. And that number does not take into consideration the probability of your parents getting together, in the first place! Your parents, in turn, had the same small odds of ever being born—and so on back through all ancestors.

If you view yourself in isolation, from the perspective of the whole universe you are insignificant, a single member of the species Homo sapiens, on a single planet, Earth, which is revolving around a single star, the sun, in a vast, vast universe. Consider yourself instead as participating in the whole of creation—that you are part of an entity with dimensions, diversities, and complexities beyond imagination. If you can experience this ultimate breadth of social support, you will realize that you are part of something very great indeed. What a good reason for high self-esteem!

There is yet another point: Properly using the resources all human beings are born with, you have a unique contribution to make to the future of the world, one that can be made by no other. And ever so slightly (at least), you will contribute to future generations. If you do that, by even the most stringent standards, you matter.

## Action

You probably cannot change your personality, but you can change your behavior. To be a winner, act like one.

## Understanding Yourself

Self-awareness constitutes an important—and absolutely necessary—first step toward self-respect.

### Identify Your Thoughts and Feelings

Happiness, sadness, fear, anger, disgust, probably contempt, surprise, and interest are universal emotions, experienced by people around the world, according to experts who study facial expressions. Still, silence—or even the censoring of facial and bodily expressions—can mask expression of these feelings. You can even hide feelings from yourself. Perhaps half our workshop participants begin unaware of one or several important emotions they're feeling. As we discussed in Chapter 5, becoming aware of your feelings is often a prerequisite for deciding when to act—and to acting effectively.

Especially when concentrating on yourself, be diligent about keeping your log of thoughts and feelings. Describe objectively the evoking situation: What are you thinking and feeling? What actions and reactions then follow?

*Scene:* Saturday night, at home watching a movie.
*Thought:* The relationships in this flick are lousy, but at least they're something.
*Feeling: Sad, lonely.*
*Action:* Stopped the video to fix popcorn. Slathered with butter.
*Feeling:* Temporarily *happy* and *satisfied.*

*Scene:* Still watching the movie.
*Thought:* My mouth feels greasy.
*Feeling: Disgusted* with myself for eating enough butter to blow my diet. Also *sadder* than before and *lonelier* too.

**Evaluate Negative Thoughts and Feelings: I AM WORTH IT!**
*Exact circumstances:* It's Saturday night, home alone with a video. Feel *sad* and *lonely.*

**I** *Is this matter important to me?*
"Yes, it's the weekend. If I don't have fun now, when?"

**A** *Are my thoughts and feelings appropriate, given the facts?*
"I think so. Most people, alone on a Saturday night for the third weekend in a row, would feel this way."

**M** *Is the situation modifiable?*
"Hard to answer. I would feel even worse without the video. But what were my other options? That guy at work did mention last month he was planning to give a party this weekend. I could have asked him if he still planned to. Or I could have gone to the ski club potluck. Or I could have asked Karen what she was doing. I don't know if any of those things would have been fun, but they might have been. I could have put a little more effort into coming up with something beyond a video."

**WORTH IT** *When I balance the needs of myself and others, is taking action worth it?*
"True, I might have felt even sadder if I had gone out and had a lousy time. But it would have been a change of pace from the last two Saturday nights. Tom might have thought that I didn't want to go to his party—maybe mentioning it was a way to see if I would be interested, without chancing rejection. And I bet Karen also is having a lousy time tonight. When I think about it, maybe I could have helped someone else have a good time at the potluck. I should have acted—it would have been worth it! Hmm— I guess I need right now to start brainstorming ideas for something to do next Saturday night."

LOW SELF-ESTEEM

© The New Yorker Collection 1996 Mike Twohy from cartoonbank.com. All Rights Reserved.

### Communicate Better

Knowing yourself—a form of self-speaking and self-listening—can be hard if your self-esteem is low. Before proceeding further, go to a private place, where you won't be interrupted for at least the next half hour. Without thinking too deeply, and writing quickly, fill in your immediate response to the following paragraphs:

I need_____

_____

_____

_____

I want_____

_____

_____

_____

In addition, I like_____

_____

_____

_____

### Empathize

Now pretend someone else—like a cousin, brother, or sister—had written these answers. Out loud, if you are comfortable with this, and silently, if you can't bring yourself to speak aloud, gently and kindly tell this stand-in why the sentiments expressed are understandable. Workshop participants tell us that adopting this perspective enables them to be much easier on themselves.

Since empathizing with yourself is probably a new perspective—and may feel a bit unnatural at first—once you have finished, repeat this entire exercise. It's a tough one—particularly if you say it out loud—but gets easier with practice.

For the next few weeks, every time you are getting ready to judge yourself harshly, substitute that cousin or sibling for yourself and try practicing empathy. Eventually, this new way of not judging yourself so harshly may start to feel natural.

Writing "I need a half hour to myself each evening" might lead you to say "Naturally you do. Everyone is tired after a hard day at work and needs a period of time to be totally free of outside demands. You just need to recharge your batteries. Yes, your spouse and children have needs, but you do too. A half-hour a day of time alone is a legitimate need."

"I want to have a voice in deciding whether we move from Dayton to Louisville" might lead you to say "Of course you do. Your friends are here. Your job too. West Presbyterian and Montgomery County Sunshares are here. You need to be sure that the importance for you of connections here is considered, along with finances, when the family decision is made."

"In addition, I like going to the state fair every October" might lead you to say "Fairs are fun. Yes, the fair costs more money than a movie, but you enjoy it a lot more. And the memory of that afternoon and evening lasts throughout the whole rest of the year. While there are other considerations, of course, having fun is important too."

## Acting Effectively

Now that you know yourself better, you're ready to act.

## Consider Acceptance

All of us need to learn to accept others on most occasions as they are—not as we would like them to be. If you can learn acceptance of others, what about of *yourself*? Try to see how often you judge yourself. Change your behavior if necessary, but separate out your core identity from the ineffectual behavior. Susan, whose story appears at the beginning of this chapter, needed to realize that she couldn't visit her mother every day, because of the length of the trip. She also needed to feel better about the amount of attention she was giving her mother—instead of letting her mother decide for her that what she was doing now was inadequate.

## Consider Assertion or Problem Solving

Recall, from the exercise above, your needs, wants, and preferences. Are they being met?

If obstacles stand in your way, identify as precisely as you can *exactly* what those obstacles are. Rather than stopping with "I don't have enough time to myself," spell out your situation: "Monday night I always go to choir practice, Tuesday night I take Janice to Scouts, Thursday night twice a month is Finance Committee, and Friday night Bill's parents come over."

Another way to help yourself meet your needs, wants, and preferences is to allocate your resources wisely: Are you using time and money in ways that result in the largest net gain? Put otherwise, are you being kept from goals because of excessive requests from others? Are you playing the martyr in areas of your life?

Whether another person is involved or not, clarify what aspects of your situation might be modifiable. What steps do you need to accomplish this? Set up an agenda for action and attach it to the same appointments calendar.

Part of translating the agenda into action involves envisioning who else might help you. What can they do? Next envision yourself asking, in very specific terms, for this aid. ("I need to get off the Finance Committee; let's talk about a deadline for replacing me," not "Please don't make so many demands of me." Or alternatively, "I feel overextended and plan to cut back. Can we talk about specific ways I can reduce my commitment? I am interested in your ideas.") As shown in Agenda 1, include plans for speaking to the identified people.

# Agenda 1

*Goal:* To get a half-hour to myself each evening

| Action | Deadline |
| --- | --- |
| Speak to Tom to request directly that he be responsible for the kids after dinner and cleanup, that is, between 8 and 8:30. | By this weekend |
| Tell Jane and Sarah that they must be home to begin homework by 5:30, so I can help them with any problems before 7. | By Wednesday |
| Check at the end of the month to see if I'm getting the half-hour. If not, devise a new action plan. | April 30th |

Getting out of the martyr role might work out as shown in Agenda 2.

# Agenda 2

*Goal:* To get off the Finance Committee

| Action | Deadline |
| --- | --- |
| Make an appointment scheduled before June 8th, to talk to Marvin Jones about resigning from the Finance Committee. | May 31st |
| Am I off the Committee? | June 30th |

# Agenda 3

*Goal:* Not to have to cook the family Thanksgiving dinner

| Action | Deadline |
| --- | --- |
| Ask Ellen and Tom—and if they refuse, Sue and Bill—to host the Thanksgiving dinner this year. | June 15th |
| Am I off the hook? If not, call Abe's, the Hilton, and Holiday Inn to check on prices, times, and whether they have private rooms for Thanksgiving meals. | August 1st |
| If we are to eat out, inform the family of the location, letting them know that each person will be expected to pay for his or her own meal. | |

## Emphasize the Positive

With yourself, just as in your relationship with everyone else, you need five times more focus on the positive than the negative. You can to a large extent get this need met, since you can learn to control your thoughts and ruminations. Monitor the messages you give yourself and adjust the ratio of positives to negatives as needed: "Nothing good is happening in my life" versus "Here are the problems I have and here is [the five times longer] list of what I am thankful for." "They wouldn't be interested" versus "My knowledge of motors would be really helpful to that group." "I can't cook very well" versus "I can create a very relaxed atmosphere that will make everyone feel at home." Not "I really gave a dumb answer in lit class," but "My answer in math class was really on the mark."

Tilly, a housewife with an "in your face" personal style, was at Duke on a weight-loss program. In a confrontational stance, she started our Lifeskills workshop. After initially announcing that she expected the workshop to enable her to be successful in weight loss, she proceeded to sabotage her chances of achieving this goal. At first she didn't do the homework assignments, announcing every day that she had been entirely too busy. When participating in small-group exercises, she would belligerently say the material was over her head, that it might be fine for people with a lot of education or psychotherapy behind them, but she was lost. (For each exercise, she had handouts with step-by-step guidelines.) As for her weight-loss program, she was only losing a pound a day—not enough for all the money she was spending.

When describing life back home, Tilly again focused on problems, though when questioned she readily admitted that she had a loving husband and two appreciative, loving children. When asked directly, she would answer yes, her daughter was a conscientious student and very loving, *but* she never listened. When pressed, she admitted that her eighteen-year-old son was a very good kid, *but* he was secretly smoking, though she had no hard evidence beyond her suspicions—just wait until she caught him.

Every time we heard Tilly bad-mouth, we asked her to name five positives, which she would do—accompanied by a shrug and upward curl of a corner of her mouth. After completing this exercise many times, Tilly started adding the mumble, "I know, you're right—I do focus on the bad."

At the same time, Tilly was getting in touch with the specific feelings of anger and hurt that were playing a big role in her overeating. In one exercise, focusing on identifying emotions, she was asked to tell us what she felt. Tilly's uncle was now living with her because of his declining health. Like a dam suddenly bursting, Tilly described in much detail how she had been taken advantage of over a number of years in the business she shared with him. Other participants expressed outrage at how her uncle had acted and was continuing to treat her. This helped Tilly admit angry, hurt feelings toward a family member who had helped and harmed her. As all of us countered her attempts to berate her first admissions of being angry, Tilly began to stop feeling so guilty. It was because of that guilt that she had had to shut down her anger.

Becoming aware of these previously unacknowledged feelings seemed to free Tilly to participate more fully in all the experiences in her life. She put some energy and interest into workshop exercises—really trying, not just going through the motions.

Then gradually Tilly began to perceive that she could direct her life much more than she had realized. She needed steps to consider her own needs as equal in importance to those of her uncle. Her agenda was as important as his—his doctor's appointments needed scheduling during times when he could be taken easily, not inconveniently. She and her husband needed to get out together occasionally, without the uncle coming along.

Why was she focusing on the negative in relationships with her husband, children, and friends—when what she primarily felt for these loved ones was appreciation? Why was it so difficult to admit this happiness? (Tilly probably needs psychotherapy to answer this last question.) Her "in your face" anger was being displaced onto strangers, family, friends.

Allowing herself to have feelings of anger and hurt, using these feelings as signals to protect herself against further mistreatment by her uncle, freeing herself up to focus most of her energy on the rest of her family, friends, and positive aspects of her business, and considering psychotherapy are what Tilly now knows she needs. In addition, she needs to focus positively.

Keeping this insight will be hard—we don't know if Tilly, now back home, is succeeding. We can say it's her best shot at the life she wants.

If you have low self-esteem, identifying your thoughts and feelings and accepting and liking yourself are among the most arduous tasks in this book. Indeed, much of psychotherapy involves trying to encourage the client to acquire these behaviors belatedly. So be gentle on yourself. And practice, practice, practice!

## Getting Real

Redford exerts more influence in the world than Virginia. News-paper reporters, magazine writers, and television producers often call to get his perspective on a recent advance in psychosomatic medi-cine. They also call when someone in the news—an irate driver or sports figure, for example—acted in anger.

Because Redford is director of the Behavioral Medicine Research Center at Duke Medical Center, his advice is sought by other medical and governmental centers, too. All of this does little to rein-force for him the message to himself "I could be wrong!"

He and his cohorts at Duke and around the world form a tight-knit, if loosely organized, professional circle that provides one another with much social and professional support. For the past three decades, these contacts have sustained him, as well as given him numerous opportunities for great professional growth.

Virginia, on the other hand, doesn't have these built-in profes-sional confidence builders, though she moves in a world with those who do. In contrast to them, she stays home alone most days to work on books. She also does all of the background planning for workshops, again largely a solitary task. Before she got in the habit of asking, "Redford or Virginia?" people would call to ask for Dr. Williams. "Speaking." "Oh, ah, sorry. I mean Redford Williams."

Add to this that Redford still, after all these years, does love to be in control. His natural first instinct is to take charge, whether it's a domestic matter, like how much pepper to put in the sauce, or a professional matter, like what belongs in a video illustrating Lifeskills.

How can Virginia maintain professional self-esteem, as well as get a fair role in making decisions about the book and workshops, when she's often everyone's second interest? Aware of her negative feel-ings about this state of affairs, she has asked her "I AM WORTH IT" questions and gotten four yeses. She needs to solve her problem.

She briefly considered always letting Redford take the profes-sional lead. The two could just establish differentiated roles. But this just hasn't been a pattern for them at home or professionally, and neither is interested in taking it up now. So she can eliminate that solution.

There's the option of devoting her energies to a different field. But Virginia loves what she does! She believes strongly that psycho-logical skills training needs to be expanded from mental illness into mental wellness, with the general public becoming educated in this field. She knows this is the perfect match for her talents and life experiences. She's seen people's lives transformed when they adopt Lifeskills. With that comes deep satisfaction and warm personal contacts. Virginia needs to keep that perspective in focus. When she does, she usually succeeds in being productive and happy.

But she needs additional strategies. She encourages Redford to let her know that he does value her highly, personally and professionally, to give both her and him that message. She asks him to stop when he's being bossy.

More often, however, the issue is not someone taking power away from her, but her needing to seize the initiative to act empowered instead of hanging back. She did this by asking the publishers that she be first author on this book. She does this in workshops she and Redford lead together by assuming an appropriately active role.

High personal self-esteem can carry over to high professional self-esteem. Her children, sister, mother, aunt- and uncle-in-law, as well as friends, provide great additional personal support, which results in added professional self-confidence. While her father is no longer living, the memory of the way he treated her sustains her forever. Scheduling time for personal pursuits, like exercise and participation in a group that meets to discuss dreams, also provides her with personal activities that are all her own, another esteem-enhancer.

So, when at the last minute she gets bumped from a previously scheduled joint appearance, in a situation she can't control, she takes it in stride. Most times, that is!

## *Exercises*

1. Over the next week, on at least three separate occasions involving different people, pick out someone to be your listener. First, make sure he or she is not in a hurry; then, without announcing what you are doing, for five minutes talk nonstop about something that interests you. If you speak nonstop, you probably can hold the floor. If the other person interjects some remarks, listen, then begin to talk nonstop again. Once you have done this, become the listener, reciprocating by giving your complete attention to the other person.

2. On day one of this week devoted to self-examination, make a list of seven features or behaviors you like about yourself.

3. On the second day, look at yourself in the bathroom mirror. Say aloud: "One of the things I like about myself is . . . " and go through the first feature or behavior on the list. Continue, throughout the week, to go through your other items in this manner.

4. Make a list of cooperative actions (being the relative who cooks the Thanksgiving dinner for the rest of the family every year), committees ("But you've done such a good job on House and Grounds this year, can't you stay on as chair?"), or favors ("I need you to lend me some money for just a little while") where you ended up feeling taken advantage of. Resolve right now to say no next time—and then do it!
5. The next time someone compliments you, simply say "Thank you" and stop right there.
6. Private meditation exercise: Ask yourself, who, of all the people you ever knew, saw your true needs most clearly and cared about you enough to try to fill those needs? (Take as much time as you want to select this individual.) As you picture this person, feel your love for this person well up in you. Re-experience as well the sustaining love he or she gave you. Continue to feel enveloped for as long as you need to. When you are ready, store away this remembering and return to the present moment.
7. Resolve right now to work out the priorities in your life. Keep adding to and, if necessary, revising your list.

# Part III

# *Intimates*

# 7. Your Partner

*Webster's Dictionary, 1828*
Marriage: the act of uniting a man and a woman for life; wedlock; the legal union of man and woman for life. A contract both civil and religious, by which the parties engage to live together in marital affection and fidelity, till death shall separate them. Marriage was instituted by God himself for the purpose of preventing the promiscuous intercourse of the sexes, for the promoting of felicity, and for securing the maintenance and education of children. Marriage is honorable in all and the bed undefiled (Hebrews 13).

*Webster's Collegiate, 1975*
Marriage: the state of being married; wedlock; institution whereby men and women are joined in a special kind of social and legal dependence . . . the wedding ceremony and attendant festivities.

*Webster's Collegiate, 1989 adds*
Any close or intimate association or union, as in "the marriage of form and content."

*S*takes are high in partnerships, as nearly everyone would like to live most intensely at home. When you get this relationship right, others become easier. While research has focused mainly on husband-wife couples, what we say applies to all caring partners.

## Vision

At first, you were swept away. After the honeymoon, you began to notice your partner's flaws. Rather than become disillusioned, you acknowledged this as an indication of getting to know each other better, a necessary step before development of deeper intimacy. You two committed yourselves to reporting many of your thoughts and feelings. You worked on acknowledging and respecting separate points of view. Gradually your intimacy has grown. Each accepts and loves the other. If your partner died tomorrow, you would have mainly pleasant memories. If you both lived forever, you would continue to respect and love each other.

You learn to share the tasks that accompany living together, supporting each other in practical ways. Each consumes only a fair share of being right, a favorite dessert, the last word, free time, and money.

If you do not currently have a partner, but yearn for a caring relationship—with mutual respect and commitment—you hone your skills, eventually finding a good match.

## *Do You Recognize Aspects of Yourself?*

Cathy and Jim, a married couple, took our workshop in different years, so we have figured out their story from bits and pieces each related. Only when we finally met Jim did we hear about their marital troubles; when Cathy took our workshop, she had focused on problems at work, speaking effusively of her happiness at home. In contrast, Jim told us he thought their marriage had been on a downward slope for several years. Cathy, he told us, vacillated between denying anything was wrong and demanding they pay great attention to improving their relationship. Jim, for his part, mouthed expressions of interest but didn't seem invested in what he was saying. He avoided fights, despite our attempts to convince him that sweeping problems under the rug was not necessarily a great virtue. Observing Cathy and Jim together outside the workshop, we noted that he also avoided much conversation with her.

Then Cathy was diagnosed with malignant melanoma. During all the radiation and chemo treatments, Jim was solicitous, supportive. When all of that was over, they went hiking along a number of trails in the Rockies—an adventure they had been talking about for years but never done.

Matters unfortunately returned to normal once their hiking boots were back in the closet. They didn't spend much time together. Yes, they lived in the same house. But they rarely talked about matters they cared about—Cathy's pottery, Jim's deep-sea diving, changing religious views, or their deep fears that Cathy's cancer would recur.

# Knowledge

Today, most of us expect historically unprecedented levels of companionship from intimate relationships—investing at the same time a larger part of ourselves outside the family. This new mix demands a great deal from us on both fronts!

## The Current Situation

Higher levels of stress in the workplace, the rising percentage of dual-income couples in the workforce, and the increasing strain of adapting to new economic realities, particularly for working mothers, have made meeting the often contradictory goals of economic success and self-fulfillment even harder for most of us to achieve.

Given the new aspirations and stressors, many marriages do not survive. Of currently existing marriages, about a third to a half are ending in divorce. Some experts expect future higher rates, suggesting that over half of first and 60 percent of second marriages will end in divorce. By the time American youth reach age eighteen, at least 50 percent will have spent some time in a single-parent household.

Despite the increased difficulty today of staying married, few widely agreed-upon new guidelines or role models have emerged. Furthermore, the new options of role-sharing, same-gender relationships, and novel living arrangements are embraced by some, decried by others. Disapproval of how others are living their lives—or advocating that we live our lives—and confusion over priorities are widespread.

## Present Wisdom

Americans are increasingly seeking new ways to improve the quality of married life. By 1995, 4.6 million couples a year, up from 1.2 million in 1980, were visiting fifty thousand licensed marriage therapists. Self-help groups abound. PAIRS (Practical Application of Intimate Relationship Skills) not only offers semester-long classes in fifty American cities; it reaches to sixteen other countries. Retrouvaille offers a church-sponsored program in which couples who have weathered marital troubles run weekend seminars for couples experiencing hard times. Another five thousand couples are members of ACME (the Association of Couples for Marriage Enrichment), where self-led groups of up-to-eight couples meet regularly.

By 1997, educators and counselors who focused on teaching couples the skills needed to maintain a good marriage had organized their first national conference. A nationwide directory of marriage-education courses is now available on the Internet (www.his.com/~cmfce/).

Marital therapists maintain that during initial courtship, you fall in love with someone you wish you were like. Then you both wake up to discover you knew only one side of the other, that you both have personalities more complex than previously realized. Worse still, neither is perfect. Annoyed at your partner's imperfections, you are worried about your own; will your partner still love you when all your warts begin to show?

Though the relationship can stop there—and most do end in early courtship—you and your partner must take a *necessary* risk if you are to know deeper love: You must let the other person explore the broader you, while at the same time trying to find out about the broader him or her.

But that's not easy! Marital therapists maintain that people fall in love with people with the same kinds and levels of problems as they have. They'll have about the same level of need to merge and be separate, the same degree of ability to see the other person beyond projections, and the same "hot buttons," though usually expressed in opposite exaggerations. (If he is overly timid, she will probably be overly bold, and so forth.) Eventually—the honeymoon over—they need to work on the very areas they most want to ignore. Furthermore, those with the fewest psychological resources and skills are matched up in kind; such a couple will need to work on their marriage overtime!

As noted in Chapter 5, during the last two decades, John Gottman, professor of psychology at the University of Washington and marriage specialist, has studied over two thousand couples—many of them in his "love lab," an efficiency apartment equipped with cameras and microphones. Marriage styles differ, Gottman observed. Some couples practice listening, persuasion, and compromise. But other couples who stay married have additional passion all around: blowups, but dramatic makeups too. And still other partners who stay married are "minimizers," who ignore differences—largely going their separate ways.

So long as a couple agrees which style is best, any of these styles can result in a stable marriage, and Gottman remarks that he has no scientific basis for favoring one type of marriage over another. He does observe that listening, persuasion, and compromise can sometimes result in a loss of romance and loss of self. Volatile couples might go too far, deteriorating into endless quarrels and bickering or even into violence. Thirty percent of minimizers have sexual problems—the husband usually wanting more sex than the wife. They also are frightened of negative emotions and do not have the skills to work out unavoidable conflicts. (We prefer the style of listening, persuasion, and compromise, the style of our marriage and the one incorporating Lifeskills.)

The big lesson from Gottman's studies is this: Those couples who stayed married maintained a ratio of at least five positive contacts for each negative encounter, whatever the marriage style. Touching, smiling, paying compliments, laughing, offering interest and curiosity in what the partner is experiencing and saying—as well as shared joys and enthusiasms—keep marriages happy. In contrast, the downward spiral of too much criticism, defensiveness, contempt, and withdrawal breeds doom. (According to Gottman, dares, taunts, making fun of the other person, stifling the other person while "winning" yourself are less harmful, but also no good.)

What differentiates happy from unhappy couples is less the number of positive affirmations than the lack of frequent negations. Such couples ignore most bait from the partner. The bait: "Why is this kitchen counter so messy!" The partner's silent thought to herself: "Oh well, he's in a bad mood. He's been under a lot of stress lately."

Couples apt to become unhappy don't seem to be able to turn off a negative cascade, once the first negative interchange occurs. When given the bait of the comment about the kitchen counter, the partner silently thinks to herself: "He is inconsiderate and selfish. That's the way he is. That's why he greeted me with such a thoughtless remark." She therefore counterattacks: "This kitchen counter is so messy because every time you come into the kitchen, you leave a mess. Last night's popcorn pan was left full of grease in the sink." If she wants to escalate further, she adds, "Do you think the classifieds should read 'A small cottage at 212 Cedar Lane. Maid service included'? Well, maid service is not included!" And if matters are really bad between them and she wants to escalate to a threat, she concludes, "If 212 has that kind of job description, maybe I shouldn't be living here."

Let's spell out a bit what Gottman labels as the cascading negative spiral. Complaints are necessary to a healthy marriage and not necessarily harmful, if balanced with five times as many positive interactions. The complaint should be aimed at solving a *specific* problem, as opposed to "you always" or "you never," and should be focused on what the speaker is feeling. Complaints voiced as global, blaming,

...gmental criticisms can be especially harmful. Defensiveness
...es: denial of responsibility for the problem; counterblam-
...g, making excuses, like "yes, but" statements; and whining.
Contempt—disapproval, judgment, derision, disdain, exasperation,
mockery, put-downs, or communicating that the other person is
absurd or incompetent—escalates the criticism cascade. Withdrawal,
often initially a final response to the ever-circling pattern of
criticism-defensiveness-contempt, is the most powerful indicator of
serious marital trouble.

Women are inclined to complain and criticize, men to withdraw.
Unfortunately, this leads to a vicious cycle. Gottman has evidence
that such couples, early in their relationship, have more extensive
physiological reactions to each other. On average, once upset, men
have a harder time calming down than women, and their
stonewalling may be an attempt to calm themselves from an uncom-
fortable level of physical arousal. Both wives and husbands, once this
pattern of negativity is established, appear to have trouble listening;
empathy and acceptance disappear. Nor can they speak convinc-
ingly, and practice assertion well. (If volatile, they no longer make
up passionately. If they are a minimizing couple, their former equi-
librium fades.)

This does not mean that couples should avoid each other. Legitimate differences need to be aired, and conflict can be helpful in
identifying and solving problems (though harmful if the partners
withdraw or behave stubbornly, defensively). Gottman advises that
if a couple do nothing to make their marriage better, but do nothing
wrong either, the marriage will still over time tend to get worse.
Gottman counsels men, "Embrace her anger," and women, "Don't
be overly compliant; rather persist in getting your husband to face
areas of continuing disagreement." "To maintain a balanced emotional ecology, you need to make an effort—think about your
spouse during the day, think about how to make a good thing even
better, and act."

## Effects on Health and Well-Being

It *is* healthier to be married. Raw statistics for any age group of both
men and women show widowed, divorced, separated, and single
people have significantly higher death rates than married persons.
For example, a large random sample of almost seven thousand adults
between the ages of thirty and sixty-nine living in Alameda County,
California, were given batteries of questionnaires. Nine years later,
almost five thousand of them could be relocated and were followed

up to see who remained alive and who had died. Non-married women were about 1.4 times more likely to die, a difference that was not statistically significant. For men, the non-married were 2.9 times more prone to die for thirty- to forty-nine-year-olds and 2.1 times more apt for fifty- to fifty-nine-year-olds, with lesser increases for men older than that—all statistically significant differences. Overall social support remained important, even when researchers tried to consider the participants' initial health.

Married people are less liable to come down with cancer or heart disease. Unmarried men and women are more likely to be diagnosed at an advanced stage of cancer, to go untreated, and to have a poorer rate of survival, even when researchers take the stage and treatment into account. Divorced people are twice as likely to develop lung cancer or stroke. Divorced males have seven times higher rates of cirrhosis of the liver and ten times higher rates of tuberculosis. (Of course in many cases, alcoholism or social problems associated with tuberculosis may have accounted for being single).

The *quality* of a marriage matters too. Experts report that in the small universe of a couple, how one partner treats the other affects mental *and* physical well-being. Aside from high self-esteem, marital happiness contributes more to a person's happiness than anything else, including work and friendships. On the other hand, persistent problems within marriages are associated with increased distress, and unmarried people are happier on average than those in troubled marriages.

Sometimes "you make me sick" can be literally true. Compared to happily married counterparts, women in bad marriages were depressed and had poorer immune function, in one study. In another study of Illinois Bell Telephone middle- and upper-level executives at the time of the breakup of AT&T, psychologist Suzanne Ouellette of the City University of New York found that being married lessened the strain—and likelihood of developing an illness—in this time of troublesome transition for most executives. The exception was "non-hardy" individuals who did not find meaning and purpose in their work and relationships; did not believe that, or behave as if, they had influence over life circumstances; and did not see problems as challenges to be overcome. Instead, the executives who had scored this way on Ouellette's tests subsequently used their spouses to reinforce their positions of alienation, passivity, and dependence. Rather than discussing their work stresses and new strategies for coping, they preferred to hear how wonderful they were. For such individuals, having a spouse actually *increased* the probability of developing illness.

Disagreements where partners behave badly can harm more than just a marriage, as indicated in a study of ninety newlywed couples by Ohio State researchers Jan Kiecolt-Glaser and Ron Glaser. All participants were in top health, with excellent health habits, and 97 percent scored high in marital happiness. The couples were observed and measured during thirty-minute discussions on sensitive topics. Researchers looked for negative behavior such as criticizing, disagreeing, denying responsibility, making excuses, interrupting, making put-downs, and trying to coerce the other into concurring. Among those with high levels of these abrasive behaviors, blood pressure and heart rate shot up higher and immune system function plummeted lower than in couples with patterns of kind, compassionate interactions. And the more negative the behavior, the greater the fall in immunological function. Since this study, the Glasers have extended their research to older couples, married on average for forty-two years. They too were asked to discuss a conflictual issue for half an hour, while being videotaped, with blood samples drawn throughout to measure endocrines. While only the women in this older group experienced many endocrine changes, the final bottom line still is similar: Treating each other badly affects bodies in ways possibly harmful to health.

The damage continues even after couples separate. These same researchers have documented suppression of immune function *lasting up to six months* following the breakup of a marriage.

Mental well-being as well is greatly influenced by the quality of a marriage. A marital problem is more likely to precede than follow depression.

RICHARD AND WENDY KOZIER, OF SADDLE RIVER, NEW JERSEY, WITH U.N. PEACEKEEPING CONTINGENT

© The New Yorker Collection 1993 Jack Ziegler from cartoonbank.com. All Rights Reserved.

Having a generally hostile personality may predispose a person to behaving in the negative ways that damage a marriage. In one study, participants were initially chosen because they scored high or low on hostility tests. They were then assigned a purposefully antagonistic partner for an experimental exercise. Individuals earlier identified by the researchers as highly hostile were more prone to rate their partners as hostile and to remember more hostile traits of this person afterwards.

Experimenters have also concluded that the verbal and physical expression of anger lowers the threshold for acting that way again. This means that frequent quarrels can lead to incessant subsequent disagreements, just because you get into an "anger habit." "Letting it all out" is *not* cathartic!

University of Utah psychologist Tim Smith and his colleagues asked married couples to solve, through discussion, a hypothetical problem. One half of the subjects were given an incentive to influence their spouse's behavior, while the other subjects were told simply to discuss the problem. When compared to the other males in the study, husbands with high hostility scores experienced larger increases in blood pressure when attempting to influence their spouses than during simple discussions. Wives' blood pressure reactivity did not relate to their own hostility levels, but did relate to their husband's.

You may be concluding that it's best just to withdraw from marital conflicts, in order to avoid problems with control and hostility. Nope. Recall that psychologist John Gottman has found that withdrawal is a frequent prelude to failure of the relationship.

An outside lover is not advised either: Primate studies among monogamous species indicate that seeing a partner being unfaithful can result in illness, and even death. Fortunately, statistically only 15 percent of American women—and slightly less than 25 percent of American men—are ever unfaithful to their partner. In a given year, only 5 percent of those married have more than one sexual partner.

Couples who improve their marital behavior enhance their physical and mental well-being. A Johns Hopkins study found that married couples taught how to communicate better had smaller blood pressure surges while discussing a hot topic than couples not trained—a finding that suggests the possibility of long-term health benefits from learning to get along better. Harvard sociologist Lisa Birkman is currently trying to help spouses of stroke victims become better caregivers—the goal being to show that this intervention aids recovery.

By acquiring Lifeskills, you and your partner can definitely improve your marriage (and presumably therefore your health). Let's illustrate with empathy. In a study of young couples together over a year, psychologists measured the degree of empathy, other desirable behaviors, and partner satisfaction. The tendency to experience feelings of sympathy and compassion for others, to share their distress and anxiety, and, especially, to see things from another's point of view correlated with warmth and having a positive outlook—which in turn correlated with partners' satisfaction. Empathetic men were better communicators, the trait most valued by the women.

## *Crossover*

A wretched childhood does not doom you to an unhappy marriage. When marriage and divorce counselor Judith Wallerstein examined fifty couples chosen for their especially happy marriages, she discovered some instances in which one or both partners had suffered "terrible, cruel childhoods, including early abandonment, sexual and physical abuse, severe mental illness in one or both parents, and other serious traumas."

The negative effects of a deprived childhood manifest themselves most often when the current environment is stressful too. Researchers who studied women reared in institutions discovered they were at much greater risk for later mental health problems—*unless* a supportive husband helped maintain a harmonious marriage.

Not surprisingly, parents who agree about child-rearing are prone to stay married. Also, their sons are more likely to be better able to express themselves, are considered by others to be interesting, and are less impulsive. Their daughters are less inhibited, less reserved—more impulsive—than girls with disagreeing parents.

Long-term follow-up studies of children of divorce indicate that many problems only surface years later. Boys are apt to act out at the time, but girls may later avoid making a serious long-term commitment to an intimate relationship. A number of research studies suggest that divorce, openly hostile and continued conflict between parents after divorce, and openly hostile discord within intact families are *all* associated with behavior problems in children. Boys may become overly aggressive and misbehaving; girls anxious, withdrawn, and goody-goody.

In some troubled marriages, parents turn to the children for allies against the other spouse—failing to support, maybe even criticizing, the partner in front of the children: "He's so strict I have to intervene, lest the kids be terrorized." "She fails to set limits, so the children are out-of-control, but I let them know what is expected in no uncertain terms." That double discipline message confuses—and thereby harms—kids.

## Action

Our generation's twin goals—of close relationships *and* personal fulfillment beyond the home front—necessitates a balancing act above and beyond that required of our parents, grandparents, and distant ancestors. To succeed in these sometimes conflicting goals demands new relationship-building tools. If we are to achieve a respecting, committed, and lasting partnership, such resources—identifying our feelings, evaluating negative feelings, listening, speaking, empathy, assertion, acceptance, and emphasis on the positive—are no longer optional niceties, but *necessities*.

## Understanding Ourselves and Others

As you recall just reading, a "status quo" marriage is probably getting worse. The continuous fine-tuning a thriving marriage needs requires you to be aware of negative feelings. In addition, positive feelings let you know what behaviors and activities to emphasize. It is important that you usually focus on these positive feelings, for the marriage to stay healthy.

### Identify Your Thoughts and Feelings

John and Jessie have been married for ten years. While generally fairly sensitive to each other, they constantly need to monitor their feelings.

*Scene:* John has just found Jessie's wet stockings and other wet underwear dripping into the tub in the bathroom they share.
*Thought:* Disgusting! This is my bathroom too.
*Feeling: Exasperated.*

*Scene:* John gets home after Jessie. She has on some perfume, apparently newly applied.
*Thought:* Ummm.
*Feeling: Amorous.*

*Scene:* Jessie begins to tell John about her mother's call.
*Thought:* Talking about her mother again!
*Feeling: Bored.*

*Evaluate Negative Thoughts and Feelings:* I AM WORTH IT!

John doesn't need to ponder how to react to Jessie's perfume, which engendered positive feelings. He hugs and kisses her, nuzzling her neck. He tells her how good she smells.

But should he mentioned the underwear? Let Jessie know he doesn't want to hear about what her mother had to say? Let's discuss the underwear first.

I    *Is this matter important to me?*
"Dammit, yes. I don't want to take a bath being dripped upon! And cold drips at that. Well, the sight of it is not too bad; it's just when I get into my bath and get dripped on."

A    *Are my thoughts and feelings appropriate, given the facts?*
"Well, yes and no. Jessie's big project may mean she needs to do her chores when she can. But I certainly deserve a pleasant hot bath."

M    *Is the situation modifiable?*
"I could ask Jessie not to put her underwear around the tub."

WORTH IT    *Balancing my needs and hers, is taking action worth it?*

"I don't want to get her in a bad mood. But I don't want to be dripped on. Hey, I'll tell her that I know she's been too busy to get to it yet, but I'd appreciate it if she could get them out before bathtime."

Then there's the call from Jessie's mother.

I    *Is this matter important to me?*
"On a scale of one to ten, this gets a five."

A    *Are my thoughts and feelings appropriate?*
"Yes and no. I'm not much invested in Jessie's mother. But on the other hand, Jessie is."

M    *Is the situation modifiable?*
"I could ask her not to tell me about it."

WORTH IT    *Balancing my needs and hers, is taking action worth it?*
"No. Jessie is concerned about her mother, so talking is a way of dealing with that. She needs me to be there for her."

## *Communicate Better*

**Listening** is one of the most important skills a partner can have. Jessie wants to talk about her mother. By listening, John communicates that he cares about Jessie's thoughts and feelings. Maybe Jessie is worried, in which case she will need to be held close. Or maybe she's exasperated at her mother and needs to ventilate, but not to her mother. John doesn't know at this point. He can find out by listening.

But only if Jessie is willing to report what she is feeling by **speaking** up. She may want to relate what her mother said. She needs also to include how that made her feel.

> "Mother called to complain about Aunt Sadie again. This is the umpteenth time. I know it doesn't do any good to suggest that she tell Aunt Sadie what she is telling me. But I now feel frustrated. Confused. I guess I also feel a little guilty for not being interested, when I think about it."
>
> "It must be hard to come home to a call like that!"
>
> "Yeah, it really is. But it's over now. And I look forward to *our* evening."

Describing incidental occurrences like the call from Jessie's mother is ongoing chatter, important but not enough by itself. This most intimate of relationships needs the nurture of "quality time" as well. Mutual deep communication requires time. Set aside twenty minutes each evening to be together, without interruptions or distractions. You may want to start with the simple exercise of letting one person speak for seven minutes only about himself or herself or a special interest (*not* comments about the other person or the relationship). Shy persons may have trouble filling the time, and more expressive types will want to jump in. But if you stick to this format, the shy person invariably gets a second wind. Trying to practice empathy, the listener reflects back either the information or the emotional content of what was heard (*not* advice, observations, analyses, or any new topic). Then the two switch roles.

When you are the speaker, remember the general guidelines of making "I" statements and speaking out of personal experiences, especially from that day. Talk about what's important to you—whether that is events or your emotional and spiritual life.

Such intimacy may feel scary at first, though less so after Chapter 6. Middle ground exists between not revealing *any* inner feelings and thoughts and obligating yourself to tell your partner *everything*. If you need to—and you probably will—acknowledge to yourself that you may have some secret recesses of your soul you still feel the need to protect. An initial blanket pledge of "complete openness" and perfect union is beyond what most of us want to—or should— promise. (During their week-long engagement, Leo Tolstoy and his young fiancée Sofia shared diaries each had long kept. But after their marriage Tolstoy soon observed, "The thought that she is there reading over my shoulder diminishes and distorts my truthfulness.' Their attempt at complete openness did not assure marital happiness, either. The relationship between the two worsened dramatically over the years, eventually poisoned by his self-righteousness and her jealousies. "Days, weeks, months pass when we say not so much as a word to one another." And when they did speak, often they drove each other mad, as no one else could.)

The rhythms in your marriage may vary, reflecting the twists and turns of each of your lives. Couples in most marriages experience times of moving away from—and toward—each other.

Boredom is a powerful enemy of a good marriage. You can stave this off in part by being sure, when speaking, that you don't ramble on in tired generalizations. Your partner should usually *not* be able to predict what you will say. In order to have something new to relate, try, for at least part of the day, to experience your world afresh. Help your partner to regard you as Shakespeare describes Cleopatra: "Age cannot wither her, not custom stale/Her infinite variety."

One last reminder: Much or most of your communication with others is nonverbal, so let your style and body language convey that you are interested in and appreciative of what both you and your partner have to say. If you avoid eye contact or look dully at your partner, stay slack-jawed, cross your arms, and perhaps curl your upper lip to the side or wrinkle your nose, your partner will get the real message quite easily.

### Empathize

In our workshops for couples, we almost always ask participants to list small irritating characteristics of their partners, which they have been unsuccessful in getting their partners to change, though good- ness knows, they have tried! (So as not to get participants overly irri- tated at their partners, we encourage participants to limit this exercise to petty annoyances.) A list might look like this:

- leaves dirty socks by the bed
- finishes something, like the potato chips, then forgets to put the missing item on the grocery list
- keeps saying "uhh"

Once lists are made, participants divide into single-sex groups. Each person selects one item on the list, then practices empathy by assuming the identity of the partner, using "I" statements, and sharing feelings to explain why the partner with the assumed identity behaves that way. If the speaker gets stuck, the rest of us add our two cents. If the speaker starts saying things like "I'm naturally inconsiderate," we ask if the partner *really* would see himself or herself that way.

> "I don't speak as fast as Martha. But I like to get my point of view heard, too. 'Uhh' enables me to keep the floor, while I think through what I want to say next. I know this irritates her and I try to stop. But I say 'uhh' at work too. And after all these years, it's part of how I think."

From our observations of participants in our workshops for couples, the members in our small group of the Association of Couples for Marriage Enrichment, and ourselves, we have concluded that everyone we have observed gets annoyed at his or her partner over a number of small personal habits. Irritations seem an inevitable part of intimate living, once a couple has lived together for a while. He likes to chew gum. She drives too slowly in the left lane. He leaves his socks on the floor. When cooking, she doesn't clean up as she goes along.

Despite everyone having differences, some couples still like each other most of the time, while other couples appear irritated often. What's the difference? In successful relationships, each party lets the other one know at least once about any irritating characteristic he or she hopes the partner will change. The partner communicates back about how easy or difficult change would be in this area. Now both parties are aware of how big an issue this particular matter is for each of them.

## Acting Effectively

From our observations, give and take also seem key. Partners in flourishing marriages work on *some* of their own irritating habits while accepting *some* of the foibles of their partners, approaching each other always with empathetic respect and often with acceptance of the other person or with a considerable effort expended to change whatever behavior irritates the other party. Achieving this balance isn't easy, so we'll continue this discussion for a bit.

For most couples, concentrating on changing behavior or accepting foibles in a specific situation proves to be a very effective way to work on big issues of control and intimacy, without ever having to get into "you always" and "you never" diatribes or deep analysis of the psychodynamics involved. When this is not enough or when one person is doing most of the giving, the other most of the taking, we advise seeking counseling from a mental health professional.

### Balance Acceptance and Assertion

Though plenty of items on his desk needed attention, Tom left work on time. Patricia arrives an hour late for supper. He is irritated, a feeling he has no trouble identifying! Now he plans to evaluate that feeling, to decide whether he wants to practice acceptance *or* assertion. He is not going to guess why she is late, nor interpret her facial expressions.

First, to get a firmer grasp of the exact circumstances, Tom listens to Patricia tell why she is late. "I was halfway through a project and knew it would take extra time tomorrow, if I carried it over. I didn't think about telephoning. Why make such a big deal!" He now has the *facts*. Patricia stayed late to convenience herself, even though they had agreed when they would be home. She did not telephone.

**I**  *Is what he is becoming irritated at important to him? (If not, he'll decide quickly to move on.)*
Tom concludes that he has wasted an hour by getting home on time. This is important to him.

**A**  *Is his irritation appropriate?*
Tom decides that expecting to be telephoned was reasonable. (He has considered only what he can see and hear, not any motives he impugns to Patricia. If he had gotten a no, he would consider the additional, positive feelings he probably would discover he has.)

**M**  *With the goal of avoiding this happening again, Tom asks if this situation is* modifiable.
Is this an area where it's reasonable to expect Patricia to change? (If not, he needs to try to learn to accept this aspect of the partner.) Tom concludes yes to both questions. Surely Patricia can become sensitive to the demands on his time—either come home on time or at least telephone.

**WORTH IT**  *What are the gains and losses for Patricia and Tom if he asks her for what he wants? (His primary goal is a good marriage.)*

"Patricia may react negatively. But if I say nothing, I am going to continue to feel dismissed. The next time she's late, I'll be even more irritated. We need to get this matter straight, before it escalates."

Tom has four yeses. "I AM WORTH IT!" he concludes.
Now he needs to practice assertion.

> "Honey, it's seven o'clock, even though we agreed to be home by six. I left unfinished work on my desk, to be here at the agreed-upon hour." [Statement of exact situation.]
> "Right now, after waiting here alone for an hour, I am feeling neglected and dismissed." [Shared feelings with "I" statements, focusing on this situation only.]
> "I don't like feeling that way. Having good evenings with you is important to me."
> "Can we agree that next time you decide to stay late, you'll telephone me right away?" [Specific request.]

Of course, if Patricia gets into the habit of telephoning that she is going to be late, Tom may need to address the new issue. If she continues to be late without telephoning, he may want to add some mild consequences to his specific request.

Let's make the situation a little harder, with larger stakes as well. Suppose Patricia and Tom were parents disagreeing about their children's bedtimes. Each had asked the four questions and gotten four yeses. One remained convinced of the wisdom of flexible bedtimes, the other of structured bedtimes. Here are two possible *compromises,* which would avoid confusing the kids and give each parent part of what was wanted:

- One parent is in charge of putting the children to bed on Monday, Wednesday, and Friday; the other on Tuesday, Thursday, and Saturday. Sunday is done the old way of both parents dealing with the children.
- The parents support each other in given tasks for a set period of time, like a week or month. Maybe she'll be in charge of bedtime, without his criticizing her approach; he'll be in charge of getting the children to pick up their toys, without her butting in.

Let's not forget the need sometimes for just plain *acceptance!* Now in touch with your feelings, you are aware that your partner has just annoyed you. You have asked the four questions, with three yeses, but have also decided that focusing further on whatever your partner has done will be counterproductive. You want to practice acceptance, but can't.

Try getting there in stages. Let's assume that you already are trying to speak in specific, personal terms about your feelings and thoughts, so that your partner should be able to figure out that a certain action would annoy you—but for whatever reason is still acting that way. You meanwhile are *listening*, so that you are becoming able to know where your partner is coming from.

As a next step, try seeing the partner's behavior from his or her perspective, along the lines discussed in the empathy exercise. (Maybe, in addition to not seeing dirty socks as a big deal, for your husband those socks symbolize freedom, not having a nag who reminds him of his mother lay down rules that must be followed. Or perhaps he has had demands placed on him all day and coming home symbolizes getting out from under unavoidable injunctions. Maybe your wife has mixed feelings about having eaten all those potato chips; forgetting to put a reminder on the grocery list is a way of removing temptation. Or maybe by the time she finished the chips, she was preoccupied with the children or finishing her report.) If you can carry empathy this far, can you go beyond empathy to accepting this aspect of your partner?

Don't get the idea this is easy. Rather than seeing it as something you practice or not, try sliding toward acceptance. Suppose, for example, that though now she calls beforehand, Patricia continues to be late for dinner—despite Tom's textbook-perfect practice of assertion. Should Tom accept Patricia as a workaholic slowpoke and arrange his life to accommodate that she will frequently call to announce she is going to be late? In this matter *only he* can balance his and her needs. And to keep the relationship balanced if he accepts her lateness, should he suggest a foible of his she might try to accept?

Even guidelines this unstinting won't always be as magnanimous as you will want to be, in this most intimate and important of all relationships. Occasional acts of special generosity will be called for! On rare occasions you will need to consider especially carefully the net gain and loss for yourself and your partner, if you practice assertion. Sometimes, when your partner has suffered a loss or is in crisis, you will want to provide extra comfort, giving of yourself unstintingly.

Will you know when a moment is one of these special times and that you're not just being a wimp? You won't always. But often you will, by knowing the other person as well as you know anybody except yourself. By reading subtle facial and body language. By knowing the other person's intimate history and special vulnerabilities and treating this special knowledge with respect and care. That

extra caring may make the difference between a good relationship—
and a great one.

And remember, whether you practice assertion or acceptance in a
given situation, it is *not* because you are being coerced. The choice
is one *you* have made freely, based on your thoughts and feelings,
your careful evaluation of the situation, and your appraisal of your
and your partner's needs.

### Emphasize the Positive

Each day, let your partner know about at least one relished feature.
Your observations can be rapturous:

> "You have incredibly sexy eyes."

Or practical:

> "I know being here by six is an effort for you—thanks for
> making the extra push."
>
> "Thanks, honey, for loading the dishwasher, even though it
> was my turn."

Keep your observations fresh and varied. (Who wants only to be
applauded as a good dishwasher loader?)

To this practical mix of positives, you need to add *delight*: Try to
touch your partner often. Squeeze or hold a hand. Give a quick hug.
Touch your partner's shoulder. Nuzzle.

If either of you is experiencing sexual difficulties, plan occasions
where you de-escalate. Set your own ground rules: On these occasions, we'll only cuddle. Or pet. The point is that the encounter not
lead to intercourse, nor threaten either partner.

You also may have to face pronounced differences in desire, aside
from any sexual problems. John Gottman found that in couples with
little contact with each other, men are more likely than woman to
want more frequent sex. Judith Wallerstein's study of fifty closely
connected happily married couples reports that in one quarter of the
couples, the woman wanted more frequent sex, in another quarter
the man; only half the couples were evenly matched.

On a special night, when you are not rushed, have one of you ask
for one single specific intimacy. Keep your request simple and easily
doable within a half-hour.

> "I'd like a back rub."
>
> "Please read to me."

"I'd like to go through one of our old picture albums together."

"Sorting through Mother's things is hard; please help me for twenty minutes."

Your partner can refuse—in which case you get to try another request the next evening. Once your request is honored, on the next night, switch roles.

On occasion, when both you and your partner feel relaxed, unpressured, and safe, bring some specialness into your bedroom too. Practicing your skills of asking for what you want on the one hand and listening and empathizing on the other hand, try to come up with some scenarios you're both comfortable with and enjoy. For some couples this may be soft background music and subtle lighting. Other couples may prefer to enjoy a feast, ending with sprayed-on whipped cream. Stay within your and your partner's comfort level. Within those limits, exercise imagination!

"Dates" can make the five-to-one ratio easier. At least once a week, plan some enjoyable time alone. If you have children, join a baby-sitting co-op if no other child care can be easily obtained. These outings need not be expensive—a picnic or walk in the park is fine. On such dates, try not to talk about the children or tasks relating to household maintenance. Instead, share new aspects of yourself—feelings, thoughts, interests, experiences. Or just have fun together.

Taking good care of your body matters in partnerships. Consider each day spent in your partner's company an unofficial date. Remember how you prepared for a date as an adolescent? You'd bathe and wash your hair. Clean and clip your fingernails and toenails too, if they were going to be on display. You'd freshen your breath. Wear clean, flattering clothes and perhaps douse on some cologne. These enhanced your attractiveness then and would now. Also, you will convey to your partner "I care about you. I want to make myself as attractive to you as possible, both to increase how much you like me and to please you, because I desire your pleasure." In sum, taking good care of yourself communicates.

For a marriage to be successful, on *most occasions,* it's better if each partner can refrain from criticizing slight misbehaviors of the other, or reacting to such criticism defensively. Recall that one sure way to get off track in a marriage is to get into the pattern of criticism leading to defensiveness, leading to contempt—with the ratio of positives-to-negatives cascading downward to about one-to-one. When this pattern gets repeated often enough, the criticized partner eventually withdraws. Such withdrawal is a powerful predictor of marital dissatisfaction, separation, and divorce. Which is not to say that you ignore mistreatment. Just choose your criticisms and defensive reactions carefully, using your skills in identifying and evaluating negative feelings.

Try to emphasize positive thoughts as well. In a marriage, each partner *on most occasions* needs to avoid generalizing about negative behavior. John has just put his junk on the counter. Does Mary think that he did that because he is basically inconsiderate ("You always . . .") or because today must have been especially hard at the office? On the other hand, generalize about positive behavior, whenever you can honestly do so. John brings Mary flowers on Valentine's Day. Does she think that he did it because all the guys at the office were getting flowers and he was just a copycat? Or did he bring flowers because generally he is a thoughtful person who wants to please her?

~

If you and your partner are experiencing serious difficulties, these skills may not be enough. If so, by all means seek professional counseling. If your partner refuses, your situation is troublesome. In our earlier book, *Anger Kills,* we recommend strongly encouraging the partner, if he or she initially rejects counseling. If your partner still refuses to see a counselor or if you two go to a counselor but still make no progress, you may be left with two choices: accept your relationship as is, or leave.

Domestic violence, child abuse, and substance abuse are never permissible—and are beyond the scope of this book. If you or your partner has these problems, seek professional help *immediately*. (Keep reading also—you'll need outside social support while you work on these thorny problems.)

## Getting Real

Our honeymoon lasted about five years. Then Redford discovered that Virginia could be perfectionistic, demanding, and self-righteous. She discovered he seemed hostile, remote, and self-centered—at times a downright control freak. The next ten years had their ups and downs, but on a descending slope. After Virginia almost left, Redford turned the corner on his own hostility control program, while she subsequently became more assertive, which diminished her need to be "holier than thou."

Once our marriage got good, we decided to go for "great." We're now each other's best friend and honestly do succeed most of the time in acting deliberately. Not always, but most of the time.

These abstractions need translation into daily life. Sometimes in being tolerant, we only partially succeed. "Must Redford say *in-*surance?" "Must Virginia keep her foot lightly on top of the brake whenever driving?" After thirty-four years of concerted effort, neither has corrected the "fault" of the other, yet we still haven't managed to give up control completely of the brake or of the pronunciation of *insurance*. But our reactions are greatly softened, and we are heading in the direction of acceptance.

Recently we had to discuss whether to keep a line of credit at our bank when we paid off a large debt in our ready-reserve automatic borrowing account. Virginia wanted the temptation of a line of credit removed; Redford wanted the safety net. Each of us thought our position more rational. We went through about five or six rounds of listening and repeating back what we heard, with no other comments. Every few rounds we would switch to the other's position for an extended expression of the other's point of view. Somehow, hearing Virginia espouse Redford's argument and vice versa was soothing. We ended up compromising by keeping the line of credit, but reducing its limit. As important as *what* we decided was that neither of us felt he or she had "lost."

Lest you worry that we've achieved marital perfection beyond the reach of mere mortals like you, here's another episode.

Just before *Anger Kills* appeared in bookstores, our publisher arranged some initial TV appearances for broadcast after book release. One of these was in Las Vegas. Scheduling was tight, as we were going to be in Europe for a meeting of the International Society of Behavioral Medicine until the day before taping the Las Vegas show. The day afterwards, Redford had to be in Williamsburg, Virginia, to give a talk at a meeting of cardiologists.

When we arrived at the Raleigh-Durham airport after the flight back from Paris, Virginia went home while Redford hopped on another plane two hours later. That got him—via Dallas—to Las Vegas at midnight. By then Redford had crossed *nine* time zones, and to say the least, his internal clock was as much in sync with the real time as the flashing "12:00" on a VCR.

About 3:00 A.M. local time, Redford's internal clock went "Boinnnggg!" and he awoke, bright-eyed and ready to go. After all, it was already noon in Paris, where his body thought he still was.

Realizing there was no chance of more sleep, Redford got up, dressed, and went down to survey the many delights of the MGM Grand Hotel, still going strong at that hour.

Hours later he headed for the TV show taping. Instead of taping one segment, they taped two. This meant rushing to the airport at the last minute for the 11:00 A.M. flight—via Dallas, again—into Norfolk at 10:00 P.M. that night (three time zones back), where Virginia waited, having driven over from Williamsburg.

Redford's plane was one hour late into Norfolk. As Redford and Virginia walked out to the car, Redford was heading for the driver's side—not trusting anyone but himself to drive safely and competently—when Virginia gently reminded him, "Now Redford, you've just crossed *twelve* time zones, and you've got to be jet-lagged out of your head. I managed to drive up here from Durham without wrecking the car, and I can get us to Williamsburg! Just get in the passenger seat and leave the driving to me."

"You're right, of course," Redford murmured, somewhat reluctantly, since even in his debilitated state he still preferred to be "in control" of the car.

Sensing his hesitation, Virginia bridled, "Now look, you know my safety record is better than yours, that I managed to get here—so I don't want to hear any instructions while I'm transporting your body to Williamsburg!"

"Right," Redford managed to say.

As they headed out of the airport, he could feel himself tensing up, thinking: "Will she make the right turn to get us on I-64?" That went okay, but he was sure Virginia barely missed hitting a road sign when she cautiously swerved as a car passed too close for *her* comfort.

Redford clenched his fist—right hand only, out of Virginia's sight—bit his tongue, and closed his eyes to meditate. Somehow they had managed to make it as far as the Colonial Parkway linking Yorktown, Williamsburg, and Jamestown, when something told Redford he needed to be on guard for danger.

Quickly becoming alert, he noticed up ahead a sign pointing to the left. It said "Colonial Williamsburg." He couldn't make out the rest, but he knew it was not the way to the Williamsburg Inn, where they were to spend the night before Redford's 9:00 A.M. talk the next morning.

Redford also knew, somehow, that Virginia was going to screw up and turn in where the sign pointed. She did! He still held his tongue, but his thoughts were racing: "I *knew* she'd blow it! Now there's no telling when I'll be able to fall into bed and collapse!"

When Virginia slowed, pulled left, and stopped in the middle of a deserted parking lot, Redford partly lost it. (If he had completely lost it, he would have pushed open the car door, jumped out, and bellowed, "I'll get myself there!" while slamming the door shut in Virginia's face.) Through tightly clenched teeth he managed to growl, "You've turned into the damned Visitors' Center!"

Stung, Virginia barked back, "I told you not to tell me how to drive. Now hush and I'll get us there as promised!"

Unable to stand it—yet not wanting to jump out of the car and tell Virginia he'd find his own way to the hotel, as he was sorely tempted to do (his mind was still working well enough to know *that* would keep him from that wonderful bed at the inn even longer)—in a flash, Redford vaulted over the seat, landing on the floor in the back, where he curled himself up into a semi-fetal position.

"Just drive, and let me know when we get there," he growled through clenched teeth.

Virginia did locate the Williamsburg Inn. It actually took only two minutes. The car stopped. Redford wordlessly uncurled himself, got out, and started in with his bags.

As they were walking along, Virginia said in a low, determined voice, "I think we need to talk about this, but we'd better wait till morning."

Nothing was said about the night before as they got up early, dressed, and went down to the elegant dining room, for a breakfast that each hoped would make things better.

About halfway through his omelet, having kept silent except for ordering, Redford glanced warily at Virginia. It was a beautiful fall morning outside, with the sun just beginning to burn off a light mist on the meadow just beyond the large window next to their table.

"About last night—" Redford began.

Virginia immediately sprang to what seemed to Redford like a fencer's *en garde* posture, even though those sitting nearby probably noticed nothing unusual.

She quietly and firmly replied, "Yesssss."

"About last night—" Redford continued, looking straight into Virginia's eyes, "How about we let me plead temporary insanity?"

Even more quickly than the sun was burning off the mist outside, it seemed as though the sun suddenly shone around the table, as Virginia curled one side of her mouth slightly upward. Reaching her hand across to take Redford's, she almost smiled at him, and said, "Okay this time. I know you must have been terribly jet-lagged."

Redford smiled back, "Thanks for understanding. Maybe after my talk, we can visit the handicraft museum?"

So, you see, even "experts" like us manage not to do it right sometimes. And so too will you, especially at those times when—like Redford's twelve-time-zone odyssey and Virginia's six-time-zone jet lag and subsequent car trips—circumstances deplete resources. Our story makes another important point: After you screw up, even royally, it's often not too late to recover poise and get your relationship back on track, as Redford did—in this case, by poking fun at his "crazy" behavior of the night before—and as Virginia did, by then smiling.

## *Exercises*

1. On some occasion when you and your partner are alone, ask for one minute to look deeply into your partner's face. Try to see your loved one afresh during this minute.
2. Set aside a period of quiet time in a place where there won't be interruptions. For several minutes, you and your partner list on a sheet of paper the physical or emotional qualities or behaviors you love or cherish in the other. Then take turns reading each item on your list. The listener does not comment in any way. At the end of the exercise, each partner gives the other the list just read. (Include some delightful items: "I adore your beautiful hair." "I like how you smell." Don't neglect the nitty-gritty of life together, either: "Your fresh tomatoes really do taste better; thanks for growing them!" "I appreciate your getting up with Tommy last night. I'll take a turn the next time."
3. Beginning once a week, and working up to once a day, find an opportunity to say to your partner, "You might be right."
4. Once a day, when you are about to return your partner's jibe, instead ignore the bait.
5. Once a day for the next six months, in the daylight and outside the bedroom, hug your partner.
6. In terms of your partnership, consider various future time frames:
   One day
   Eternity
   Some length of time in between

**One Day**
If you subscribe to a newspaper that reports most deaths in the community, we recommend you and your partner read the obituaries for the next week, as a means of reminding yourselves that life is a precious, potentially capricious, temporary gift. None of us knows if

we have a day, a year, a decade, or longer to live. We do know that none of us has forever.

If one of you dies unexpectedly, your marriage will be over. As viewed from the present moment, you might try writing an obituary of your marriage, highlighting the major information about your collective life together.

_____

_____

_____

_____

_____

_____

Next ask yourself, "In what ways am I satisfied with my marriage? dissatisfied?"

Satisfied: _____

_____

Dissatisfied:_____

_____

## Eternity

The death-tomorrow supposition takes you only so far. Try the reverse. In *No Exit,* a one-act play by Jean-Paul Sartre, three previously unacquainted characters who have just died find themselves sharing a room with no mirrors, no windows, and a locked door. Gradually they realize that they reside in hell:

> You'll see how simple it is. Childishly simple. Obviously there aren't any physical torments—you agree, don't you? And yet we're in hell. And no one else will come here. We'll stay in this room together, the three of us, for ever and ever. . . . Each of us will act as torturer of the two others.

Finally one of the characters bangs open the door. But neither he nor the other two leave. By then, they've become inseparable. But being together still is hellish.

> So this is hell. I'd never have believed it. You remember all we were told about the torture-chambers, the fire and brimstone, the "burning marl." Old wives' tales! There's no need for red-hot pokers. Hell is—other people!

Suppose your partnership continued throughout eternity. Forever, you two must endure each other's close and continual company. What is your first reaction to that prospect? What would be
best about having your partner around forever? Given your present
relationship, in what areas of your marriage would eternity be a *very*
long time?

First reaction: _____

_____

_____

Best features:_____

_____

_____

_____

Worst features:_____

_____

_____

_____

## Some Length of Time in Between

For four years, we have belonged to a group of eight couples in a
local chapter of the Association for Couples in Marriage Enrichment
(ACME). Along with partners of other ages, we have observed
almost-newlyweds and three couples each married about fifty years.
The group meets twice a month to practice a specific assigned exercise designed to improve communication or otherwise enrich
couple life. Everyone speaks with his or her partner; some dialogues
are private, others take place before the group. During the course of
these structured communications and during free-wheeling general
dialogues, couples discover problems, try to listen to each other's
point of view—and sometimes, but not always, resolve differences.
We have learned much from the dialogues of couples married half a
century on how to live together successfully.

How many weekends a month should Tom and Mary hit the
road in their new RV? Later, doesn't Mary want them to have some
fun this weekend; why doesn't Tom realize she is too drained by
chemotherapy to go?

Why does Adrienne need to hear Paul say he loves her, if she knows that already?

Why doesn't Patrick dig up the flower bed so Susan can get the new bulbs in; why doesn't Susan realize he'd like to dig it up at his convenience?

When we first became privy to such dialogues, our initial reaction was: Fifty years of deep commitment to each other, yet these couples still had problems to work out! How disappointing! The ACME slogan promised "to make a good marriage better." These marriages didn't seem all that hot. Indeed, these couples seemed to have greater difficulties than we.

No, but they were more aware of differences between them than we were.

Gradually, disappointment changed to encouragement. Neither partner was suppressing feelings or giving up autonomy. Most problems seemed insoluble from either single perspective; usually compromises left each partner okay, if not elated.

"I hear you saying even though you really know I love you, you want to hear me say it. Hey, you mean I can make you feel good just by letting you know I love you?"

"So it's not that you don't want to dig up the flower bed; you just don't want to do it on Sunday."

"That's not exactly it. What I don't want is to be tied down to a schedule. I'll get it done next week, I promise."

Occasionally, telling the other person what was wanted led to a gift.

"I hear you saying you don't feel up to a trip this weekend. Thank you for letting me know."

Watching these couples over the course of years, we have observed that they gain a lot of satisfaction from their marriages, and some delight. One partner has now died; the other two older couples survive. Not surprisingly, these partners continue usually to enjoy living together. For after fifty years of marriage, they are still practicing and perfecting the art of learning to express feelings, listen, compromise, and when necessary, give the other what was asked for, out of respect for special needs.

One day.
Eternity.
Some length of time in between.

# 8. Your Young Child

Family life not only educates in general but its quality ultimately determines the individual's capacity to love. The institution of the family is decisive in determining not only if a person has the capacity to love another individual but in the larger social sense whether he is capable of loving his fellow men collectively. The whole of society rests on this foundation for stability, understanding and social peace.

*Martin Luther King, Jr.*

All of us with children aspire to be good parents—not an easy goal! An ongoing relationship with an ever-growing young person fascinates us one minute, stretches us to the limit the next. The unique personality of your child, her stage of development, your needs and values—as well as the new Lifeskills you are developing—must all be juggled at once!

Fortunately—and unfortunately—children are natural mimics. Children of parents who smoke, swear, eat sweets, drink, ignore others, or often criticize their children are more apt to behave the same way when they grow up.

Being a good role model will not be easy. Yogesh Gandhi tells the story of a mother distressed by her son's resistance to changing his poor eating habits. Knowing his admiration for Mahatma Gandhi, with her son she traveled three hundred miles on foot, in the hope that the Mahatma would counsel him not to eat sugar. When he learned their purpose, the Mahatma told them to return in two weeks. Despite her weariness and disappointment, she obeyed. Upon their return, the Mahatma met with her son, and it is said that out of devotion to this great leader, the child changed his ways. The mother, however, asked the Mahatma why he chose not to speak with her son on the first visit. It is said that the Mahatma replied, "Two weeks ago I was eating sugar."

You, with a young child, will get all the reverence older persons reserve for sages like Gandhi. In no other relationship are you so admired. With no other tie do you have as great a chance to influence what another human being will be like in the future. You can model Lifeskills and encourage moral and spiritual values that will last a lifetime. Also you can help your child to feel good about herself forever, to have the high self-esteem advocated in Chapter 6. Listen, empathize, accept your child for the unique person she is, focus on the positive, and probably you will have someone who treats you well for life. (Except perhaps during those toddler and teenage years, of course!)

## *Vision*

You and your partner have the child you both wanted so much. Each of you has sufficient opportunities to get to know your newborn, so the expanded family can enjoy each other. Later, your toddler's struggles between dependency and autonomy do not threaten you too deeply. Building on this strong base, you provide your older child with a good mix of independence and a structured life based on moral expectations and spiritual values. Above all, you enjoy your child and most of the time emphasize the positive.

## *Do You Recognize Aspects of Yourself?*

Dylan was not only planned—his parents had spent years deciding whether to have a child. Daniel had two daughters from an earlier marriage. They were almost grown, and starting all over required surrendering a lot of new-found freedom. Still, his two daughters were not turning out all that well, which he blamed on their mother. The idea of rearing a perfect child, to demonstrate that the girls' problems were her—not his—fault appealed to him a great deal. He did not expect to reduce his hours at work nor modify his personal style, which many acquaintances found abrasive.

Nita had no children and, as she put it, didn't want later to regret not having "done that." Both parents were highly educated, held responsible, demanding jobs, and were devoted to self-improvement— exercise, cooking, travel, entertaining graciously. Nita also did not expect to reduce her hours at work nor modify her highly competitive, perfectionistic approach to life.

Nita worked up until the day Dylan was born, and was back at work within a week—a state of affairs which had a slight touch of "Look at me!" about it. The finest of child care centers was found for Dylan, and neither parent adjusted hours at work. Dylan was given educational toys and coached at home in the evenings with the mind-stimulating exercises described in erudite books. Little time was spent just being together.

By age three, he was enrolled in the most progressive preschool. But the teacher reported that Dylan was having trouble fitting in and seemed unusually nervous. He was promptly sent to the best child psychiatrist in the area. But today, now seven years of age, Dylan still seems highly nervous and does not get along well with other children. His parents still seem very busy.

# Knowledge

According to the editor of the state-of-the-science handbook on parenting sponsored by the National Institute of Child Health and Human Development, "The family generally and parenting specifically are today in a greater state of flux and re-definition than perhaps at any other time." What does this mean for child-rearing? Under these unprecedented circumstances, how can we be good fathers? Good mothers?

## The Current Situation

In these difficult times for rearing children, Americans are searching for guidelines. In at least eight states—including California, Delaware, Michigan, New Jersey, New York, Tennessee, Vermont, and Virginia—classes in parenting are a high school graduation requirement, taught as part of home economics classes. (Baking a cherry pie is being replaced by focus on consumer science and the family.) Other child-rearing advice is plentiful. By 1997, *Books in Print* listed 1,697 books about "parenting" in the subject index—more than double the number available fifteen years earlier.

On a more personal level, and as part of the expanded psychological expectations characteristic of the present generation of Americans, most parents want a warm and loving relationship with their children. Yet in one large survey, 40 percent said they spend an inadequate amount of time with their kids, though a significant percentage of parents, especially among fathers but even among working mothers and single parents, feel that they spend more time, not less, with their children than their own mothers and fathers spent with them. Forty-four percent of parents feel that the family as a whole does not spend enough time together either. Another estimate, cited by the Department of Education, put the figure of working parents who said they did not have enough time for their children at two-thirds.

Despite the entry of more mothers into the workplace, individuals in America are less supportive of parents and less involved with other people's children than ever before, in terms of volunteering to spend time with them. Nor have we instructed our governmental officials to legislate much greater tax credit for children, a shorter work week, paid parental leave, subsidized child care, flextime, or shared jobs, either. (We document this state of affairs in Chapter 15.)

The resulting bottom line: Expectations for a good relationship with your child are high, yet free time is probably limited. At the same time, few community resources exist to support parents.

## Present Wisdom

In a 1994 national survey sponsored by Massachusetts Mutual Life Insurance Company of a thousand children aged eight to twelve, 94 percent said their families are happy. (Ninety-three percent of parents also are satisfied with the quality of their family lives; only parents not living with their children report dissatisfaction very often.) The children, when asked to account for family happiness, emphasized:

- family togetherness—doing activities together, going places together, spending time together
- communication and affection—talking, loving, caring, and helping
- no or few arguments or fights, and being able to get along with one another

Eighty-nine percent of these children reported that they spent enough time with their mother. Children whose mothers work, whether full- or part-time, are just as prone as children whose mothers are not employed outside the home to report spending enough time with them. The reasons why children felt they spend enough time with their mothers were most often based on three key perceptions:

- Mom is home—whether it's before school, after school, during the evenings, or even on the weekends.
- Mom does things with me—going places, shopping together.
- Mom supports me—talking, being there when needed, helping with homework.

Sixty-seven percent of this same group of children felt they spent enough time with their father, while 24 percent felt they never got enough time with him. The following distinctions are notable:

- Of the 19 percent of the children surveyed who did not live with their father, 58 percent reported not spending enough time with him.
- Girls were more likely than boys to say they do not get to spend enough time with their fathers—37 percent to 27 percent, respectively.
- Only 57 percent residing in the western United States and 58 percent in families earning less than $25,000 a year were satisfied.

(We do not know from this survey how the children's answers were influenced by their need to be part of a caring family and to feel adequately cared for by their parents or, in the case of single-parent households, by the message about the other parent conveyed by the resident parent.)

In this same survey, half of the sample were asked to describe, in their own words, the primary thing their parents had taught them about life. They most often cited values—such as "acts of kindness and helping others, showing respect, telling the truth, being responsible, following religious teachings, discipline, and saving money."

Expectations for behavior and rules are the next significant lesson cited: "Using manners, not fighting, not talking to strangers, and not using swear words, drugs or alcohol." The third most frequently cited category concerned the importance of an education: "Getting good grades, parental assistance with math, reading, and spelling, and doing your homework." Chores or skills constituted the fourth major area: "Cleaning, cooking, baking, sewing, yard-work, care of pets, and how to fix or build things." These children averaged two chores—some of which, like yard work, were not daily responsibilities.

Parents matter a great deal to their children. In psychologist Kenneth Pelletier's study of fifty-three prominent individuals who had ideal mental and physical health, almost all of them had strikingly strong fathers who took a deep interest in them. On the other side of the coin, mothers of "troublemakers" have been studied, to see if they have any special behaviors. They do! When shown videotapes, they are more inclined than other mothers to see children as misbehaving on purpose, rather than attributing the misbehavior to the situation or the child's lack of knowledge or skill. Overly aggressive "problem" children don't perceive themselves that way. On the other hand, like their mothers, they view other kids as out to get them. Such misperceptions are in part what lead to the arguments and fights such kids are prone to, so that eventually the kids' perceptions about the "misbehavior" of others become self-fulfilling. While this evidence once again gives fathers the good lines, mothers the problems, let's not lose sight of the broader message: How you treat your child *now* matters *forever*!

And you can succeed in successfully parenting your child, even if you do not have any support from the child's other parent. When researching her book on families, writer Maggie Scarf originally planned to organize her materials on the basis of whether any given family was traditional, single-parent, blended, and so forth. But after an observation period, she concluded that—more than family structure—how power, intimacy, conflict, and individuality are handled within a family counts.

Just as parental neglect exacts a toll on the child's later development and performance, so also can parental involvement be the largest positive influence in a child's school performance. A British study has followed a large sample of children—born during one week in 1946—since their births. Examining such a large group, observed over such a long period of time, has enabled the national Medical Research Council to see the effects of social class, sex differences, health, and family structure on various aspects of well-being, including academic achievement. When these children were given achievement tests at age eight, the most powerful influence on test scores was parental interest, as measured by teachers' and parents' reports of mothers' and fathers' visits to the schools for discussion. Parental influence continued throughout childhood.

The same conclusion has been reached after three decades of research in the United States: parental participation improves students' learning. This is true whether the child is in preschool or the upper school.

The kind of attention given is important too. Berkeley child psychologist Diana Baumrind has been carefully observing parents and their children for a couple of decades, trying to determine what styles of parenting produce the best-adjusted, most self-fulfilled children. She concludes that parents who demonstrate warmth *and* also set limits have children more socially and academically skilled than do parents who emphasize either mainly the warmth or mainly the rules. Parents need to provide structure, control, and regimen, in acknowledgement of the child's immaturity. But they also need to provide stimulation, warmth, and respect for individuality, in acknowledgment of the child's emergence as a confident, competent person. *Balance is key*.

In 1981 some members of the National Association of School Psychologists gathered long-term data on seven hundred children in thirty-eight states, in a study comparing children in divorced and intact families. Among the points made in the resulting president's report was an endorsement of structure: "Children who had regular bedtimes, less TV, hobbies, and after-school activities—children who are in households that are orderly and predictable—do better than children who [did] not. I don't think we can escape the conclusion that children need structure."

Creating structure sufficient to nurture a child requires more careful effort today than ever before, especially for single or remarried parents. In earlier times, families often were disrupted by the death of one parent, followed by the remarriage of the other. Today, disruption is more likely to be occasioned by divorce, with remarriage still frequent. But given current geographic and social mobility, both men and women are more inclined today to remarry across class, ethnic, and religious lines; remarriage will therefore often produce extraordinarily complex and socially diverse families. Such newly formed families may need to work especially hard to create the consistent structure children need.

With all our focus on environment, let's not forget the other side of the coin. Each child has a unique innate personality. Studies of identical twins reared apart indicate that children are born with a portion of their intelligence, personality and temperament, occupational and leisure-time interests, and social attitudes determined by genes.

One child in ten provides parents with special challenges; she is a child who especially needs you. She stresses easily, reacts extensively, and adapts slowly. With such a child, be patient, loving, and consistent, and don't let self-confidence waiver. Eventually her intensity may make her an exciting, vibrant, and enthusiastic adult.

## Effects on Health and Well-Being

Remember from Chapter 4 unlucky Tom Smith, who grew up haphazardly, and lucky Edward Jones, who grew up in a caring family? Here is a similar, this time historical, example. Neuroscientist Robert Sapolsky describes studies of children reared in two separate German orphanages just after World War II. Both orphanages were run by the government, so the children had the same general diet and health care.

One orphanage was supervised by Fräulein Grun—a warm, nurturing woman who played with the children, comforted them, and spent all day singing and laughing.

Fräulein Schwarz, the other head, minimized contact with the children. She frequently criticized and berated, typically in the presence of assembled peers.

Physical growth rates at the two orphanages differed: children in the orphanage that treated them positively grew more. Then Fräulein Grun left, and Fräulein Schwarz was transferred to the other orphanage. Growth rates at her former orphanage promptly increased; those at her new facility decreased.

In another study, this time in Oklahoma, expectations of a flu epidemic led medical researchers to administer psychological tests measuring family functioning and well-being to a group of 246 husbands, wives, and children. Also determined was that pre-existing levels of flu antibodies were not altered as a function of the psychological tests results. By the end of the flu season that year, physicians knew that good family cohesion and adaptability had been protective. Those families in the mid range between disengagement (being too loosely attached) and enmeshment (being too closely attached) had experienced less severe flu symptoms than enmeshed families, though disconnected families seemed protected too, probably because they avoided one another when infected as they did at other times. In addition, families who could change the power structure, role relationships, and relationships to fit the situation—avoiding the extremes of rigidity or chaos—also were less likely to get the flu.

The correlation between good parenting and good health lasts longer than one flu season. Back in the early 1950s, as part of a more general study on reactions to stressful laboratory tests, a representative sample of Harvard undergraduates were given psychological tests in which they rated their mothers and fathers separately in terms of positive caring (loving, just, fair, strong, clever, and hardworking) and negative characteristics (severe, stingy, brutal, mean, nervous, poor, punished frequently, and drunk). Thirty-five years later, the original subjects were contacted again. Eighty-seven percent of subjects with low positive perceptions of both parents had illnesses such as coronary artery disease, hypertension, duodenal ulcer, and alcoholism. In contrast, only 25 percent of those subjects with positive perceptions of both mothers and fathers were as sick in mid-life.

Mental well-being also is affected by the quality of family life. You will recall from Chapter 4 the Kansas study in which for an hour each month for over two years, developmental psychologists

Betty Hart and Todd Risley had their research team observe 42 one- to three-year-old children and their parents in their homes, to examine the effects of talking to children. They found that the more the children are talked to by their parents, the greater the children's intelligence, capacity to deal with change as well as opportunities, and sociability at age three and at ages nine to ten. Most important for later achievement is the ratio of positive-to-negative talk. While low-accomplishing children received slightly more negative feedback ("Don't," "Stop," "Quit," "Shut up," or "Bad" and "Wrong"), high-achieving children received much more positive feedback (parent repetitions, expansions, extensions of child utterances, plus explicit approval of the child's words and actions: "Good," "Right"). You may be thinking, "Maybe positive talk is just coincidental: Smart professional parents talk more because they are smart and sociable. They may have smart kids only because of their good genes, without any contribution from environment." Nope. Even when these Kansas psychologists controlled for the I.Q. of these blue- and white-collar parents, how much talk, especially positive talk, children get still correlates strongly to later achievement.

In a pilot study of the relationships with the parents of children in the Los Angeles school system, positive parental attitudes were associated with academic success. Successful children and their parents performed rituals like braiding hair, rubbing the scalp or massaging the skin, or eating ice cream together. Successful children had nicknames like "Tiger" or "Wizard," less successful children "Snake," "Fatso," or "Dumbbell." Parents of successful children would remark "He can really make it, as long as he puts his mind to it," as compared to "He's always had trouble" or "She just really is slow, you know."

Not surprisingly, parents affect a child's long-term personality. As mentioned in Chapter 4, psychologist Karen Matthews and her colleagues at the University of Pittsburgh observed fourth- and fifth-grade boys with their parents, evaluating the quality of their interactions. The more positive the tone of the parent-child relationship, the lower the boy's hostility level, when measured two to three years later.

## Crossover

Children are influenced by the quality of their parents' marriage. Over the past twenty years, numerous studies have linked processes within the family to children's physical and psychological well-being. Social scientists can even predict—from what a marriage is like *before* children arrive—how well-adjusted the offspring will be in preschool!

Marital satisfaction, division of housework and care-giving, and parental stress appear to be interrelated.

In a study of two middle-class suburbs of Milwaukee, adults who were "mostly happy" with parenthood rated their marriages better than adults who were unhappy as parents. The majority of all parents interviewed were not only "mostly happy" as parents, but claimed their families to be the most important aspect of their lives.

Present-day parenting can bring great rewards. As a parent, you learn to put above your own needs those of your child—to be fed, put to bed, played with, changed, stimulated, comforted, taken many places, and provided with a good mix of structure and independence. Your habit of flexibility in considering the needs of another persists long after the child is grown. (Think about it: Among a group of older persons, can't you usually tell which ones have been parents, by their greater flexibility? And let's not leave out their added layer of humility!)

If you establish a positive relationship with your young child, you may find it easier to deal with inevitable future problems as your child matures.

Having a child brings you her love now and throughout your life.

Helping your child become a caring adult enables you to influence the planet's future.

# Action

Practicing Lifeskills with your child affects not only the present moment, but your child's future interactions with you and the rest of the world as well.

## Understanding Yourself and Others

Since you are the grownup, with enormously more resources at your disposal, your focus needs to be first on *listening to* and *emphathizing with* your child and, only after that, on identifying and evaluating your feelings to decide on courses of action.

### Communicate Better and Empathize

Children often cannot identify, let alone say, what they are thinking and feeling. To encourage your child in these directions, be as gentle and perceptive a listener as possible. Pay close attention to your child. Even infants require this. Close contact with her caregiver is pleasurable to a baby, but after a while sensory overload can elevate her heartbeat suddenly and dramatically. By looking away, she takes a breather. The sensitive caregiver will respect the baby's need, in order to calm down, for this temporary break, instead of insisting that the baby again pay close attention right away.

Even when you are "listening" carefully, you may often need to consult a development chart or apply sensitive intuition, to see how the world seems from the child's perspective. What does the world seem like, when a child is one year old, or two, three, four, or five? Once you have this important information, you will be better able to *empathize* with her. This will also help you to decide when your child needs limits set.

Do remember that a child is unique and may develop slowly in some areas. This is normal; your attempts to speed up this timetable can possibly be harmful for her or you.

As your child grows older and more talkative, you can help her learn to identify and evaluate her feelings by practicing good reflective listening.

"Ms. Fletcher is dumb."
"Oh?"
"She's the stupidest teacher I ever saw!"
"That bad, huh?"
"The test wasn't fair."
"Oh?"
"I studied vocabulary, and she asked about the story."
"That must have been a shock!"

By remaining interested, but not adding information, advising, judging, or grilling, you are helping your daughter get in touch with her feelings. Continue your interest—but not anything else—and your daughter will probably evaluate her own situation.

"I felt so mad . . . A little scared, too . . . And dumb . . . Ms. Fletcher *had* said to get the big picture."
"Oh, dear!"
"I really felt mad . . . At Ms. Fletcher . . . But mainly at me."
"That can feel mighty down."
"Yeah . . . It's part my fault, I guess."

When the parent remains focused on the child, but silent, chances are the child will come to her own insights.

"Next time I'm going to write down what she says."
"That sounds like a really good idea!"

Should you wish to assume a more active role than the one described here, we suggest you read *The Heart of Parenting* by psychologist John Gottman. In addition to careful listening, he recommends helping your child to identify emotions by labeling them for her. He also recommends actively encouraging problem solving.

### Identify Your Thoughts and Feelings, and Evaluate How to Handle Any Misbehavior

Let's assume your child has misbehaved. First take a moment to calm yourself. (Remember that your instinctive reaction may be a fight-or-flight response to a perceived threat.) Focus in objective terms on *exactly* what the child has just done. Then ask your questions.

### I   *Is this matter important?*

Note "to me" is dropped from this question, as you are putting the interests of the young child first. If your child is having a lot of problems in a number of areas, try to select one at a time to react to; for example, hitting another person. Otherwise, correcting misbehavior could be all you do! Most children are going to misbehave rather often; be prepared to answer yes only infrequently. When observers on site in homes of nondistressed families watched closely, on average perfectly normal young children behaved poorly three or more times an hour in interacting with their parents.

In a study of eighty-five "problem-free" families in Oregon, parents' reports of children's misbehaviors included arguing, defiance, noncompliance, talking back, whining, and complaining.

### A   *Are my thoughts and feelings appropriate, given the facts?*

Are your expectations reasonable, *given the age of the child*? Temper tantrums are normal for a two-year-old, not for a first-grader. All parents need to be familiar with child-development charts, as an aid in understanding their child.

Also consider whether you are reacting only to the current situation, as your child's actions may have reawakened an old problem with your own parents in the past.

**M**   *Is the situation modifiable?*

As you are so much more powerful in every way, this question is often answered yes. Remember to focus on a *specific* behavior, like "Can I get Tommy to stop pulling out the magazines?" not "Can I get Tommy to stop misbehaving?"

**Worth It**   *When I balance the needs of myself and my child, is taking action worth it?*

You have numerous options. You can ignore the situation, play the scene at medium pitch, or make a major deal. Figuring out the ideal response requires effort and relates to the child's age. The tumultuous years between ages one and three, for example, are the times that especially try parents' and toddlers' souls. One minute, your toddler will demand and deeply need your involvement. Five minutes later, she may be loudly yelling "No!" Try not to be oversensitive to these early attempts to achieve autonomy. Equally important is not feeling that you are being a bad parent or that your child has a sorry future.

When you set age-appropriate behavior guidelines and follow through on enforcing them, you encourage your child to take early steps toward developing self-discipline. This active involvement also conveys to your child that you care about her.

## Acting Effectively

You will always want to consider your actions from the perspectives of both short-term and long-term effects.

### Consider Acceptance

Accepting your child "as is" becomes easier when you familiarize yourself with developmental charts. Many "problems" are natural stages later easily outgrown. When our sixteen-month-old grandson, Will, chooses to use a bowel movement as fingerpaint to decorate himself and the wall beside his crib, it is, of course, quite annoying to his mother. But Jennifer knows that toddlers Will's age do this, and she makes a joke of the situation. If Will were still using his feces as an artistic medium at age five, she would feel quite different!

### Consider Assertion

If you have decided to practice assertion—not acceptance—in a gentle but insistent manner, quietly tell your child what behavior you expect. Be specific about the physical behavior you want, rather than trying to influence your child's attitudes or motives. Maybe your typical three- or four-year-old has just hit her brother. State *specifically* what behavior you disapprove of, rather than labeling her: Say "No, I don't like it when you hit!" rather than "Naughty girl!" With young children, you may observe the misbehavior on the spot; if so, react immediately (after thinking through what your response will be).

When you suggest a behavioral change to a young child and the child refuses, gently but firmly insist that the child go right then into timeout, away from everyone else. One minute for each year of the child's age is about right, with double the child's age as the upper limit and five minutes as the maximum for any age, since young children easily forget. You may need to repeatedly place a two-year-old in a chair, empty playpen, or crib; older children may understand they must stay there until told timeout is over, or they may need to be placed in a safe room, like their first-floor bedroom (*not* a second-floor room with windows that open, an ill-lit place, or somewhere the size of a closet).

Timeout gives your child time to get herself back under control; you have saved her from behaving even worse than she did. (She needs to learn to be on the receiving *and* giving end of that five-to-one ratio!) You may have accomplished this for yourself as well! Once timeout is over and if your child has become silent (four to five seconds of silence for a two-year-old, ten seconds for a three-year-old), don't moralize—the incident is over. Repeat timeout as needed, several times if necessary. If the child doesn't become silent within the suggested time limits, ask her if she's ready to rejoin others. If she answers yes, consider the incident over. If she indicates no, tell her to let you know when she's ready. If she doesn't respond in a minute or two, ask her again.

Sometimes your child will have completed the dastardly deed before you discover the mess. Let her know you expect more, that you do intend to impose limits. "No. Liquid soap is not for emptying on the bathroom floor. I expect you to not do that. I expect you to help me clean up this mess."

Finding new locations for forbidden objects, which avoids potential future problems, can ease the stress for everybody and help keep your child safe. That liquid soap would have been better put up, away from your three-year-old. Putting a low barrier, like a footstool, between her and the TV may keep your one-year-old at a distance from those interesting knobs. Your vanity, with its fascinating pots of makeup or shaving cream, may be better shut down when you aren't around.

For older children, loss of privileges sufficiently disciplines them—as you will learn in the next chapter, on teenagers.

### Emphasize the Positive

A child gives you a fresh take—on the four seasons, holidays, water and sand, watermelons, soccer, and cuddling. Above all, take pleasure from your child. Forty percent of parents enjoy sports with their children, 33 percent enjoy board games, 15 percent card games, 12 percent reading. If you invite a young child to engage in your favorite activities and if on these occasions you can avoid a goal-oriented, high-achievement attitude toward performance, your child may eventually come to share the enthusiasm.

Hugging communicates.

In surveys, both parents and children place high value on sharing breakfast, as well as the whole family's sitting down to a full dinner and sharing events of the day.

Listening carefully to the still-hesitant speech of your child communicates that the child is an interesting person, with important things to say. Simply a moment of your exclusive interest, a com-

"I'm not hungry, or thirsty, or any of that stuff. What I'd REALLY like is a hug."

Reprinted with special permission of King Features Syndicate.

ment, or a repetition of what your child says invites your child to continue.

Positive reinforcement works. Focus whenever you can on rewarding a child for acting well rather than punishing for misbehavior. Children want the attention above all else of their parents, so be deliberate about what you respond to. Ignore small misbehaviors and reward small good behaviors: "Good job! I really like it when you dress yourself!" "Thanks a lot for unloading the dishwasher without my having to remind you!" "You are doing a wonderful job of picking up and putting away your blocks!" When you focus on the positive, you are teaching her to receive support by acting well. Apply this approach consistently, and she'll get the message.

Want a smart child? A prominent Yale child psychologist and educator tops his list of guidelines with "Teach children that the main limitations on what they *can* do is what they tell themselves they *can't* do." He cites one famous study, where teachers were told that testing revealed that some of the students were going to bloom during the next year and other children were not. In fact, the children identified as potential "bloomers" were chosen at random. You guessed it—the prediction came true.

Young children are quite distractible. Often you can get a toddler and even an older child to stop misbehaving simply by offering a new focus.

Remember, you won't be the perfect parent always. Congratulate yourself when you deal well with a situation. When you don't, try to improve next time. Your child will learn about persistence, self-improvement.

The one exception: If you succumb to using physical punishment with your child as a rather regular means of control, be aware that in addition to whatever message you think you may be getting across, you are also surely teaching her that it's okay to use force and violence to gain desired ends. Not all spanking constitutes physical abuse, of course, but many child development experts consider spanking close enough to abuse to condemn it as a form of discipline. Therefore, if you're unable to keep from regularly using physical forms of punishment, we urge you to seek advice and help from your pediatrician, a child psychologist, or another qualified professional.

## Divorce and Your Child

After an acrimonious hearing in a divorce case, Judge Michael Haas of Walker, Minnesota, delivered these words in the Cass County Courthouse to the divorcing couple:

Your children have come into this world because of the two of you. Perhaps you two made lousy choices as to who you decided to be the other parent. If so, that is YOUR problem and YOUR fault.

No matter what you think of the other party—or what your family thinks of the other party—those children are one half of each of you. Remember that, because every time you tell your child what an idiot his father is, or what a fool his mother is, or how bad the absent parent is, or what terrible things that person has done, you are telling the child that half of HIM is bad.

That is an unforgivable thing to do to a child. That is not love; it is possession. If you do that to your children, you will destroy them as surely as if you had cut them into pieces, because that is what you are doing to their emotions.

I sincerely hope you don't do that to your children. Think more about your children and less of yourselves, and make yours a selfless kind of love, not foolish or selfish, or THEY will suffer.

## *Getting Real*

After marrying in their mid-thirties, Sally and Thad immediately tried to conceive a child. When Cal arrived two years later, after a difficult pregnancy, both parents were thrilled. They cut back on their extensive social life and tried to spend as much time as possible with him. As a baby, he cried a lot, so they held him frequently. The terrible twos were stressful, too. When Cal became three years old, he began to attend morning preschool. To both parents' dismay, his teachers reported that Cal had a shorter attention span than the other children.

Sally and Thad redoubled their efforts to be good parents to him and his little sister. But problems at school continued. The family sought professional help, picking up some useful skills on imposing rules, practicing consistency, and using timeout as punishment. Despite his parents' best efforts, Cal continues to have adjustment problems at school and home. He has a short attention span. He picks fights with his sister and children at school. Most of the other children don't like him. He is accident-prone.

Sally and Thad continue to seek counseling, which does help. They continue to practice their Lifeskills. They have enrolled Cal in a school noted for its relaxed environment. But they still worry.

What is to become of Cal? And, for another matter, how long can they themselves remain patient, involved, and caring?

Probably Sally and Thad can continue this way for as long as needed. Parenting Cal will remain a challenge. But they are laying down a strong foundation both they and Cal can draw on as Cal grows up. If they can persevere, parenting their "special" child may eventually get easier.

## *Exercises*

1. Put your child's hand in yours and compare sizes.
2. Figure out how many times taller and heavier adults are than your child, and try to empathize with how this probably feels. For example, if your child is two years old, imagine your world populated by people twelve feet tall.
3. At least three times a day for the next six months, hug your child.
4. Think over all contacts with your child during the last twenty-four hours. Make a list with "positive" and "negative" columns of how you must have seemed, seen from the child's perspective. (When you yelled at your two-year-old child, you may have seemed angry. When you praised her, you may have seemed proud. When you raced over as she toddled to the staircase, you may have seemed scared.) Once you complete both columns, reflect on how you are coloring your child's world.

   Also observe the ratio of positives-to-negatives. Is it at or above that magic five-to-one ratio? If not, think about tomorrow—positives you can add and negatives you can avoid.

# 9. Your Teenager

*Let thy speech be better than silence, or be silent.*

*Dionysius the Elder*

Between childhood and adulthood, the teen years are a watershed period. You are concerned about your child's safety and future habits. Your teen is focused on himself: his rapidly changing body; being accepted by his friends; becoming independent; figuring out what kind of person he wants to grow into. He also will be busy searching for values that feel worthwhile and answers to his questions about the meaning of life.

## Vision

Teenage years provide an extraordinary opportunity to set the stage for a lifetime of closeness, health, and happiness. As he breaks away to become his own adult person, you don't overreact, eventually conquering feelings of rejection and fear that your sacrifices are unappreciated. You still provide sufficient structure to encourage your teen to continue to develop ethically and spiritually. Once he grows up, the respect and commitment he absorbed, but often couldn't acknowledge at the time, are given back.

## Do You Recognize Aspects of Yourself?

As those who know them attest, Patrick and Lisa are amiable. They get along well with each other and care deeply for their two children. Patrick, employed by a large company, successfully manages his entire division. Lisa works for a private school, teaching art—arranging to be available when the children need her.

Lately that's less often. Greg comes in from school close to suppertime. During dinner, in between enormous bites he may grunt assent or growl disagreement, but he rarely initiates conversa-

*"Whenever Mother's Day rolls around, I regret having eaten my young."*

©The New Yorker Collection 1994 Edward Frascino from cartoonbank.com. All Rights Reserved.

tion. Immediately afterwards, he disappears to his room. He spends hours talking on the telephone, though his parents don't know how he can carry on a conversation above the din of the nonstop rock music. He is expected to keep his things picked up in the rest of the house and allowed to keep his room any way he wishes. Apparently he wants to cover the floor wall-to-wall with books and clothes.

About six months ago, he let his hair grow longer, fashioning a number of small braids. Recently, he has applied a green rinse.

Patricia, a couple of years younger, likes her parents, and at suppertime happily shares information about happenings. The only person she appears actively to dislike is Greg. She recently has begun to talk on the telephone for hours. And sweet Susan Carrington, her best friend since third grade, now plaits her hair in numerous little braids.

When we first met Patrick and Lisa they wanted to provide the correct mix of structure and freedom for their children. They also longed for a close relationship with them. Practicing Lifeskills has helped them achieve both these goals.

~

Cynthia was the ideal daughter, much smarter and more cooperative than her older brother. When still in high school, she won a governor's medal as one of the outstanding teenagers in Illinois. She became an equally outstanding college student. When in high school and college, she still liked vacations with her parents. During her senior year, she became engaged to someone her parents were lukewarm about. A year later, she broke the engagement. She became engaged again, but broke off that one too—again to her parents' relief. Eventually she did marry in a private ceremony, someone her parents had met only briefly. These days, she rarely visits, though she maintains close contact with her brother.

Though we only knew about the situation later, it's clear to us that Cynthia did not break away from her family as a teenager. When she finally did, at a later stage of her life, the process was much more painful for everybody.

## Knowledge

In colonial times, children worked beside their parents, as junior partners who assumed ever greater responsibilities, yet still deferred to parents. During the nineteenth century, work shifted to outside the home, undermining parental authority and children's usefulness. Early in this century, in acknowledgement of this economic reality, psychologists "discovered" adolescence as a separate and important life stage.

## The Current Situation

In the last decade or so, a growing number of experts have begun to raise questions about the extent to which youth still remain free from career pressures. American middle-class teens today need to prepare for a successful future career. This trend is centuries old, but stakes are higher than ever before and the pathway to success newly arduous. Teens are presented with a wide and possibly bewildering array of career choices, yet cautioned that they need to become broadly skilled. In the future, jobs with high social status and pay will require technical expertise—so today's middle-class teens are under more pressure than previous generations to become highly educated. Yet entry slots—to accelerated high school classes, colleges, and graduate schools—are limited. Once trained, young adults face new rounds of competition for initial jobs and subsequent promotions.

Meanwhile, lower-class teens—children of both the working poor and the unemployed—can envision few realistic career opportunities. A growing number find illegal careers and teenage pregnancy more attractive than alternatives. Thus many teens of all social circumstances may feel almost overwhelmed.

Current opportunities are a problem, too. Continuing a trend already over a century old, today's teens have few ways likely to be attractive to them to be useful and earn adult respect. The partial fiscal dependence of middle-class teens and many young adults has become pronounced.

All of us are vulnerable to manipulation by media images, but probably those most affected are teenagers, whose self-confidence is just developing, fragile. Many teenage girls still feel evaluated on appearance, so they are especially susceptible to judging themselves inadequate. Given the emphasis on near-unattainable physical perfection, it is not surprising that the United States is experiencing an epidemic of eating disorders among young women.

Teenage girls, maybe even more than boys, are subjected to pressures to conform to the expectations of peers, to stifle the verve and curiosity they expressed so naturally when younger. In *Reviving Ophelia,* clinical psychologist Mary Pipher chronicles the shocking tales of young women seen in her practice, girls—more often than society is comfortable acknowledging—manhandled, frequently rejected if too smart, sensitive, plump, or individualistic, who have reacted to the enormous stresses in their lives by resorting to drugs, alcohol, premature sex, violence, even self-mutilation.

At the same time that today's teens are under new career and appearance pressures, they are also subjected to an unprecedented lack of healthy support from family and community. Parents now have less time for their teens than a generation or two ago and community supports are greatly weakened, while the often unhealthy influences of peers, the general culture, and the specialized youth subculture are greater than ever.

Twenty-eight percent of high school seniors recently reported that they had had at least five drinks in a row during the previous two weeks. While drug use in the United States has been on the decline for several years, recent statistics indicate that the number of secondary school students using illicit drugs is increasing, while the number of students who believe that drug use poses a significant risk is decreasing. Data from the University of Michigan's Monitoring the Future study indicates that slightly over one-quarter of high school seniors, almost one-fifth of tenth-graders, and almost one-tenth of eighth-graders reported some use of marijuana in 1993. After declining for several years, the use of other drugs—such as inhalants, LSD, and stimulants—is also on the rise.

In the present-day United States, between 15 percent and 35 percent of all males are arrested before the age of eighteen for a variety of offenses, though the majority only once. More than 50 percent of adolescents admit to theft, 35 percent to assault, 45 percent to property destruction. Sixty percent of adolescents engage in other undesirable antisocial behavior.

## Present Wisdom

Eventually, in their own marriages and with their own children, teens usually mimic their parents' behaviors. How you treat your teen is not only important for today but surely will affect how your teen behaves when grown.

Teens can be too hard to live with for their own good. By the time young people with the highest hostility scores reach college, the world has already closed in on all sides. They have chronically high levels of anger and hostility. They aren't experiencing much satisfaction from relationships with others. They report a greater level of family conflict and increased levels of stress in jobs with supervisors. They also report more negative life events and more frequent day-to-day hassles.

Being *somewhat* difficult to live with is a necessary developmental stage for most teenagers. Teens who don't rebel often catch up later, in their twenties and thirties—frequently with serious repercussions. All of us need to become our own grownup person so that as adults we can question authority and seize initiative. A prerequisite is to stop—as your primary role—being the child in your first family.

Another major area of concern relates to values. Consider the possibility that teenagers need moral and spiritual guidance beyond the levels that most are currently receiving. In *Greater Expectations,* developmental psychologist William Damon sounds the alarm:

> The legacy for many young people includes a cynical attitude toward moral values and goals; a defeatist attitude toward life; a lack of hope in the future; a thinning of courage; and a distrust of others as well as of the self. Above all, many show an absence of purpose, of commitment, of dedication—in a phrase, a failure of spirit.

We are misguidedly protecting our children from the very things they need, in our exclusive focus on their self-esteem and our concern to not overly stress them. "The valid insights of science have been degraded by polarizing debates that have set child-centered approaches in opposition to adult-centered ones." In schools, self-expression is seen in opposition to academic rigor. Within families, some parents never establish guidelines, others discipline too harshly.

Damon tells us that everything we know about children indicates they need structure *and* freedom. He advises parents to emphasize both communication *and* control, respect for the child's perspective *and* commitment to the adult's standards.

In addition, teenagers need moral dimensions to their lives:

> Sparing children from demanding challenges, and in particular from all expectations of service to others, does *them* a disservice, because it robs them of opportunities to establish their sense of competence and the sense of social responsibility. It imparts to children exactly the wrong pair of messages: (1) that they are incapable of accomplishing anything and (2) that they are living only for themselves. The first message belies the child's natural endowment of intelligence, hardiness, and energy. The second goes against the grain of what it means to be a fully developed human.

Despite how teens may sometimes seem to regard their parents, teens really do value parental involvement. Among students aged ten to thirteen, 72 percent of those polled said they would like to talk more with their parents about schoolwork; of older adolescents (ages fourteen to seventeen), 48 percent agreed.

## Effects on Health and Well-Being

Is personality a product of nature or nurture? Both, though scientists do not know enough yet to assign percentages. We can say with confidence that many teens are much like their parents. In one study, for example, family members were given a battery of tests to measure hostility. Mothers scoring high had children who also scored high. The same correlation held for fathers, for certain kinds of anger.

It is axiomatic that living and coping with teenagers can be stressful for both alike. One of our friends recently told us, "I hadn't experienced another year in my life as stressful as when I was fourteen—until the year my daughter was fourteen." It should come as no surprise, therefore, that in a study at the University of Rochester of heart attack victims, internist William Greene found that one of the most common situations cited by patients as precipitating a heart attack was an argument with a teenage child.

It is the teenagers themselves, however, whose health is most

often affected if their antisocial behaviors get out ⊘
and accidents are the most common cause of de⸌
boys. It is normal for teenagers to be impulsive a⸍
tempers—teenagers are the group with the highest record
scores—but many are going over the edge.

It is clearly desirable for teenagers to have relationships that can
help buffer them against the many health problems to which they
are predisposed.

## *Crossover*

For better and worse, and at the same time he or she is breaking
away, your teen will copy many of your behaviors, including—if
you model them—the eight Lifeskills needed for successful living in
the modern world. Model self-confident assertion, for example, and
your teen will have an easier time saying no to drugs, smoking, carrying weapons, and thwarting unwanted sexual advances.

Teens can express themselves more clearly than young children.
They can also carry on increasingly complex conversations. To
establish good communication with your teen means your world
view, interests, even tastes in music will expand.

If you can successfully practice tolerance with your teen, the rest
of the world may seem like a piece of cake!

## *Action*

Well-meaning friends and relatives may be inclined to express concern as your young person acts like the typical, outrageous teenager.
They may even provide suggestions to keep your teen in line—
implying that unless you agree, you are a bad parent.

On the other hand, the unsolicited advice you receive may concern your attempts to establish structure and standards in a society
predisposed to neither. You may be told that you are demanding
too much—given the stresses of modern life—of your teen by
asking him to balance his needs with yours and to contribute to the
welfare of others.

Resist letting others make you question your relationship with
your teen. This is an opportunity to cash in on all of your efforts at
having high self-esteem. You—and your teen—do not need to perform for others. If others interfere too much, practice assertion—
you are the parent, and how you treat your child is your

...ponsibility. You need to do what is best for your teen, not what others think is best.

# Understanding Yourself and Others

Teenagers often are not easily understood, even by themselves. You will probably experience complex emotions as you observe your child traveling—with starts and stops, over bumpy and smooth terrain—the road toward adulthood.

### Identify Your Thoughts and Feelings

Your teen probably will provide many opportunities for you to hone your skills for identifying your negative thoughts and feelings. Harder will be keeping in touch with your positive feelings. As most teenagers are insecure and—despite appearances to the contrary—still need your approval, this is important.

### Evaluate Negative Thoughts and Feelings

Let's say your teen has just behaved in a way you disapprove of. Always identify—and then evaluate—your thoughts and feelings before taking action. What *exactly* has he done? (Try to ignore his scowl.) Then ask these questions.

**I**  *Is this matter important to me?*
Criticizing your teen's appearance and friends uses up potential influence you may prefer to save. On the other hand, he does need to do his fair share of the work of running the household and does need to be civil to other members of the family.

**A**  *Are my thoughts and feelings appropriate, given the facts?*
You may be reliving a sensitive issue between you and your parents, or you may be trying to live out your own dreams. Answering this question may be easier if you have been frequently listening to whatever your teen has to say.

**M**  *Is the situation modifiable?*
Criticizing your teen's friends probably will increase their attractiveness to him. Forbidding makeup means your daughter will apply it after leaving the house. Demanding that your teen be less generally surly, without pointing out a particular behavior, is unenforceable. (Stick to explicit behaviors that could be used as testimony in a court of law!) On the other hand, you can expect him to do his fair share of work, with privileges withdrawn if chores are

not done. Expect to be treated with the respect he would accord a stranger.

WORTH IT  *When I balance the needs of myself and my teen, is taking action worth it?*

You *can* realistically expect your teen to keep curfews, perform chores, and obey family rules, for your own sake and that of your teen. And you can take away allowances, special privileges, and the use of the family car if these expectations are not met. (We suggest you keep any car you pay for in your name.) Be sure that household standards are clearly stated, well understood. Then invest your energy in ensuring that they are consistently followed. Always explicitly state beforehand the consequences of breaking these standards: "If you are late for supper we won't wait. You will have to reheat your cold supper and clean up any resulting mess." "Each day you do not make your bed, your allowance will be docked five percent for that week."

Almost every teen will find some house rules a problem and on occasion will break established guidelines in a major way. Believe us, to deal with your teen, you are going to need to use all the Lifeskills in this book!

Never use physical force with a teenager. Not only is it sure to fail, but soon he'll be as big as you! If you cannot refrain, we urge you to seek counseling immediately.

### Communicate Better and Empathize

Be available when your teen wants to talk. *Listening skills are paramount,* as often speaking to you is a safe way for your teen to talk aloud, *not* a means of seeking advice. It's better with teens most of the time just to listen. Try not to improve on their statements; you'll block the flow. As much as you are able, follow the cardinal mantra: **You are not truly listening unless you are prepared to be changed by what you hear.**

Try to remember what you felt when you were a teen: "I was crushed whenever I felt inadequate, which was frequently."

If you decide to speak about a problem between you, be honest. Share your feelings, with "I" statements, around a specific incident.

"What do you mean I can't go! That's ridiculous! Sam, Molly, Peter, Sally, George, Kristie, Will, Kate, and Janice—their parents are all going to let them go. Myrtle Beach is just another beach. We'll just be swimming a lot. And it wouldn't cost you that much. No one around here ever trusts me to do anything."

You might trust your son to behave responsibly in lots of settings, but not while he's spending a week at Myrtle Beach with paired-off friends, probably illegal I.D.'s, and no chaperone!

> "In my judgment, it's unsafe and inappropriate for a person your age to be in this situation unchaperoned. I would be very worried. So no, I don't trust you in this situation!" [Note the "I" statements and sharing of feelings. Avoid made-up reasons, like "We can't afford it," "The beach will be too cold in May," or "Your grandmother needs you to visit then."]
>
> "What do you mean, you don't trust me? You don't think I'm honest? What kind of mother are you? The other parents trust their kids. I bring home straight A's—don't I deserve a reward?"
>
> "I am very proud that you do so well in school." [An affirmation.] "That does not cancel out that I feel responsible for your well-being and am saying no." [Your feelings of fear for his safety and well-being are important and appropriate. You can modify the situation. When you consider the needs of yourself and your son, assertion is worth it. You therefore are saying no.]

Then there's the matter of letting your teen know your expectations: a few simple rules ("You must be home by 11:30") or only some guidelines ("Always come home at a reasonable hour; call us with information if you are going to be late").

Some teens may be ready to listen to you talk about your own youth and your dreams, realized and unfulfilled. Suitable genuine sharing can increase closeness. One possible topic for a mother might be how she sees herself in relation to changes in the roles of women. Both parents might want to share how they made career choices. Or where their current spiritual journeys are taking them. However, your child needs to be able to count on you as a rock of stability, so don't confide a deep psychological crisis of your own, problems between you and the other parent, or between you and another child.

## Acting Effectively

### Consider Acceptance and Assertion

Especially with teens, aim for a win-win situation (whenever possible). In an article entitled "You've Got Yourself a Deal," Florence Littauer describes a conflict with her junior high school–aged daughter Marita, back in the era of tie-dyed T-shirts and frayed jeans. Florence had grown up in the Depression and could not understand how her daughter could prefer to dress in old T-shirts and low-slung jeans, capable of defying gravity only because of how tight they fit. As Florence was constantly criticizing her daughter's appearance, her daughter persisted in dressing the same way, even distressing new jeans to make them look worn.

One day when Florence drove to the junior high to pick up her daughter, she observed how other girls were dressed. The same or "worse," of course.

She had overreacted, she admitted to Marita, on the way home. She compromised: "From now on, you can wear anything you want to school and with your friends, and I won't bug you about it."

"That'll be a relief."

"But when I take you to church or out shopping or to my friends, I'd like you to dress in something you know I like, without my having to say a word. That means you get ninety-five percent your way and I get five percent. What do you think?"

"Mother, you've got yourself a deal!"

From then on, in the morning Frances gave her daughter a happy farewell. When they went out together, Marita dressed "properly."

This is a classic case of basic Lifeskills in action, to keep a relationship positive:

- getting additional information about how other girls in junior high were dressing
- empathizing with Marita's perspective
- proposing a compromise, which was part assertion, part acceptance

### Emphasize the Positive

Above all, focus on the five-to-one ratio. To an extent you probably will not be aware of at the time, you are sending a positive message when you let your teen know that you love him unconditionally. Also, he will highly value any good opinions you have of him. (He probably won't tell you so—at the time he may not even be aware of this himself.)

Helen Mrosla, a Franciscan nun in Little Falls, Minnesota, taught Mark Eklund in the third grade and again for ninth-grade math. One Friday, after a week of working hard on a new math concept, she sensed the students growing frustrated with themselves and edgy. To stop the growing crankiness, she asked each student to list the names of the others and then write down the nicest thing they could think to say about that person.

© 1994 Lynn Johnston/Dist. by Universal Press Syndicate

FOR BETTER OR FOR WORSE © Lynn Johnston Productions, Inc.
Distributed by United Features Syndicate

Next Monday, Sister Helen gave each compilation to the student in question. Afterwards, she recalls, the students were again pleased with themselves and one another.

Several years later, Mark's parents called Sister Helen, to report he had been killed in Vietnam. After the funeral, Mark's parents pulled her aside. "We want to show you something," Mark's father said, taking a wallet out of his pocket. "They found this on Mark when he was killed. We thought you might recognize it."

Opening the billfold, he carefully removed two worn pieces of notebook paper, that had obviously been taped, folded, and refolded many times.

Mark's classmates started to gather round.

"I still have my list. It's in the top drawer of my desk at home."

"Charlie asked me to put his in our wedding album."

"I have mine too, in my diary."

Another classmate reached into her pocketbook, took out her wallet, and showed her worn and frazzled list. "I think we all saved ours."

## Getting Real

When our daughter Jennifer was a teenager, we could have used more Lifeskills than we possessed at the time. For example, if we had known then what we know now, we would have reacted differently to her speeding ticket.

Jennifer initially told us she needed fifty dollars for an additional team suit to wear when she played on her school volleyball team. We did not give her the money, explaining that we thought her existing outfit looked fine and was after all washable. She would have to earn her own money or use allowance money if she wanted a new outfit. She then was forced to explain why she really needed the money. She had gotten a speeding ticket for driving seventy miles per hour in a fifty-five-mile-per-hour zone. The ticket needed to be paid by tomorrow.

We were shocked and disappointed. Suppose she had been in an accident! How many other times had she driven that fast? Besides that, she had lied about the volleyball outfit to avoid telling us about the incident! And we had an agreement that she wouldn't drive over the speed limit!

Instead of listening first to gather more information, enable Jennifer to share her feelings, give ourselves a chance to calm down, and increase the likelihood that we could empathize with her, both Redford and Virginia began long tirades that we were massively disappointed in her and deeply concerned about her safety, given what she just had done.

Jennifer reacted defensively, saying that we were making a mountain out of a molehill.

We decided to give her the money—she was too busy with schoolwork to get a part-time job, we reasoned—but take away car privileges for a month. Since we lived in the country, this effectively grounded her. Upon notification of what her punishment would be, she burst out sobbing, explaining how terrible life at school was and how driving was the only thing that kept her life from being completely miserable.

Having blown the situation already, we then overreacted in the other direction, reinstating car privileges. In exchange, she agreed to read Scott Peck's *The Road Less Travelled,* an advice book about relationships and spirituality, which we would subsequently discuss as a family. (These "discussions" consisted of a belligerent Jennifer speaking in monosyllables while casting us dirty looks. As this went on, we became belligerent too.)

If we had practiced Lifeskills at the time, we would first have listened to Jennifer describe how she had come to be driving seventy in a fifty-five zone. Limiting ourselves to "umms" and "hmms," we would have let her tell us how bad she felt about what she had done and then explain why she had then lied about the matter. She might even have shared as well how miserably the rest of her life was going.

Once she finished, we would have reminded her of our agreement. In addition, we would have expressed our disappointment that she had lied to us. We would have explained that breaking rules has consequences. We would then have shut up again to let her react to that.

Our suspicion, with hindsight, is that she would have agreed that this matter was serious. We like to think that we could have worked out consequences that discouraged such behavior in the future rather than imposing one punishment and then substituting a too lenient and silly one. Perhaps she could have come up with a plan for repaying our loan for the fine.

~

While Redford was growing up, Redford Sr.—despite problems with alcohol abuse—worked for the migrant labor division of the Farm Bureau, in two counties on Virginia's Eastern Shore. Included in his responsibilities were four "labor camps," where migrant farm workers—following the ripening crops of beans, tomatoes, and potatoes—would live when they stopped on their northward migration. Redford and his parents lived in a modest rent-free house at the largest camp.

From the time Redford Jr. was twelve years old, his father would rouse him from his bed at 3:00 A.M. to sell breakfast snacks in the camp's small store to potato-digging crews, who had to be up this early to get all the potatoes out of the field before the blistering sun rose too high. Since he usually stayed up each evening until midnight or later, he went back to bed about 5:30, after the last customer trudged out of the store. He had to get up again to reopen the store in late morning, when crews returned.

Redford *hated* this job. The summer before his fifteenth birthday—driving age under Virginia law—Redford began to think he had identified a means of emancipation.

The thousand people living at the camp—men, women, children—generated a lot of trash and garbage. At least twice a week—three times when the camp was filled—that garbage had to be collected and hauled to the county dump five miles away. This job was done by Alfred Gunter, the maintenance man. Redford Sr. hired a young migrant crew member to drive the 1936 camp truck—Alfred had never learned to drive—up and down the rows of cabins, while Alfred would muscle the garbage cans onto the truck. When the truck bed was full, they would drive to the dump, empty the cans, then return for another load, making two or three round trips.

Redford thought, "Here is my ticket out of that damn store! As soon as I get my driver's license, I can get Daddy to pay *me* to be the driver. I can sleep till noon, then haul the garbage in the afternoon! And only two afternoons, maybe sometimes three, a week."

So Redford began to lobby his father in a concerted campaign to get the garbage truck driver's job for next summer. Redford Sr.'s first reaction was discouraging: "You don't want this job—you don't realize how nasty that garbage is."

"I don't care. Anything's got to be better than working in that junky store!"

"You may be saying that now, but after two days of hauling garbage I know you'll be back in here, begging to go back to the store."

"I *guarantee* you I'll stick on that job all summer and never ask to get off!"

And so it went, during those waning days of summer. Redford Jr. would even postpone his nap after closing the store in the mornings to stop by the office or track his father down wherever he might be around the camp, so he could plead to be garbage truck driver next summer. He kept up the pressure all fall. With spring, Redford stepped up his campaign, even agreeing to sign a contract that he would stick with his new driving job all summer and never, ever ask to be let off.

Finally, Redford Sr. relented. As the first migrant crews began to arrive late in the spring of 1956, he agreed to make Redford garbage truck driver for the summer.

At first the job was everything Redford had hoped for. He drove, while Alfred loaded the cans and emptied them at the dump.

By the end of June, the garbage stunk worse, as summer's temperatures rose above 90 degrees. The camp population surpassed twelve hundred for the first time. With the camp generating more garbage, it was now taking Redford and Alfred nearly all day to get the garbage to the dump. And the garbage had to be hauled three times a week, instead of two, which cut into the time Alfred needed to complete his other work.

Redford would probably still have been satisfied that he was better off, if Alfred had not thought of buying used 100-gallon barrels to fill up the back of the truck. Smaller garbage cans emptied into larger reservoirs meant fewer trips, cutting work time to a half-day or less each garbage pickup. Unfortunately, this did not end morning work, since waiting until the hotter afternoon would make the smell yet fouler.

The routine of emptying cans into large drums meant that Redford no longer stayed in the driver's seat. Instead, one person carried a can to the truck, passing it up to the other, who would dump it into the large drums, then pass it back.

Having tried to be the one who carried the cans to the truck, Redford had to admit that they were too heavy. On the other hand, Alfred had done hard work all his life—running back and forth with 100-pound loads fazed him not in the least. Redford was now stuck in the back of the truck.

You cannot imagine how nasty, foul, and stomach-turning that garbage was! Even now, forty years later, Redford becomes nauseated when he remembers the back of that truck. When he would dump each can—all too often filled with disgusting, maggot-ridden, decaying animal and vegetable matter—into the large drums, the contents would be mixed and aerated as they tumbled down, stirring and releasing an ungodly mixture of fetid, putrid aromas. Sometimes the goop spattered upward, spraying Redford.

Redford now tried to convince Redford Sr. to let him transfer—

even to the camp store. (Redford did need some job, for money was essential to his growing social life.)

"Daddy, I can't stand this garbage any longer. I want to do something else."

"You can stop right there! I warned you hauling garbage was a filthy job, but you kept after me to let you do it."

"I never realized it was going to be this bad. Besides, none of the other drivers had to get up in the back and dump that [expletive deleted] into those drums!" Redford retaliated, with just a hint of a whine creeping into his voice.

"Alfred's got too much work to do around here to spend three full days hauling garbage. Now don't come whining to me about this again!"

Redford beat a tactical retreat, but only so he could return to fight another day. At first, he tried logic: "I promised I wouldn't try to get out of this, I know, but this job, the way we are doing it now, is entirely different from what I agreed to."

Redford Sr. pulled out the contract. "Do you see anything on this that says anything about what happens to your commitment if the job changes?"

"No, but I say it's not fair to—," Redford began.

"That's enough!" his father stopped him. "You can just quit trying to weasel out of what you promised."

Another retreat. Redford began to use heavier artillery. "Okay, that's it! I quit! I'm not going to haul that damned garbage, and you can't make me!"

Redford Sr. remained long silent before replying. "I may not be able to 'make' you do anything, but the first day you aren't in that truck when Alfred's ready to start will be the last day this summer and fall you get the keys to *my* car."

Redford was stymied. No car for the rest of the summer *and* fall! Even hauling garbage was better than no car!

Desperate, Redford tried one last assault, "I don't have to do what you say! You're nothing but a drunk!"

"That may be, but you promised to stick with the garbage job all summer."

Redford had to quit the field. He sulked and glared—especially on garbage days—but haul garbage he did, all the rest of that long, hot, odoriferous summer.

That summer's battle with his father taught Redford that when you take on any responsibility, you finish the job, even if it means that all summer long you smell like garbage.

Redford also learned that summer, though he wasn't fully aware of it until much later, that his father was not always the drunken failure he had thought. He was an exceptionally strong and loving father, who cared enough for his son to hang in there, despite strong pressures, to see that his son learned an important lesson.

## *Exercises*

1. During the next day, praise your teen for one particular good characteristic or action. (Don't expect your teen to acknowledge your compliment graciously!)
2. The next time your teen tells you something, listen with total attention. Do not interrupt, judge, grill, or offer advice. When he finishes, summarize the content or feelings of what you heard. Then listen again. Once the interchange is over, compare it to other conversations you two have had.
3. How good is your present relationship with your teen? Circle the number that fits best:

|  | Never | Sometimes | Always |
|---|---|---|---|
| I program into my schedule each day time exclusively reserved for talking with my teen. No one else can interrupt or participate. | 1 | 2 | 3 |
| I listen more often than I lecture. | 1 | 2 | 3 |
| Sometimes my teen surprises me by the subjects he's willing to bring up. | 1 | 2 | 3 |
| At least half the time, my teen and I talk about positive subjects. | 1 | 2 | 3 |
| I try to practice empathy. | 1 | 2 | 3 |
| I set realistic and clear guidelines about family expectations and then I enforce these standards. | 1 | 2 | 3 |
| If I am expressing concern about his behavior, I limit myself to a specific incident. | 1 | 2 | 3 |
| I don't yell, belittle, or interrupt. | 1 | 2 | 3 |
| I don't exaggerate the importance of issues. | 1 | 2 | 3 |
| I am prepared to be changed by what I hear. | 1 | 2 | 3 |

| | Never | Sometimes | Always |
|---|---|---|---|
| I'm willing to be persuaded. | 1 | 2 | 3 |
| My teen and I make decisions together. | 1 | 2 | 3 |

Rescore yourself periodically, aiming to tally at least in the upper 20s or low 30s.

4. If you need a further reference for normal problems, we recommend Louise Felton Tracy, *Grounded for Life?: Stop Blowing Your Fuse and Start Communicating with Your Teenager* (Seattle, Wash.: Parenting Press, 1994). A middle-school counselor, Tracy is refreshingly honest about her own experiences as the mother of six.

# 10. Your Parents

Once, long ago, there was a farmer, who, when his father had reached seventy years of age (a very ripe old age in those days), knew the old man was no longer productive and it was time to send him to the barn to live, where he would most certainly die from exposure and lack of food. The farmer, being a gentle sort in his own way, called for his own son and told him to bring his grandfather out to the barn with a meager blanket to cover him. After about fifteen minutes the son returned, carrying half of the blanket. The farmer, aghast at what he saw, asked, "Why did you leave that poor old man out there with only half of a blanket to cover him?" "Father, I felt it important to save some of the blanket for you," the son replied.

*Folktale, retold by*
*Mark A. Edinberg*
*in* Talking with Your Aging Parents

Your parents remain with you always, in memories and feelings, so you need to work through any conflicts with them. If they are still living, you probably can establish at least a reasonable relationship and maybe a good one, based on mutual respect and admiration of your present selves.

## *Vision*

For the remaining days of your parents' lives, you help them have a good relationship with you. Each of them eventually dies, comforted by the intimacy and love between you.

You in turn sense that each parent loves you. You value the good aspects of what they have given you over the years and let them know.

You accept their imperfections. When they behave badly, with assertion you protect yourself. You realize that self-esteem now must come from within. You stop blaming them for your limitations and set about instead taking charge of your own life.

As an infant, you worshipped your parents. As a child, you copied them. As an adolescent, you analyzed and rebelled against them. As a young adult, you at first overcompensated, behaving exactly the opposite of characteristics about your parents you disliked. Now, in maturity, you have freed yourself to act rationally.

Rather than only going through the motions of having a good relationship with your parents—conversations full of dutiful declarations but little substance, in which each of you is only half-listening—you genuinely try to practice *mutual* communication, empathy, acceptance, assertion, and emphasis on the positive. In all cases and especially if your parents are hard of hearing or have limited sight, you hold their hand and hug them a lot. Like relations with your partner and children, this intimate a relationship with your parents may not be easy, but is definitely worth the effort—both for you and for them!

## *Do You Recognize Aspects of Yourself?*

Doug, now twenty-eight years old and living on the West Coast for the last five years, is doing rather well as an engineer, despite the general economic malaise in his field. He spends enjoyable hours with a number of good friends. One Saturday a month he works with City Cares of Seattle, and he has dated a number of women he's met this way. So far, he hasn't encountered anyone he wants to marry, though. He is pleased by a recent promotion at work and the active role he is playing in his community. So this is what being a grownup is like—not bad, actually!

Then why does he revert to being a nineteen-year-old whenever he returns to Houston? His parents ask where he is going every time he leaves their house—and he tells them! His mother invites over this bimbo of a neighbor, obviously trying to fix him up with her—he's insulted that she thinks he would be interested in someone that light-headed! To tell the truth, he's glad when the "vacation"—call that obligation—in Houston is over and it's time to escape back to Seattle.

Elton and Denise's last child is in the tenth grade, so in another three years, they'll be alone together at home for the first time in over two decades. (Anchovies on the pizza at last, spontaneous decision to go to the movies, not preparing breakfast unless they want to, everything picked up in the playroom. Maybe one Sunday afternoon they'll build a fire in the fireplace and lie in front of it with all their clothes off.) They won't in three years be financially free, of course, but they can even see the light at the end of that long tunnel.

Except for Denise's mother. Mom hasn't seemed the same since Dad died last year. She says, "Now don't worry about me, dear." But living alone, anything could happen. Suppose she has a stroke in the night? And why does she look so downcast when Denise visits? Is the look on her face one of accusation? sadness? Or do older faces just look that way?

## *Knowledge*

More people are surviving into old age than ever before. Many Americans live long distances from their parents. A grown child who is a parent himself, part of a two-career household, or the designated family caretaker may feel stretched too thin—with too little time, money, and energy—to be always as available to his parents as he would like.

## The Current Situation

Only about 5 percent of American children see a grandparent regularly. In a 1994 national survey of one thousand children aged eight to twelve, 56 percent of the children said they did not get to spend enough time with their grandparents. In a similar survey of parents the previous year, 53 percent said their children didn't get to spend enough time with their grandparents.

Forty-seven percent of Americans in a national survey regard respecting one's parents as one of the most important values, and 36 percent extend this to taking care of them in old age.

## Present Wisdom

Many current conflicts with your partner, boss, employees, and own children may be re-enactments in part of problems originating in an early troublesome relation with a parent. Touchy areas for you—issues of control, sexuality, an extreme sensitivity to criticism, preferences for extremes of authoritarianism or unlimited freedom, difficulty considering your own needs, whatever—are of course most tender when dealing with the problem parent.

Our relationship with our parents—whether they were absent or present, loving or rejecting, accepting or authoritarian—remains important to us all the days of our lives. Sons and daughters, no matter what indifference they proclaim or how cold they act, always care about their parents and what they think and feel.

You may or may not be able to change your parents' behaviors. You can give it your best shot, and you definitely can change how you react, thereby improving your parents' lives *and* your own.

When your parents die before you, as they probably will, you can feel that you have helped them to achieve a good closure on their life, to have died in a state of grace. And you will feel their continued blessing upon you.

## Effects on Health and Well-Being

Your parents will probably enjoy reasonably good health most of their lives. On any given day, only 5 percent of the nation's sixty-five-and-over population are living in a nursing home. But 25 percent of the elderly will spend some time in that setting, even if it's only for a brief convalescence.

When parents become extremely ill, real problems arise. Psychologist Jan Kiecolt-Glaser and immunologist Ron Glaser report that caretakers of family members with Alzheimer's suffer isolation, a weakening of immunity, and a variety of other illnesses.

## Crossover

Getting along better with your parents can be a practical way of improving all relationships. If you can recognize that your parents accept and love you—imperfections and all—as well as vice versa, your self-esteem will rise. Report your feelings with them, and you probably will be able to report feelings to almost everyone. Practice deep intimacy with your parents; your spouse will then possibly find you more open and trusting.

## Action

If you have children of your own, you already know how highly parents value their children. If you don't, take our word for it! And you know how deeply you care about your parents. From both perspectives, it's important to have this relationship as good as it can be.

# Understanding Yourself and Others

Your present relationship with your parents is overlaid by how you've treated one another in the past. This history of being together sometimes enriches and other times complicates getting along in the current moment.

### Identify Your Thoughts and Feelings, and
### Evaluate Any Negative Ones

With some parents, you may need to walk a delicate tightrope between acceptance of still being treated like a disobedient child and overreacting like an adolescent or young adult to minor slights. When in doubt about your true feelings and best course of action, ask your now–usual I AM WORTH IT questions:

**I**  *Is this matter important to me?*
If you have just been put down or told what to do in an important area of your life, the answer probably is yes. If it concerns an idiosyncrasy of your parent, possibly not. "You never did have an ear for music" is a put-down. "I need to go to the store *tomorrow*" may not be a convenient time for you. On the other hand, only a teen would rise to the bait of debating political or religious views with a parent convinced he or she is right—though you may need to state what your opinions are in order to let the parent get to know the real current you.

**A**  *Are my thoughts and feelings appropriate, given the facts?*
You are a grownup who doesn't need to rebel to prove separateness. Even if you've been mistreated in the past, focus on the present.

**M**  *Is the situation modifiable?*
Remember that you now have a separate life, so you do not always need to get in the last word. On the other hand, if you are being put down in a significant way, you do need to practice assertion, for everyone's well being. And there will be times when you'll need to just say no.

**WORTH IT**  *When I balance the needs of myself and my parent, is taking action worth it?*
What will be the net gain or loss for me and my parent? You probably play a big role in your parent's life, so consider what effect any action you take will have. Yes, you probably can get your aging mother to stop telling you once again about her intestinal problems,

By permission of Johnny Hart and Creators Syndicate, Inc.

but you may decide it's not worth the cost, in terms of her hurt feelings.

### Communicate Better and Empathize

You and your parents have a history of your being the child, they the grownups. It's possible to get so stuck there that no one focuses on the present reality. Begin by trying to report your true present thoughts and feelings to your parents (not past resentments against them or personal matters they don't need to know). Truly listen when your parent speaks and reflect back what you think you heard. Proceed from there to empathize, and in turn tell your parents enough about yourself so they can empathize with you.

When your parent seems not to listen to you, ask, "So that I am sure you understand, what do you think I am saying?" You may want to preface your remarks: "Concerning [whatever], I have had some new experiences in the last few years, and I want to share with you what I'm thinking and feeling right now, so you can know me better."

Parents naturally love their children, and most parents give high priority to getting along well with them. Chances are, your parents will be interested in learning about your life and touched that you are giving them the gift of sharing your true self.

Once your relationship with each parent gets real, you will have an easier time getting out of the forever-child role we all have a tendency to fall back into. Instead, your parents will see the counterpart, grownup person you presently are, which will be healthy for both of you.

# Acting Effectively

No matter how difficult a parent may seem, almost always, deep down, that parent very much wants to have a good relationship with you. So give your parent an excellent opportunity to achieve that!

## Consider Acceptance and Assertion

When you choose to practice assertion, it's especially important to state exact circumstances, speak in "I" statements, share feelings, and make specific requests:

> You have just said that I don't have an ear for music.
> This makes me feel inadequate and irritated.
> I do want our time together to be pleasant.
> So I am asking you not to say that again. Is that something you think you could do for me?

If your parent proceeds to try to argue that, indeed, you don't have an ear for music, gently remind him or her that that is not the issue at hand.

Once you have established your boundaries, you may find yourself less frequently upset by a difficult parent. Gradually you will find yourself increasingly often practicing acceptance of him or her as is. As long as that situation arises from a growth in your self-esteem, not from caving in, it's all to the good!

For some, these suggestions will seem glib, as some parents *are* extremely hard to deal with. In his helpful book, *Making Peace with Your Parents,* psychiatrist Harold Bloomfield singles out martyrs and dictators as special challenges.

If you have mixed feelings toward your parents—and most of us do—Bloomfield suggests the following steps as a means of making peace with your parents:

1. First make a list of specific resentments.
2. Next, in a secluded private place, visualize the parent you've decided to work on, and for at least a half hour, visualize items on that list, describing your feelings. This heavily emotional

experience—if cathartic—can feel overwhelming. At the end of the exercise, visualize yourself and your parents together in a safe place.

3. Then write a letter to each parent, again describing specific resentments and especially your feelings about that. *Do not mail the letter!*

4. Instead, select a friend, spouse, or sibling (not a parent) whom you trust. Instruct this person to listen only. When seated face to face, read your list of resentments or describe your feelings.

5. As a last exercise, divide a piece of paper into two columns. Write in the left column "I forgive you" and in the right column your immediate next thoughts, like "For being so self-righteous." Continue this until you have three "I forgive you's," followed by blanks, because you've run out of things that need to be forgiven.

After Bloomfield's suggested exercises, you may be ready to bring present, true feelings to getting along with a difficult parent. Probably, you will need to read Bloomfield's book. If after that you still feel troubled, by all means seek professional help. Then do your best to establish a real relationship with your parents.

Once you have forgiven for the past a parent who seems to you to have been a martyr or dictator, you still have to deal with that person in the present. Chances are his or her personality remains generally the same and you are going to have to work hard to create a mutually satisfying relationship. Begin by being sensitive to your own feelings, so you know when you are hurt, irritated, angry—whatever. Determine the exact circumstances that occasioned your feelings; then ask your usual I AM WORTH IT questions and choose the best course of action available to you.

### Emphasize the Positive

As part of the realness you've brought to your relationship with your parents and your efforts to emphasize the positive, try to plan some activities with them that aren't part of a regular routine. If you live nearby and share only holiday dinners, try adding a spontaneous buy-the-food-and-eat-together picnic. If you live far away, call at an unexpected time and report what is happening in your life. Send a small present, for no occasion at all. Order a second set of snapshots when you have film developed.

Laughing together creates good bonds. So does having fun together. A relationship can be important without always being solemn. (It helps if in addition to funerals, you celebrate together joyous occasions: birthdays, anniversaries, bar mitzvahs. Even better is getting together for no occasion at all other than to have fun.)

If you have children of your own, you have built-in allies. Here is an opportunity for your parents to see you in a favorable light. Which is it, your good genes or your good nurturance, that makes their grandchildren so wonderful?

Providing access to their grandchildren is an excellent way for you to care for parents; at the same time, you are exposing your children to additional grownups who are apt to esteem them deeply, a win-win way to care about both generations simultaneously.

Hug your parents frequently. Loving touch is especially important when one of your parents has died, leaving the other to live alone.

## When Parents Are Infirm

Middle ground exists between giving up your entire personal life to care for an aging, increasingly infirm parent and distancing yourself from your parents as far as you can. Honestly try to establish your and your partner's comfort level. Then, *within those limits,* make yourself as available as possible. Notwithstanding their increasing infirmities, your parents probably still most want to feel that you cherish and love them.

If your parent is infirm, you may need additional help. As a next step, we recommend the informative and compassionate book by Mark A. Edinberg, *Talking with Your Aging Parents* (Boston: Shambhala, 1987). A psychologist, Dr. Edinberg is director of the Center for the Study of Aging at the University of Bridgeport, Connecticut.

## *Getting Real*

After Redford's father's death, his seventy-two-year-old mother, Virginia, chose to stay on in the house where she and her late husband had lived for almost twenty years. This residence was located only an hour and a half from our home, and she liked our nightly calls, as long as we didn't call during her favorite TV shows or sports events. She also liked weekly visits, as long as we only conversed during commercials if the Atlanta Braves baseball team or any North Carolina college team were playing. Special-occasion extravaganzas, flowers, and candy also were positively received. Otherwise, she preferred to remain alone, where she could watch her TV quiz and sports shows, play solitaire nonstop, take long walks, smoke numerous cigarettes, and dine on TV dinners, without having to readjust her schedule and longtime habits.

Observing her over the years before the death of her husband, listening to her describe how she wanted to continue to live, observing how scheduling upsets made her lose her usually excellent sense of humor, and then trying to see her situation from her perspective resulted in a different stance toward her widowhood than we would have practiced with our other three parents. Over the years, she had been very accepting of us and genuinely interested in our activities. On the other hand, she wanted us to be accepting of her too and to understand that regimentation, too many structured activities, and situations which placed even small demands on her were not what she liked. Over the ensuing nine years when she lived alone, she became more forgetful, but still could drive her car and enjoy life, lived on her own terms.

Then in September 1996, Virginia Sr.'s health began to decline.

As an inkling of problems to come, on her regular Saturday visit, Virginia Jr. noticed that her mother-in-law's knee looked quite inflamed. Virginia felt alarmed. This matter was *important,* her concern was *appropriate,* she ought to be able to persuade Virginia Sr. to go to an urgent care center (*modifiable*), and that trip was clearly *worth it* for everybody. So Virginia Jr. behaved assertively, finally getting her mother-in-law to agree to go. After several hours of waiting at the urgent care center, Virginia Sr. was seen and then referred to the hospital for more tests, followed by treatment with antibiotics. The two Virginias returned home late that night.

Always a casual housekeeper, Virginia Sr. probably had not vacuumed in nine years and had been deeply insulted each time a cleaning service or family help had been mentioned. (No, making an issue of that had not been *worth it!*) Despite the thick tobacco haze and other allergens, Virginia Jr. spent the night to be sure that the medications her mother-in-law had just received had controlled the problem. (This *worth it* question had led to a yes.)

One week later, Redford's mother collapsed in the parking lot in front of the grocery store, suffering what was later diagnosed as a heart attack. At that time, she also suffered numerous small strokes in her brain, which left her short-term memory heavily impaired.

Redford, spelled by Virginia Jr. and Virginia Sr.'s sister Lucille, spent most of the ensuing ten days with her in the hospital, arranging her transfer, when her medical condition stabilized, to a continuing care facility located near us. Redford got to practice his problem-solving skills *a lot* during this period, when it wasn't so clear from one day to the next what level of care—assisted living or full nursing care—Virginia Sr. was going to need.

The next seven months were hard on everybody, especially Virginia Sr. She was appalled by her loss of memory. When occasionally she would notice, she resented her loss of freedom. Still relishing her cigarettes—Virginia and Redford turned over that decision to her doctor, who limited her intake to five a day—she always managed to wheedle the nurses out of more than her allotment.

Once the initial crisis was over, the general approach outlined in Chapter 6 helped us to decide how much time to devote to being with her, without feeling guilty that we weren't doing enough. We each went by for a visit once a day. While we cut back on travel, whenever we started feeling full of remorse when we were away, we would ask the *I AM WORTH IT* questions, get some noes, and then practice deflection to get over our negative feelings about not being there for her that day. (Guilt is a stuck, actionless—and therefore useless—emotion, unless it leads directly or indirectly to changed behavior.)

Communication with Virginia Sr. actually sometimes was quite satisfactory during this time. We needed to do most of the talking much of the time. We explained her medical situation to her over and over, which helped Virginia Sr. to become oriented, at least temporarily. We read and reread her cards to her. We repeated previously expressed thanks for the best aspects of our relationship with her over the years. Listening on our part was mostly nonverbal—did she look comfortable or in pain? Was she agitated or calm? She still maintained her sense of humor over the compromised state she was in, and we would sometimes laugh together over that.

When it came to increasing the "positives," we tried to remember to hug her a lot and to hold her hand.

It was too late to get many additional benefits from all of the pictures and the scrapbook we are going to recommend at the end of this chapter.

We planned for her to come along on holiday outings, though she could only last a short time before becoming mentally and physically frazzled. We ended up that way too, but the sacrifice seemed *worth it*.

Our own relationship suffered. Redford, especially, felt strained and helpless, which gave him less resources for other relationships. (During this period, he broke his wrist going after an impossible tennis shot and was involved in an automobile accident, which was his fault.) Finally, we just hunkered down. We began to recognize that we often were not practicing Lifeskills with each other and probably weren't likely to improve at that very much, as long as so much of our emotional energy was going toward Virginia Sr. Easier to declare a moratorium on "improving our relationship." Practicing empathy and acceptance, we tried to give each other some slack, usually choosing acceptance over assertion.

Then Virginia Sr. broke her hip. In consultation with her physicians, we made the decision not to operate, because, given her tenuous circulation, she might suffer even more brain damage. Medications, including steroids injected into the hip, were prescribed to control her pain. Her hip still hurt, especially in the last minutes before the next pill. Helplessly observing this felt awful. Looking back, we think not operating was the better—or less worse—decision, but we are not sure. (Lifeskills don't solve all dilemmas!)

She died soon thereafter, probably of a recently diagnosed lung cancer. In retrospect, we do not feel bad about how we had treated her or each other during her illness. But Virginia Sr.'s ill health only lasted for seven months. We did not face the choice of keeping her in her own community or relocating her near us. We had already ourselves been married for almost thirty-four years, so we could afford some "down time." We both thought of her as our parent. Given different circumstances, we might have needed to come to different accommodations. For one example, we probably would have needed to take our relationship out of dry dock and to work on increasing the positives directed toward each other.

## Exercises

1. If your parents live nearby, invite them to an evening out. If they live far away, write them a real letter, enclosing several snapshots.
2. Make a list of aspects of your upbringing you genuinely value. Select one item each month and tell your parent several times during that month how much you applaud some specific thing he or she did for you.

   *Easy case, with a giving, affirming parent:* "Remember how crushed I was in the fourth grade when I didn't make the softball team? I really appreciate that you then played pitch and catch with me every evening, so my pitching arm would strengthen and I would drop the ball less often. Playing softball felt so important, and you helped a lot."

*Difficult case, with a parent who has been a prickly personality, inflicting much harm along with the good:* "Today some of my friends with crooked teeth are having a lot of cavities and gum disease. Your willingness to pay those orthodontist bills really has saved me a lot of later pain and aggravation. Thank you."

3. Consider giving each parent a scrapbook as a Christmas or Hanukkah present, in which each close relative, children included, writes up a positive reminiscence ("Grandpa, remember that cold Saturday you took me to the zoo?"). Snapshots make a wonderful addition.

4. Some schoolteachers can be persuaded to give students the assignment of interviewing an older relative and then writing a short biography of that person—complete with snapshots. The process is a valuable history lesson for the student and an excellent opportunity for the separate generations to get to know each other. If author and subject get to keep copies of the biography, so much the better!

5. The next ten times you see your parents, give them hugs. (If your parent lives with you, substitute "once a day for the next six months.")

# 11. Your Friends

A friend is someone you feel comfortable calling on the telephone, even when you have nothing to say.

*Anonymous*

The benefits of friendship are obvious, behaving well being easiest in friendships. With friends (excluding roommates), we don't share finances, chores, or perhaps painful memories of past wrongs. Contact is limited, so we only need to behave well for short stretches. Yet you still can easily care about a friend, since you probably share interests, world view, and a history of past experiences together.

## Vision

Through time spent yapping on the telephone—or better yet, face-to-face—you and at least one good friend relish laughing together each day.

Friends usually share your interests, and you spend time with them at the same time you are enjoying favorite activities. Both the activity and friendship are enhanced.

Friends provide practical support. In addition to enhancing your enjoyment of work, companions there make a commute less onerous, inform you about pending decisions and re-shufflings, assist you with projects when you are snowed under, give you an opportunity to expand your skills when you help them with projects, and provide an initial sounding board for new ideas.

Intimate friends know you well enough to sense what you are feeling—sometimes before you can—and vice versa, an aid in identifying thoughts and feelings. You two can reach out to meet expressed or unexpressed needs. When you or your confidant lose a family member through illness, death, or divorce, the other consoles the bereaved.

# *Do You Recognize Aspects of Yourself?*

Our daughter Jennifer, busily employed as a research assistant, has two sons, ages one and three. Pam, a bank officer, is the divorced mother of two daughters, ages four and six. Pam and Jennifer met three years ago, when Jennifer and her husband, Mel, applied for a loan to buy a house. They began to see each other first occasionally, then often. Pam lent Jennifer maternity clothes, a big savings. They supported each other on long walks preparatory to starting an exercise program, pushing younger children in strollers, while supervising the two older ones. The women trade baby-sitting, giving each a chance to shop alone. Sometimes Pam leaves her two daughters with Jennifer when she has a date.

Their friendship is not limited to mutual services. Jennifer and Pam went to the beach together once. They and their children occasionally get together on the weekend for breakfast. Their enjoyment of life is enhanced because of their friendship.

❧

Lorraine arrived in Philadelphia six months ago. She and her husband of twenty years relocated because of his promotion, and she hasn't found a satisfactory new job yet. Most people in her new neighborhood work, so she hasn't gotten to know neighbors well. She and Paul don't belong to any religious community. She writes and calls old friends, but she misses day-to-day, face-to-face contact. For the first time in twenty-five years, Lorraine is experiencing deep-enough depression that recently she began weekly psychotherapy.

## *Knowledge*

When Americans move around the country, they leave behind former friends, ties which may have taken years to cultivate. If they juggle a job and family, their unscheduled time is scarce.

## The Current Situation

More than ever before, middle-class Americans today need close friends as a kind of adoptive family. As you will recall from Chapter 1, the relatives of present-generation Americans are likely to live far away, thus being unable to help with kids on a week-to-week basis or be there during those small crises inevitable in every household. Yet parents of the current generation probably work outside the home and need such social support. Single parents obviously are especially needful, as are the large number of families who face ever-tighter budgets. Who is to care for you when you get the flu? Where can Johnny go if both Mom and Dad have to work late one evening? For many of us, the answer—if there is to be any positive answer at all—must be friends.

## Present Wisdom

As families and communities deteriorate for some people, friendships become especially important, since having another person to count on may make the critical difference between feeling totally isolated and feeling cared about.

## Effects on Health and Well-Being

Numerous studies document the proposition that having good friends improves health. We already have mentioned the large study in Alameda County of adults who were asked a battery of questions and then re-contacted later. Among the questions initially asked were "How many close friends do you have?" "How many relatives do you have that you feel close to?" "How often each month do you see these people?" When answers are considered together, for all ages and both sexes, people who reported having fewer friends and relatives and/or who saw them infrequently were much more likely to be dead nine years later. The health advantages of social support held true, even when initial health status was considered.

Recall the study of Duke heart patients, where Redford and his colleagues found that those with no one to confide in—neither spouse nor friend—died within five years three times more frequently than those with a spouse or other confidant.

Building on the initial work of psychologist James Pennebaker, many other researchers have provided individuals with new opportunities to express themselves and then measured the effect on their health of doing this. These scientists have documented that people who recount previously unreported intimate thoughts and feelings to at least one other person subsequently enjoy better health than individuals who do not express themselves in this way. This holds true whether the confider speaks or writes, and whether the confidant is a friend or stranger.

## *Crossover*

Most other intimate relationships benefit from good friendships, as you will be shored up by the shared emotions, interests, and practical help.

Your self-esteem always rises when someone likes you.

When you share enjoyable activities with another couple, you increase the number of good times in your marriage. Also, you get to observe which of their behaviors succeed in improving their marriage, which ones fail.

When you socialize with another couple with children the age of yours, you avoid the expense and effort of finding a sitter. You'll get a chance to watch in action another set of parents. You'll probably feel good about how you're handling some aspects of parenting. Chances are, you'll pick up some useful hints in other areas. Both couples possibly may grow to care about each other's children and hence become an additional source of social support for them.

## *Action*

Friendships are to be savored. As often as possible, make the actions connected with them pleasurable.

## Understanding Yourself and Others

Friendships provide excellent opportunities for developing your Lifeskills: identifying your thoughts and feelings; evaluating negative thoughts, negative feelings, and options; communicating better; and empathizing to understand others' behavior.

### *Identify Your Thoughts and Feelings*
The process of talking to a supportive friend about life situations sometimes can help you to become aware of previously unidentified thoughts and feelings. While the conversation probably doesn't officially lead you to ask your I AM WORTH IT questions, often the answers to them will come up spontaneously. When this happens, your friend becomes a good sounding board for helping you to clarify, then evaluate critically, exact circumstances and options.

### *Communicate Better and Empathize*
You can usually easily concentrate on what a friend is saying, interested in the subject at hand. Even when you can't, you care about

*"Oh, Stanford, I'm touched. Trust is <u>such</u> an important first step."*

© The New Yorker Collection 1993 Charles Barsotti from cartoonbank.com. All Rights Reserved.

that person, which makes listening easier. When your turn comes to speak, you have an easy-to-talk-to, usually supportive audience. When reporting thoughts and feelings even to close friends becomes difficult, you know you have a problem, either with the particular situation you are keeping to yourself or with speaking up.

A conversation with a friend provides the perfect setting to practice speaking up: Use "I" statements; be specific; report feelings and thoughts. Since this situation is relatively easy, stretch as much as you can, to improve communication. Once you're comfortable in this supportive situation, try the same approach elsewhere.

Listening also is relatively easy, since you and your friend are apt to be similar in ways important to you both. Receive compliments graciously. When you don't, you insult your friend's judgment!

If either speaking up or listening to a particular friend frequently is hard, try to determine if the problem is yours, or if your friend needs to be aware of something that's being ignored.

Once you each have spoken and listened, you both should be able to take the next step, of empathy. After all, you know each other well enough to figure out where the other is coming from!

## Acting Effectively

Since friendships provide you with a safe setting and an audience predisposed to accepting and liking you, try practicing your new skills here as often as you can.

### Consider Acceptance and Assertion

Practicing acceptance usually is relatively easy also, as you presumably choose as friends persons you generally approve of. If not, you need to examine the pattern of your relationships, to see if you are usually judgmental or choosing friends unwisely. You also need to find additional friends, people whose actions generally meet with your approval.

Friendships provide built-in testing grounds for assertion, though usually of the variety of asking for a favor rather than trying to get the friend to stop some behavior. Try asking for what you need in both simple *and* complex ways. Your needs probably will get met, and you will gain important experience. Men and women probably will go about this with distinct styles. You'll have no trouble identifying the sex of these speakers!

> "May I borrow your shawl this Saturday to wear to Tom's wedding?"

> "Looks like the boat will hold us too!"

> "I must address 300 envelopes before next Monday. When I think about it I get tired. If I fixed a special lunch for us, would you come over to help? I know this means that I need to volunteer to help you the next time you're in a jam."

> "Tom dumped his desk onto mine. I'm furious, but you know how he can't handle refusals. Would you take over the Smith project?"

Unlike relatives, you *choose* friends. When a friendship isn't working you can apply all the Lifeskills you've learned to improve it. When you've done your best, yet problems persist, you have the option of withdrawing.

### Emphasize the Positive

You may find you exceed the suggested five-to-one ratio with good friends. (If you don't, examine yourself, as well as choices of friends.) Your biggest challenge may be creating time for current friendships to thrive. To start you thinking, here are some possibilities:

- Arrange your schedule to spend time with a friend during an activity you both would in any case be engaged in (at your child's school, your church, exercising, eating lunch). You'll like the activity more and probably perform better—or at least digest your food better!

- Invite a friend along to share the community activity we recommend in Chapter 13. This could be either in connection with volunteer work or through your church, synagogue, or temple.
- Share a favorite book with your friend.

Sometimes, an important friendship can become strained and you would like to get back to the good feelings you and your friend formerly had toward each other. At times, this estrangement results from a specific unpleasant incident or a misunderstanding. When that happens, treat the situation as you would any other log entry. What are the *exact circumstances* that created the strain in your relationship? What are you *thinking* and *feeling*? Once you determine this, ask your *I AM WORTH IT* questions to find out if you want to try to get over your negative feelings or, alternatively, to take some action to undo the damage.

Laverne, one of our workshop participants, reported to one of us in a private conversation an incident from the previous weekend where subsequent application of Lifeskills made a big difference. Laverne adored her son and daughter, despite their being "ne'er-do-wells" in some people's eyes. She also adored her friend Lonna, who was outspoken, witty, and adventuresome, a nice balance to her own reserve.

Needing to tell someone, Laverne had described to Lonna the latest scrape her daughter had gotten into. All she had wanted was a little sympathy. Well, to tell the truth, she really had hoped that Lonna would declare the situation not her daughter's fault.

Instead, Lonna expressed her outrage at the daughter's behavior. Worse yet, she advised Laverne that she should attach consequences to such disgraceful conduct. Laverne didn't say anything at the time, though as far as she was concerned the rest of the day spent together was ruined. During all of the week, she waited for Lonna to call to apologize. That didn't happen.

"So the exact facts of the situation are that you reported the scrape your daughter was in, expecting support. Instead, Lonna reacted by becoming outraged?"

"Yes. And I had thought she was such a good friend."

"What else are you thinking?"

"I think Lonna is inconsiderate, judgmental, a poor listener, and meddlesome."

"And what are you feeling?"

"Angry. Hurt."

"Anything else?"

"Well, lonely too."

"These are negative feelings, all right. So ask your *I AM WORTH IT* questions."

"It's important. I think what I am feeling is appropriate. I don't know if I could change the situation or not."

"What is it you want to change? Lonna has said what she has said."

"Maybe she didn't mean it. Maybe I misunderstood her. Maybe she didn't realize that what I really wanted was her support, not advice."

"Had you told her before describing the scrape that what you wanted was support, not advice?"

"Well, no."

"So she might have responded differently if she had known what you wanted. In fact, might she be responding differently now, if she knew how upset you were at her?"

"Well, yes."

"Would getting this misunderstanding between you cleared up be worth it, from your and her perspectives."

"Yes."

"So what is to prevent you from inviting her over, describing to her how her remarks made you feel, and asking her if next time she could just listen?"

"Nothing."

Of course, Laverne also could have practiced empathy, to see how different the situation may have seemed from Lonna's perspective. But communication probably will succeed, and Laverne and Lonna can get back together. Maybe, even most of the time, the communication between them will be better than before.

Here are some strategies for developing new friendships:

- You and your partner can get together with another couple and both sets of children. This does not, of course, give anyone undivided attention, but the children may have a good time too, if well matched in ages and interests.
- Try to develop real friendships at work.
- Consider starting a reading group or a group that meets regularly to report on and discuss dreams. (If you are thinking about setting up a dream group, we recommend reading Jeremy Taylor's *Where People Fly and Water Runs Uphill* (New York: Warner Books, 1992).

We acknowledge finding friends sometimes requires considerable effort.

If you are a new parent who has chosen to stay home and whose previous friends were mostly from work, you may suddenly feel isolated. Consider baby-sitting co-ops. On-site child care at community interest associations or religious groups provide another option.

Being single can be lonely, recent divorce devastating. If your partner is gone and you two spent a lot of time with other couples, you may experience diminished opportunities, in addition to the very painful loss of your spouse. A partner who had spent most free time with a now-lost mate also will need to branch out. Or maybe you have always been by yourself, and this is a problem for you because you want to feel connected with others. Whatever your circumstance, if you feel disconnected, try to get to know better someone in a similar situation.

Also focus on the old standbys—community activities and a religious group. Or join an organization focused around an interest you share—a choir, a sports club with team sports, a group that fixes and eats gourmet meals. Check the weekly supplement in your newspaper or in throwaway magazines for a listing of community activities (from nature hikes to skydiving to quilting circles to stamp-collectors clubs).

If you are shy and need friends, practice your new skill of speaking up. Also, invite persons you meet and like to an additional activity.

Sometimes seeming-shyness may mask underlying depression. A person may feel too down to get out into the community. The resulting lack of social contacts may lead to deeper depression. In such a case, professional help is needed: a trusted religious figure may be a good start. When this is not enough, seek out a mental-health professional.

## Getting Real

Frankly, we can't illustrate very well systematic application of Lifeskills to friendships—except problem solving to find time and ways to be together—because friendships seem usually to glide along without much effort required. Nonetheless, friendships are a wonderful illustration of Lifeskills in action. Often friendships provide you with all the benefits of social support, without much fine-tuning required.

Since we have relocated five times, we share day-to-day contacts with some current friends, yet lack shared histories going back to childhood with these people. Other friendships are the opposite, like Virginia's friendship with Sandy.

Virginia met Sandy in the eighth grade, when both attended the same countywide high school and spent much of their time in the same group of girlfriends. During college, they kept in touch, while concentrating on new college friends. After college, when Virginia resided in Rhode Island and Sandy in Connecticut, Virginia would hitch a ride home to Virginia with Sandy, who had a car. Virginia introduced Sandy to some of Redford's friends and, since she had an apartment, invited her to visit some weekends. Sandy came home for Redford and Virginia's wedding. She gave a party beforehand, but had to get back to her job before the day of the wedding.

Virginia served as a bridesmaid when Sandy got married. They corresponded through Christmas notes and occasional letters. Sandy's sons were just a bit younger than Virginia's daughter. While Sandy's husband was serving in Vietnam, she and the older boy visited the Williamses in Washington, D.C., exchanging advice on child rearing and catching up on mutual friends.

Sandy moved to Maine, Virginia to North Carolina. Sandy got divorced, then remarried; she had another son and then divorced a second time. She returned to her girlhood community. When Virginia came to see her parents, she would visit Sandy and Sandy's parents as well. Sandy and her boys would in turn visit in North Carolina, as a way station on longer trips.

Virginia's parents became more frail. Sandy would visit them, bringing baked goods and cheer. Virginia and Sandy would occasionally talk on the phone.

Sandy came down for Virginia's fiftieth-birthday party.

Both women were now older. Less time spent talking about kids, more about personal and spiritual matters. The friendship deepened.

They supported each other through family funerals. Now occasionally Virginia stays with Sandy—there is no room at her mother's retirement community. Planning together a sleep-over for the women from their little high school class, Virginia will provide the place to stay and the meals, Sandy will contact everybody and set up the arrangements.

Meanwhile, Sandy's son Piet has begun a career as a cartoonist. You will find one of his cartoons, designed especially for this book, in Chapter 13.

Obviously this friendship would have been different—and more sustaining on a day-to-day basis—if we'd lived in the same community. Yet observe how closely it fulfills all the definitions of social support:

- a sense of being accepted by others
- the support believed to be available, if needed
- support actually received
- the recipients' perceptions of that support and their satisfaction with it

## *Exercises*

1. Write down a list of your good friends. Next ask how often you have connected with them during the last (typical) week. Are you averaging one or more contacts per day with at least one of them?
2. If you discovered in Exercise 1 that you have only limited interchanges with friends, ask yourself if you can take some simple, easily doable steps to increase the frequency with which you touch base with the friends listed.
3. If you still need extra friends, review the potential activities suggested under *"Action"* in this chapter. Next make a brainstorming list of potential actions *you* could take to develop additional friendships. Rank the items on your list; then select a specific action to be taken next week. Repeat this process once a week for a month, each time deciding on some new action.

# Part IV

# Acquaintances

## CLOSE TO HOME

### BY JOHN MCPHERSON

"Joyce, get that idiot who gave the
stress-management seminar on the phone!"

CLOSE TO HOME © 1997 John McPherson. Dist. by UNIVERSAL PRESS SYNDICATE.
Reprinted with permission. All rights reserved.

# 12. Your Coworkers

To love what you do and feel that it matters—how could anything be more fun?

*Katharine Graham*

The trouble with a rat race is that even if you win, you're still a rat.

*Lily Tomlin*

Most of us spend a large portion of our time working—so we should make work as fulfilling as possible, as well as keeping it in fitting balance with the rest of our life.

## Vision

You like your work.

While not necessarily lavish, your recompense suffices to meet your needs, especially now that you no longer substitute things for relationships nor use possessions to shore up self-esteem.

You cast off job problems once you walk out that office door. The balance you've struck between challenging work, time alone, and leisure spent with family, friends, and the wider community feels right.

You and your boss communicate freely. In a mix of assertion and acceptance, each speaks and listens with empathy. You have equally good relationships with those you supervise. You and coworkers help and support each other. When you survey work relations as a whole, you conclude that you feel part of a team.

At all life stages, you continue to learn and grow on the job.

You help to shape the workplace.

You usually put in good effort and use all of your faculties to the fullest. As a result, you contribute a great deal.

This in some way makes the world a better place: You are not only carrying out assigned tasks, but significantly involved in something important.

## *Do You Recognize Aspects of Yourself?*

At first, Miriam loved her job as administrative coordinator for the battered women's center. She felt helpful and liked the responsibility of her new position. But that was thirteen years ago. Now she could perform her job with one eye closed. She seems to spend endless hours typing. The truth is, she's bored. Well, maybe a lot of the problem is the young, hot-shot new director, who says she wants to initiate vast changes, but then doesn't follow through. Miriam is forty-five years old and not pleased by the prospect of another twenty years in her present position.

⌒

Sam would never savor the luxury of being bored. He switched companies two years ago, a major promotion for him. Now his present company is downsizing, and all the employees in sales worry about losing their commission rate or even their jobs. Sam is fifty-two years old, and way up on the pay scale. What can he do to make himself indispensable? Is his relationship with his supervisor satisfactory? How about his relationships with those under him? He tries to make a joke about having to go on welfare, but he's anxious. In truth, he's feeling insecure about the future and very tired.

⌒

Lloyd, a junior in college, needs to choose his life's work. He began in engineering, but discovered he disliked the lack of contact with people. One night he had to take a friend to the emergency room and found himself really turned on by the idea of becoming a doctor. But now that he's seen the projection figures for the number of physicians and taken several pre-med courses, he's no longer so sure medicine is what he wants to do. There's the ministry, but the multiple demands, relatively low compensation, and need to relocate any family he might have a series of times makes that problematic too. Advertising looks exciting, but will that be satisfying? What's he going to do with his life?

⌒

Ralph expected to work fifty- to sixty-hour weeks at the *beginning* of his career. But now that he's a director, he's still working those hours. A stack of message slips lies beside his phone—he has come to hate the color pink. Another pile of letters requires answers. But his calendar indicates six appointments or meetings today. Excited by what he's doing, he finds it stressful, too. And he is interested in making more time for other, personal aspects of his life. What are his priorities? He's not sure.

# *Knowledge*

## The Current Situation

Americans are working longer hours, an average increase from 40.6 hours per week in 1973 to 48.8 hours per week for men and 41.7 hours for women by 1993. Workers in better-paying, more prestigious jobs on average put in longer hours still. Entrepreneurs in small businesses are now working 57.3 hours a week; professionals, 52.2 hours a week; male executives 54 hours a week; female executives, 56 hours a week. Workers with incomes over $50,000 a year spend 52.4 hours a week at work. On average for all workers, domestic responsibilities take up sixteen additional hours per week for men, while women add on twenty-seven more hours.

Though 75 percent of children are now brought up in two-job households—a recent development—many, perhaps most, Americans do not have opportunities for paid parental leave or even unpaid parental leave beyond six weeks; flextime; shared jobs; opportunities to work at home; or time to participate as volunteers and managers in child care centers. How can they successfully juggle both job and family?

Despite longer hours and the entry of large numbers of women into the workforce, the real income—the goods and services that can be purchased with a week's pay—of families with children has dropped in the last couple of decades, especially for families in the lower two-fifths of the income distribution, and most especially for the very poor. (Almost 50 percent more children live in poverty today compared to fifteen years ago.)

Sixty-four percent of workers in one recent survey reported experiencing poor communication between management and workers, the biggest complaint. Seventy percent of workers polled experienced stress on the job.

Unfortunately, a growing number of jobs are now routinized, commercialized, and bureaucratized—with no self-pacing or self-initiated improvements possible. There's little opportunity sometimes to be face to face with the person helped, or even ever to see the final product. A telephone service representative usually operates under rules that rigidly limit possible responses to an irate customer. He—or usually she—must sit and take it. And then receive another call. And another. Meanwhile, her performance is perhaps being monitored by random electronic eavesdropping. Three wrong responses and she's fired.

Bosses endure different pressures. Some CEOs face newly fierce international competition. Other executives worry their business may become outdated. In the future, will more citizens scan the Internet instead of *The Washington Post*? Is downsizing inevitable? If profits plummet, will the executive be able to weigh the needs of stockholders and employees fairly, without getting fired?

## Present Wisdom

Today, most workers, especially managers, need to be able to get along with others in order to perform well. The summary study of *New York Times* reporter for behavioral and brain sciences Daniel Goleman emphasizes the importance of what he entitles *emotional intelligence* to success in most aspects of life. In addition to his focus on intimates and health, Goleman devotes a full chapter to business,

*"Hank, when you're finished firing this gentleman I have some rather unfortunate news for you as well."*

© The New Yorker Collection 1996 J. B. Handelsman from cartoonbank.com. All Rights Reserved.

arguing that succeeding in a growing number of jobs depends on working well with others. Many projects today are too complex to be completed by any single individual, even if exceptionally talented, Goleman argues, so teamwork is essential. The ability to motivate others, network, value diversity, and share control are no longer considered just niceties, but increasingly recognized as *necessary* business skills.

### Effects on Health and Well-Being

A Chicago study sampled twenty-three hundred representative adults to determine the problems and challenges in their lives. Among the top ten life stressors, five concerned work—being fired or laid off; becoming unemployed because of health problems; being demoted; losing a job to take up homemaking; and having depersonalized work relations.

Certain jobs are quite stressful. A job that couples boring work with routinized high demands—with little control over how these demands are met—places a worker at risk of becoming fatigued, anxious, and depressed. That's not all the bad news. Two pioneers in workplace health, industrial sociologist Robert Karasek and physician of industrial medicine Tores Theorell, have demonstrated that jobs with high demands *and* low control are hazardous to physical health, especially to coronary well-being. Their research suggests that people in high-demand/low-control jobs have a two to three times increased risk of heart disease. After they adjusted for known physical risk factors—age, education, race, region, urban/ non-urban residence, and self-employment—the risk remained about 1.5 times greater than for other workers.

The research of Redford and his colleagues at Duke shows that women who report high demands *and* low control in their jobs are more depressed, anxious, and angry than those reporting lower strain. They also report lower levels of social support.

A number of other studies cited by Karasek and Theorell yield the similar finding that stressful workplaces can be unsafe. Among Swedish construction workers, any job difficulty or important job change within the year imposed a 1.6 times excess risk of a heart attack over the next two years.

Overwork appears to be hazardous also. In the United States, Bell Telephone workers who attended college at night, in combination with full-time work, also were at increased risk for heart trouble. In the Framingham, Massachusetts, study female clerical workers who had at least three children at home were much more prone to heart attacks.

In a comparison of two Belgium bank organizations, workers in the bank with a less hectic work pace and greater employment security had fewer heart attacks. In a United States study, workers at Western Electric who reported high job pressures subsequently had more heart attacks, regardless of conventional risk factors.

German sociologists Johannes Siegrist and Karen Siegrist have yet another framework that correlates with worse health: High effort/low rewards. The worker who tries hard, but is "stuck"— with little possibility of advancement—is in a frustrating position, indeed. Small wonder that on average, people in "stuck" jobs are less healthy.

## *Crossover*

Problems at work spill over. Not just obvious ones, as when your boss yells at you and you in turn yell at your kids. Suppose your job doesn't use all your skills; eventually you won't have those skills.

Injury doesn't stop there: The less challenged you are at work, the less variety of leisure activities you probably enjoy. Researchers have found that workers who aren't challenged limit their leisure activities to only one out of seven possible areas (culture, sports, entertainment, religion, home activities, and political activity as leaders or participants in mass actions). This narrowing of interests holds true, despite controls for a variety of demographic and social class measures.

Monotonous work leading to monotonous leisure clearly is a problem for the unlucky worker with the stressful, dead-end job. But it's also a problem for the rest of us. What kind of spouse, parent, neighbor, or citizen is such a created dullard inclined to be? Think of the myriad ways that affects you!

Working longer hours means less time off. This affects every other relationship. Will there be time each day to be alone, simply listening to one's inner self? Will there be time to be—we mean *truly* be—with your partner? A marriage that's not being worked on—time sharing thoughts and feelings, time giving and getting, time devoted to ensuring the ratio of positives-to-negatives exceeds five-to-one—is probably getting worse. Even a good sex life, especially for women, requires time for pillow talk, as an accompaniment. Many surveys indicate that most women prefer intimate talk first, extended foreplay second, and intercourse last.

Work affects relationships with children and vice versa. Two in three working parents say they spend more than enough time at work, while only one in three says the time spent at home is the right amount. If asked to choose, three-quarters of the employees surveyed said they would pick a child's event over an important function at work; two-thirds said the choice would be easy. Fifty-four percent of moms have turned down a promotion so as not to cut into time spent with children, while 29 percent of dads have done so. To the extent that management positions are perceived as associated with extra demands, our society may thereby be excluding from management parents who put families first, hence eliminating disproportionately many of the young and those responsive to the needs of others.

And how about time for parents? friends? connections beyond our circle of intimates?

But enough of such a negative focus—for work benefits can carry over as well. By working, we earn a living. We also perform useful tasks that benefit others and help to get the work of the world done. In addition, the right number of work hours, high decision latitude, supportive social connections at work, and engagement devoid of stress, with opportunities for skill enhancement, have been found in several studies to be healthful, to raise self-esteem, and to be life-enhancing.

Research has also demonstrated that among employed mothers, those satisfied with their jobs are better parents.

Lifeskills do help workers to cope better. Redford and his colleagues at Duke recently found that women workers who received training in stress management skills, like those described in this book, were more prone to report afterwards higher levels of social support across the board than women who attended lectures on stress or who got no intervention at all.

## Action

In terms of applying your Lifeskills, we encourage you to be more cautious in the workplace than with family or friends. Monitor your feelings, evaluate carefully, and plan out any action before proceeding further.

## Understanding Yourself and Others

If you are not already concentrating on other relationships, try for one week to devote your thoughts and feelings log to work. This will help you clarify how you are feeling during interactions with

your boss, your subordinates, and other coworkers. Are any relationships especially satisfying? problematic? Can you detect patterns
in how you respond? Are your responses leading to results you
want? Can you relate trials or triumphs during the workday to how
you behave after-hours?

## Identify Your Thoughts and Feelings

This particular morning Robert, a researcher in the marketing division of a telecommunications company, has something to write up
in his log. But first he fumes that his immediate supervisor, Suzanne,
head of the research section, is a jerk. Well, maybe not a jerk, but
certainly not a "people" person. But Robert knows that thinking
Suzanne is a jerk won't get him anywhere. What *exactly* has Suzanne
done? Robert asks himself. He then answers that this morning,
Suzanne showed no interest in the clever idea he had for marketing
their new telephone. Instead she emphasized the importance of his
routine report about that telephone, a report not due until next
Thursday. Robert feels dejected and annoyed.

### Evaluate Negative Thoughts and Feelings

Robert decides to use his negative thoughts and feelings as a signal
that he needs to evaluate this situation by asking his usual I AM
WORTH IT questions.

I   *Is this matter important to me?*
   Yes. Robert decides that being able to think about new possibilities is central to how much he likes—or doesn't like—his job. And
he knows he will increase his chances of getting promoted if he can
make unique contributions.

A   *Are my thoughts and feelings appropriate, given the facts?*
   Yes.

M   *Is the situation modifiable?*
   Official company policy is to welcome new ideas. The answer
should be yes.

WORTH IT   *When I balance the needs of myself and Suzanne, is taking
action worth it?*
   Yes, though I am going to have to be careful to go about this in a
way that doesn't threaten Suzanne. Actually, Suzanne would be better
off also if my idea were incorporated into the new marketing plan.
(Clearly, as we shall delineate below, careful assertion is called for!)

### Communicate Better

To communicate well with Suzanne, Robert tries listening first, by asking:

> "Suzanne, so that I'm sure that I incorporate everything expected in that report, please review for me what you're looking for."

Robert is careful to listen attentively to Suzanne's answer and then responds:

> "Let me go over this so I'm sure I've got it right. You want a report that's at least ten pages long, with proposed distribution figures for the entire Southeast, based on sales figures for the last year, as well as the reports of each regional supervisor and our in-house guess of how well this telephone will sell. I am to track down any missing reports or sales figures. I am also to include all ideas for advertising presented to date from any source, whether these ideas have been officially approved or not. You want the report by next Thursday."

After getting all of this straight, Robert needs to try to figure out Suzanne's concerns and motivation.

### Empathize

Robert thinks to himself, "Suzanne wants to be sure that the report is well done, as it will reflect badly on her if it's not. Also, I may be a little threatening to her—is she worried that she might be replaced by me?" Robert concludes that he needs to present his idea in a way that enables both him and Suzanne to look good. If he can't get Suzanne's cooperation, he'll have to decide between further assertion or acceptance of her stonewalling. But a win-win situation is obviously in both their best interests.

### Acting Effectively

Emotional intelligence is essential to being successful at your job. You spend a large portion of your waking hours at work. It follows that acting effectively in this area of your life is crucially important.

### Consider Acceptance and Assertion

Robert responds to Suzanne:

> "I'm confident that I can satisfactorily meet your expectations. I'm also still interested in what I think is an exciting idea for

advertising strategy, involving direct mailing. I know that you
have concerns about keeping costs down, but I think those
concerns will lessen when you learn more about how we
would come up with our mailing list. I'd like to incorporate
this idea into the report, alongside the other advertising possibilities under consideration. Is that acceptable to you?"

Note that Robert is asking his boss point-blank if this is acceptable
to her. Note that he has lightly implied a consequence—that he'll
get this idea on the table somehow, in this report or otherwise. He is
giving Suzanne a chance to cooperate and look good too—a potential win-win situation for both of them. If Suzanne says no, he could
drop the matter, but he already has decided that he will try to find
another way to present his idea.

We have assumed that Robert has partial control over his fate at
work. That will usually be true. But you can't make that assumption
for all situations. You will need to evaluate whether your level of
effort matches your circumstances in the long run. Will working
harder than your cohorts lead to greater job security, better working conditions, or additional money? On the other hand, does your
present level of effort put you at risk of losing your job? If you are
working hard, yet still stymied at your present work site, can you
find another comparable position elsewhere?

It's not easy to answer these possibly painful questions honestly.
Because you may find that you are stuck. Or you may discover you
are a slacker. Such awareness would be upsetting, but ultimately lib-
erating, if you use it to guide you in changing your behavior.

### Emphasize the Positive

Through empathizing with Suzanne, Robert has already figured out
that she is most focused on getting out a good report. He decides
that he will keep her informed of his progress on this front—which
will be a positive interaction, from her perspective. Since Suzanne
has never stolen any of his ideas, in the next day or so he will inform
her in more detail of his new marketing proposal. (She, in turn, may
be able to help him fine-tune his idea.) He realizes that it's important that the report be finished on time, another positive. He plans
to thank Suzanne for any direct help given—yet another potential
positive.

Situations involving subordinates are different, as you will need
both to affirm your subordinates' efforts *and* give them ongoing
honest performance evaluations. A number of investigators have

concluded that workers perform better when supervisors appraise their efforts *immediately*.

But before you open your mouth, evaluate for yourself both the positive and negative aspects of the work. Along the lines of your I AM WORTH IT road map, you will want to keep to yourself criticisms that are unimportant, not related to the problem at hand, out of the employee's control, or not worth it, considering everyone's needs.

Consider whether your directions were clear. If they were not, when you make your other comments, you will want to let your subordinate know you have realized this, so you two share the problem. Considering how you probably will come across *from your subordinate's perspective* often helps you to word what you say effectively.

As always, five affirmations are needed for each negation. Specific comments are likely to be more effective than general ones:

> "I am so relieved that you are starting on that report right away. You really allot your time well."
>
> "Your extra research on the research and development plans of those Asian companies will enable us to position ourselves well there."
>
> "Thanks for helping Fred with that Helmsley report."
>
> "I understand that you think that a better product name would help. You want us to call a special meeting to brain-storm about that."
>
> "What I'm hearing is that you are concerned that our support staff isn't large enough to get that mailing out in a week."

Immediate specific negative feedback also is necessary:

> "All of the slogans but the first one need to be more attention-getting. Also, try to keep a clearer focus on key aspects of the product. Please come up with an additional list of possible slogans. Will you be able to have that new list for us to go over by Thursday morning?"

Next ask the subordinate to summarize what you've said so you're both clear about what to do next.

Unfortunately, some supervisors have trouble giving negative feedback, saving up grievances until they're annoyed beyond endurance, then delivering harsh criticism that is often inconsiderate in tone, threatening, blaming, and too general to be helpful.

"I don't think you are at all original. This is dull stuff. I wasn't impressed at all. The whole thing needs to be fixed. Did you try? Or was this your best effort? If your work doesn't improve, I'll get someone else to do it."

The effects of such destructive criticism are devastating, according to industrial psychologists. The recipient often feels angry and tense, reacting with excuses or refusal to change. Such a worker is less prone to set his or her own goals or to feel effectual.

You will need to fine-tune all of these suggestions along lines appropriate for your title and the nature of your work.

## Special Circumstances

Some problems are particular to the workplace. Your Lifeskills will still hold you in good stead.

### Your Friend, Not You, Gets That Promotion

You and Joe are both up for the same promotion. Joe, your friend, gets it, even though you have more experience. You are furious. What do you say to Joe and the supervisors who chose him over you?

First, you need to determine the exact facts of the situation. Find out who made this decision, and schedule an appointment to see that person or persons. Then, ask for more information, following your Lifeskills guidelines for speaking assertively.

"Joe and I were both up for that promotion. Since I had more experience, I expected to get it." [Exact facts.] "When I didn't, I was disappointed, to say the least." [Sharing your feelings.] "I would like to know why you chose him over me." [Specific request.]

Under the circumstances, you may have a hard time listening carefully to the reply, but give it your best effort. You may want to take a few notes to help you remember what is said. Then repeat back what you are told.

After leaving your supervisor's office, ponder for at least the rest of the day and evening what you were told. Stay in touch with whatever thoughts and feelings come up.

Next go through your I AM WORTH IT road map. You can skip the importance question—of course this is important! Now that you have more information, was Joe a more reasonable choice, given the objective facts of the situation? (For example, if he has a stronger background in marketing and your supervisor has told you that's what they were looking for, their decision to choose him over you may have been reasonable, and your inappropriate fury may change to appropriate disappointment only. On the other hand, maybe you *were* more qualified.)

When you ask whether you can change this situation, consider potential future promotions with this company. You may want to ask your supervisor to advise you about how best to position yourself for advancement within the company. Consider opportunities in other divisions and with other companies as well, especially if at least part of the problem is your supervisor.

If you are truly stuck now and probably in the future, try some more general problem solving before concluding that the situation is hopeless and that you therefore should switch into trying to deflect your negative feelings. Are other related fields more open to advancement? (If you are in sales, for example, would a job selling hospital equipment be better than your current position as a drug rep? You will need to research the pros and cons of such a potential move before you answer that question.)

Of course, you may in fact be stuck in your present position, with no opportunities within your company or elsewhere. Better to know this, so you can switch into reasoning with yourself, telling yourself "stop," distracting yourself, and meditating, to keep your bad situation at work from ruining your life.

Meanwhile, you still must deal with your feelings toward Joe. Did he behave badly toward you or anyone else in his quest for the promotion? If he did behave badly, can you change this situation, either to rectify what happened in the past or to prevent its recurrence? If he didn't behave badly, are you angry at him or just envious? If it's only envy and you and Joe have been good friends for a while, you may be able to share with him that you are disappointed yourself, but want to keep his friendship. Indeed, Joe may be an effective future ally in helping you also to advance in the company.

### A Coworker Consistently Undermines Your Efforts

Sally sees herself as an idea rather than a detail person. In your opinion, she is lazy, arriving at work late and leaving on time every day, with long coffee breaks in between. You get stuck with all the details, like researching and writing up a project assigned to both of you. Sally does devote a lot of effort to one thing—putting down your ideas behind your back. You stay in a slow burn, a negative feeling you have no trouble identifying.

Wait for the next time Sally puts you down. Then identify *exactly* what she has done *on this occasion,* sticking to facts that would hold up in a court of law.

> "She agreed that I, not she, would write up our report, saying she'd leave all the details to me. Now she has gone behind my back to our supervisor to bad-mouth my idea for exporting our product to England, in favor of her idea for stepping up our efforts in the Midwest."

You feel angry! So ask your four I AM WORTH IT questions. Of course the matter is important to you and your anger is appropriate. But what are you angry about? That half of the time Sally doesn't write up your joint reports? That Sally went to the supervisor instead of coming directly to you? That Sally has pushed her own plan, while criticizing yours? That you and Sally still have comparable jobs, when you have worked so hard and she hasn't? (In the latter case, you may be mainly angry at the system or your supervisor, not Sally.)

Let's say that you decide that you like writing the reports, because that's your best chance of getting promoted. What upsets you is that Sally went to the boss instead of coming to you. You may be able to get that changed, a situation in her and your best interests, given that you must work together.

> "Sally, we had agreed that I would write up our joint report. I have found out that you went to Marie, not me, with your marketing ideas. I had no idea you were unhappy with marketing to England, or that you wanted to focus on the Midwest, so of course our joint report contains none of this. [Exact facts.] Your going to Marie instead of discussing this with me first makes me feel disappointed and irritated. [Sharing your feelings.] Next time I am writing up a report for both of us, will you come to me first, so we can discuss it between ourselves?" [Specific request.]

If Sally answers yes, commit her to a timetable.

> "Since it takes me two days to write the final report and get it typed, it's best if we talk before then."

The next time the two of you agree that you, not she, will write up your joint report, remind her of your agreement, including the suggested timetable.

# Your Job Is Overwhelming You

You realize you can't handle your present workload. If you ask for help, will your coworkers and supervisors think you're a wimp? It depends on circumstances and how you go about asking.

First, carefully document what hours you are working during days and evenings.

> "On Monday, I worked nine to seven, with an extra hour at home. Tuesday was nine to around nine. Wednesday was nine to six. Thursday was eight to six. Friday was eight to around five. But then I had to come in Saturday morning for three hours and Sunday afternoon I worked an extra two and a half hours at home, for around fifty hours total."

That is much more likely to be effective than "I have too much to do!"

Depending on your situation, you may want to document what you were working on.

> "Monday: nine to twelve, the Smith project; one to three, marketing meeting with the regional reps; three to six, worked on the April budget; six to seven, looked at incoming mail and dictated correspondence."

Armed with the facts, identify as precisely as you can your negative thoughts and feelings. Tired? Unappreciated? Overwhelmed?

Let's say you feel overwhelmed. Of course it's *important*. Have you been assigned an unreasonable workload, so that your feeling overwhelmed is *appropriate*? If you find yourself making excuses for your company, consider how you would feel if the person involved were not you, but a cousin or sibling. If you still answer no, your feeling overwhelmed is not appropriate, you have identified a different problem you need to deal with—depression, problems at home, or whatever. On the other hand, you should be able to get this situation *modified* if you answered yes. (Remember that options may include switching jobs, if you can't improve the situation in your present workplace.)

An overwhelmed employee is not in the company's best interests, either, so the *worth it* answer is usually straightforward.

Let's say that now you have four yeses to your I AM WORTH IT questions. Before you can make a request to be given less work, you need to have a very clear idea of what you want and who has the power to give it to you: Do you want your supervisor to assign certain specific projects to someone else? (It will be useful to have a list, so if your first idea for what you would like removed isn't satisfactory, you can move down your list.) Do you want your supervisor to give you less work—it doesn't matter what is taken away? Or is the workload not the problem, but that your coworker needs to take half of the stack of work to be done, instead of both of you drawing from the same pile? (In this case, you will need first to try to solve this problem with your coworker rather than going to your supervisor.) Is overwork an ongoing problem of long duration or a recent development? If it's the latter, is the new situation likely to be a permanent or temporary problem?

Now you are in a position to ask for what you want. Make a specific appointment with your supervisor. Arrive at your meeting with documentation of how you are spending your workdays and work evenings. Share that you are feeling overwhelmed, a feeling you don't like having, as you want to perform well, get along with your coworker, or continue to like your job—whatever relates to your specific circumstances. Then ask for what you want. If the other party agrees but can't change the situation right then, ask him to assign a timetable of when the changes agreed upon will go into effect. Mark that date in your calendar, so you can follow up if what was agreed to hasn't happened. If it has, thank him or her.

If upon meeting with your supervisor you learn that this person is not empowered to reduce your workload, get your supervisor's permission for you next to speak to whomever can make such a change and schedule that next appointment.

## *Getting Real*

When Beverly entered our Lifeskills workshop, she was at the end of her tether. She works at a law firm. When clients first arrive at the office, she is responsible for logging in relevant information about their visit. She also schedules all the appointments for three lawyers, including their court appearances. As she described her situation to us, sometimes as many as five attorneys, interns, paralegals, and clients are around her desk, each in a hurry, each wanting her attention *right now*. When matters calm down at her desk, she types letters, sends out and monitors the payment of all bills for her attorneys, and calls clients to inform them about schedules and the results of their cases. These calls can be stressful, too, especially when a client loses! She and another woman share the front reception area, taking turns answering the phone and responding to special requests from all of the firm's lawyers and paralegals. More often than not, Beverly is the one who gets around to solving a lawyer's problem first. But then this coworker, who has a slightly more important title, deals with the lawyer, claiming the credit. By the end of most days, Beverly fells frazzled, angry, spent. She aches all over, and has been troubled by multiple illnesses over the last few years.

A pleasant woman with large sparkling eyes, a wide smile, and regal bearing, Beverly brought more hopes to our workshop than we could ever fill. We couldn't cure Beverly of her very real medical problems. We couldn't change the nature of her job. (She has already looked into a number of opportunities elsewhere, but has been unable to find a more or even equally lucrative situation; she needs all the money she currently makes.)

What we could offer her were coping skills. What about her job was potentially under her control? Not the telephones. Not the five people circling her desk. But when she analyzed her situation, she realized that she was layering on additional stresses.

Beverly now keeps a thoughts and feelings log, which has helped her to recognize sooner her negative reactions to job situations. Now when five people crowd around her desk, and one of them makes a slighting remark in the heat of the moment, she realizes much more quickly that she is becoming irritated. So right then she asks her I AM WORTH IT questions. She reports to us that usually this leads to an early no, and she switches into deflection strategies, which help somewhat. Mainly, she avoids working herself up into a lather that leads to a headache, backache, and other muscle aches lasting the rest of the day.

Beverly also now practices assertion with her office mate and has been able to get her to stop taking credit for Beverly's work. She is experimenting with a few minutes of meditation each evening— well, most evenings, anyway. She and a friend who also has serious medical problems try to spend some time together—after all, each understands what the other is going through.

As the case load in the law firm continues to mount, Beverly's job is unlikely to get any easier. Still, Beverly reports to us that practicing Lifeskills has made her feel more in control of her life.

Recently Beverly filled out some questionnaires at her community college guidance department that led her counselor to suggest some additional career pathways. She's thinking about beginning an evening program that would eventually qualify her for a less stressful job. And maybe someday, her doctors will identify and treat the source of her multiple medical symptoms. Meanwhile, life is better than before she took the workshop.

# *Exercises*

1. For the next month, each day log in roughly how many hours of office and home time you devote to your job and how many to family, friends, community, and other leisure activities. Also log how much time is left for yourself.

   When the month is up, evaluate. Consider:
   - your need to keep or improve your job and how extra effort at work may or may not contribute to those goals;
   - your desire to improve nonwork relationships;
   - your need for unscheduled time alone.

   Does the present balance feel right?

   If it doesn't, ink into your calendar additional activities in the deficit area, while scratching that much time out of the over-committed area. Now stick to the new schedule! Re-evaluate after the second month is up.

2. Do you have any close friends at work? If not, resolve to have lunch or several coffee breaks with a few coworkers. If that goes well, invite them to some additional social activity outside the office.

3. One by one, meet with all the people you *directly* supervise. Ask for their opinions and ideas concerning the workplace. If some key areas are important to you, have questions in mind to refer to after your subordinate finishes speaking spontaneously, if he or she doesn't cover that aspect of the job situation. (Possible questions to consider: What do they like about their jobs? What are the least favorite aspects? Does the workload feel about right? Are they satisfied with their career path? Are there any addi-tional skills they wish they had? How, in general, do they feel about working there?) Except for these possible questions at the end, just listen. When the person finishes speaking, reflect back *only* what you heard. After each person leaves, make a few notes to help you remember what was said. You will need to tailor this interchange to fit the formality of your workplace, the number of group and individual responsibilities, and your posi-tion in the company.

4. Have second individual meetings with these same subordinates. This time, address any concerns expressed in the previous

meeting. Also share pertinent, nonconfidential information about how each person's job fits into the overall picture.

5. Think about what frustrates you about your job. Is it reasonable to expect this could be changed? If you think yes, brainstorm solutions, choosing what you consider to be the best option. Then ask your supervisor for an appointment (not over the water cooler, a real appointment).

At the meeting, first thank your supervisor for this time (positive feedback). Practicing assertion, ask in specific terms for what you need. If the boss refuses—and tries to explain why your request is impossible—listen carefully. Later ponder what was said. Is a compromise or partial solution possible? If so, you may want to give the matter a second chance by carefully documenting the conversation and then giving this, plus your follow-up suggestion, to your boss in a concise, tactful memo.

# 13. Community

I am very hostile! Very angry. My teen wishes to move
out. My husband always is working. I have no support systems.
My family all live in another country. I am overworked,
overwhelmed with responsibility. I have no social life or outlets
(or money). How do I control this hostility and loss of direction before I become a victim of heart disease or attack?

—*Anonymous question submitted after*
*Redford gave a lecture in Edmonton,*
*Canada, October 28, 1994*
*Redford's answer:*
Become involved in your community by volunteering.


You cannot shake hands with a clenched fist.

*Indira Gandhi*


What America needs now is a major social movement dedicated to enhancing social responsibilities, public and private
morality, and the public interest.

*Amitai Etzioni*

*W*hen you think about it, isn't the phrase *private citizen* a
contradiction in terms?

In recent years, *private* has been winning over *citizen.* The traditional American community was relatively homogeneous. In a small town or rural area, people knew each other by
name—sharing often, if not always, some aspects of their cultural
histories. Even within big cities, ethnic neighborhoods frequently
functioned as separate communities.

Today many communities are quite diverse, containing people of
different races, ethnic groups, educations, incomes, religions, political affiliations, senses of humor, sexual orientations, and lifestyles.
Since so many of us move so frequently, we are a nation of new-
comers, a further disconnection.

We—and most others on our planet—are challenged to re-create
some measure of wholeness in this complex setting, to find, for our

physical and mental well-being, ways once again to care about and support our entire community.

When such caring happens, we humans seem programmed to value it. Citizens of Seattle who attended a few years ago their Special Olympics for the physically handicapped or mentally retarded are still writing and talking about one event. Nine contestants competed in the 100-yard dash. At the sound of the bell, they took off, but a single boy fell immediately. One by one, the other runners realized this. Each then turned around and went back to the fallen contestant. A girl with Down's syndrome gave him a kiss, saying, "This will make it better." Linking arms, the nine participants next walked together across the finish line. Spectators then stood and cheered the runners for ten minutes.

## *Vision*

Imagine a time when it will have been possible to reduce the role of the state—especially its policing role—by enhancing each person's sense of moral obligation to the community. Since most drivers voluntarily obey traffic laws, fewer state troopers patrol highways. Most motorists don't litter, so roadsides stay clean, without higher taxes. Tougher penalties, extra police, and additional prisons are no longer called for, because a larger percentage of citizens voluntarily refrain from committing crimes.

Imagine caring neighborhoods throughout your city. Mail gets picked up when residents are away, the elderly are looked in on, each adult keeps an eye out for all the children in the neighborhood, providing them with warmth and occasional scoldings. The young people in turn provide grownups with chances to buy Girl Scout cookies and get their cars washed for a dollar.

Imagine a school where you know your children's teachers well and have an active voice in determining curriculum and school standards. A place of worship that truly embodies the core teachings of the sacred texts. A larger community where *every person* remains an individual, instead of being grouped into a category on the basis of sex, skin color, ethnic background, sexual orientation, speech, or amount of money possessed. A place where almost *every person* contributed at least an hour a week helping those in need (as we all are), so that social problems gradually began ever so slightly to diminish.

Imagine full participation by every citizen in governing the community, where each citizen felt a sense of responsibility equal to or exceeding his or her sense of entitlement.

"Yeah," you say, "I'd like to be part of such a place. If I lived in an all-Anglo (or all-African-American, all-Chicano—plug in whoever you are) largely middle-class (working-class, whatever) village with no traffic jams, malls, or sources of entertainment except other villagers, I would be part of a caring community. I would participate in government. But the community I call home has the diversity of a UN meeting, the efficiency of an L.A. thruway at rush hour, and a level of child abuse, sniper fire, and misunderstandings reminiscent of Vietnam in the sixties."

That new complexity is here to stay, and the problems are not going to disappear by themselves, so stretch a little. Acquire the Lifeskills you need to be part of the solution. Begin the task of reestablishing the community we all need.

## *Do You Recognize Aspects of Yourself?*

Maggie grew up in Belle Haven, a small town of two thousand people on the Eastern Shore of Virginia. All the residents knew each other. At least those of European descent knew those of European descent, as did all African Americans. Her daddy was on the town council and in the Lions Club; her mother was active in the PTA at the grammar school. Each week, *The Eastern Shore News* printed all the news fit to print. Some critics were known to add "And then some." Each of the twenty or so towns that dotted the Shore had a special column in that newspaper, with details about the community: bridge parties, who had gone to Norfolk, who was away visiting relatives, and who was at home convalescing.

When Maggie turned eighteen, she attended Old Dominion College, where she trained to be a nurse and married a classmate. She followed her husband from place to place for medical school, internship, residency, and army—finally settling in Atlanta, which was 650 miles from Belle Haven.

Maggie commutes for forty-five minutes from her home in Marietta to her school nursing job in Atlanta each morning, back again each evening to her pleasant development. She has some close connections in her development and occasional contact with the broader community, outside that neighborhood. Within her development, turnover is high—there's always a FOR SALE sign somewhere.

Except for work, she and her husband rarely go into the central city—they're scared of being mugged or robbed. She does keep up a bit—most days, she reads *The Journal,* concentrating on national news, advertisements of sales, and matters directly relating to her family.

## Knowledge

We live in an era of individual entitlement; "personal growth" is our mantra. Skydiving, palm-reading, step aerobics—go for it. At the same time, we count on the community to support our individualism. Citizens expect society through its schools and handicapped access to foster opportunities for personal growth. They want laws and consumer protections that maximize choices.

## The Current Situation

Choice and entitlement have expanded, but our sense of personal responsibility has diminished. A city bus crashes into pedestrians, a drug produces unexpected side effects, a doctor bungles an operation—all of these can touch off litigation. Surely someone else—usually government, a large institution, the "other guy"—is responsible!

Since 1974, each General Social Survey, a sampling designed to gauge the habits of Americans, has asked respondents, "How often do you spend a social evening with a neighbor?" Attendance even once a year at such an event has declined from 72 percent in 1974 to 61 percent in 1993. Since 1973, the number of Americans who report that in the past year they have attended a public meeting on town or school affairs has fallen—from 22 percent in 1973 to 13 percent in 1993. Similar declines have occurred for attendance at political rallies or speeches, serving on a committee of some local organization, or working for a political party. Regarding attendance at religious services and membership in church-related groups, the decline is perhaps a sixth since the 1960s.

Participation in voluntary associations also is down. In 1974, 24 percent of adults engaged in some regular civic volunteer work; by 1989, only 20 percent did so. Participation in parent-teacher organizations declined—from over twelve million in 1964 to five million in 1982, before recovering to seven million by 1995. Since 1970, the number of adult volunteers in the Boy Scouts has declined by 26 percent; in the Red Cross, by 61 percent.

Likewise, in fellowship groups: The Federation of Women's Clubs, League of Women Voters, Lions, Elks, Shriners, Jaycees, and Masons all have experienced declines in membership. One whimsical yet discomforting bit of social disengagement in contemporary America: In 1993 compared to 1980, 10 percent more Americans went bowling, but participation in league bowling was down 40 percent.

A sense of community is something many of us yearn for, albeit vainly. In a 1991 survey commissioned by the Massachusetts Mutual Life Insurance Company, 73 percent of respondents believed that "to take care of elderly parents today, people need to look outside their immediate families for help." About half say people need to look beyond immediate families for help in raising children. Despite perceived needs, as shown in Table 13-1, relatively few people have actually sought help from many outside institutions.

## Table 13-1

| Individual or Group | Percentage of Respondents Asking an Individual or a Group for Help |
|---|---|
| Church or synagogue | 40% |
| Social worker, doctor, other professional | 36 |
| School | 24 |
| Place of employment | 12 |
| Parents' support group | 11 |
| Government | 10 |
| Community center | 8 |

According to the same survey, lack of usage correlates with people's beliefs that these groups or individuals would not be effective if asked to help. At the same time, as shown in Table 13-2, people want these institutions to be doing much more than they are now to help families.

## Table 13-2

| Individual or Group | Percentage of Respondents Saying Individual and Groups Should Do More to Help |
|---|---|
| Schools | 62% |
| Government | 57 |
| Community centers | 46 |
| Places of employment | 45 |
| Social workers, doctors, other professionals | 42 |
| Parents' support groups | 39 |
| Churches or synagogues | 38 |

The physical evidence is no less discouraging. Often prisons are our major new public architecture. Town centers, with churches, a town hall, or at least a thriving downtown shopping district, are being usurped by malls on the perimeter.

### Present Wisdom

Cognitive psychologists tell us that divisions into "us" and "them"—they call these divisions the "in-group" and "out-group"—interfere with our ability to perceive the world accurately.

- Whenever people are divided, members of the same category are perceived as being more similar to one another, while members of other categories become more dissimilar, than when groups are viewed simply as aggregates of individuals.
- People assume that persons similar to them in some way—for example with similar artistic preferences—are like them in presumably irrelevant other ways too.
- Out-groups are perceived as being more homogeneous than in-groups: "The girls in *their* sorority are all alike, while in *our* sorority we are quite diverse."
- In-group members are perceived more favorably than out-group members. For example, responsibility for an accident is more likely to be blamed on someone from an out-group.
- Once stereotyped, behaviors that fit the stereotype are recalled more easily than other behaviors. (The only good news is that behavior inconsistent with the stereotype is easily recalled too.)

Cognitive psychologists hold that these cognitive processes operate regardless of the basis of the grouping. (The features just described are derived from studies of such diverse groups as women, the elderly, librarians, British private school students, Muslims of India, and African Americans.)

Probably the leading basis for grouping people in the United States at present is race. This "us" and "them" serves all citizens badly, as many current community problems cannot be explained away as reflections only of our history of troubled racial relations. Where social class is comparable, there are no differences between blacks and whites in divorce rates, proportion of births to unmarried mothers, proportions of children living in female-headed families, and proportions of women working outside the home.

In numerous studies, small groups often outperform individuals on a wide variety of tasks involving thinking and problem solving. The wider the talents and experiences group members bring, the better. The bottom line: Social networks help both workers and companies and also result in better schools; faster economic development; lower crime; efficient, responsive government.

### Effects on Health and Well-Being

Two additional conclusions from the already mentioned Alameda County study: Individuals who belong to a church or temple have lower mortality rates than those who do not. With the exception of older men, both men and women who belong to at least one formal or informal group have lower mortality rates than individuals who did not. This risk holds true even after researchers took initial health status into account.

In another study—of 232 patients fifty-five years of age or older undergoing elective open heart surgery—lack of group participation in an organized, regular social activity, such as local government, a church supper group, a service center, or an historical society was associated with over a threefold risk of dying within six months, even after controlling for other physical risk factors. (Absence of strength and comfort from religion also resulted in an additional threefold increase in mortality within six months. The risk was increased threefold again among patients who didn't participate in groups *and* derived no strength or comfort from religion.)

Phyllis Moen, of the Life Course Institute at Cornell, began to study 427 married women with children in 1956. They ranged in ages from twenty-five to fifty, and she examined them in their roles as worker, friend, neighbor, relative, church member, and member of a volunteer club or organization. When she and her colleagues re-examined 313 of these women thirty years later in 1986, only two of the characteristics measured were associated with longevity. The first was engaging in multiple roles beyond those of wife and mother. The second was being a member of volunteer organizations. Fifty-two percent of the women not belonging to volunteer clubs or organizations in 1956 had experienced a major illness by 1986, compared with only 36 percent of women who had been active in their communities. This health benefit held true, whether the women volunteered intermittently or continuously. Active women also showed significantly higher self-esteem thirty years later. These results held up when Moen took into consideration the women's education, husband's occupational status, social class, number of children, level of social support, social class, general life satisfaction, self-esteem, and sex role traditionalism. Moen has since found that the more roles and helping activities in which a woman is engaged, the better her health.

Certain religious groups, most notably Seventh-Day Adventists and Mormons, and ethnic groups such as Japanese Americans, are at reduced risk for a wide variety of disease, suggesting that they are buffered or protected in some way. These reduced-risk groups are notable for their cohesive and well-integrated communities. In contrast, widowers, people living in environments characterized by social disorganization and poverty, and people who are highly mobile either occupationally or geographically are at increased risk. Such groups lack many contacts, either intimate or community. While diet and lifestyle certainly account for part of these health differences, the web of social relationships also seems to play a role.

In one study from the early 1980s, a group of devout strangers agreed to pray in a systematic way for heart patients they did not know. For ten months, all 393 patients admitted to the coronary care unit of San Francisco General Medical Center were randomly assigned to one of two groups. In one group, the first names, diagnoses, and ongoing general condition of the patients were given to a previously selected group of Christians—active members of one of several Protestant churches or of the Roman Catholic church—accustomed to daily devotionals. The intercessors prayed daily for their assigned patient. The control group received the same medical care but no assigned outside prayer. No one within the hospital knew which group a patient had been assigned to. When the two records were subsequently compared, the control patients had required ventilatory assistance, antibiotics, and diuretics more frequently than patients in the intercessory prayer group.

## Crossover

One way to help our community in the future is to teach our children to care. A 1992 survey asked what respondents considered the most important family value learned in childhood. Among the 48 percent who chose being responsible for one's actions (surely a community value also), over half said they learned this lesson through the expectations of and examples set by parents and elders:

> I can remember taking my children back into the dime store
> for stealing and making them pay for something they stole. I
> turned around and taught them what my parents taught me. I
> took my children to a demonstration in Washington. It taught

them that we must be responsible for what our country does. When it is wrong, we have to say so.

> *Ohio pig farmer, married mother,*
> *more than sixty years old*

A total of 26 percent of those surveyed said that respecting others for who they are had been the top family value when they were growing up (again, surely also a community value). According to about three-fourths of this group, they learned this from the role-modeling and expectations of parents.

The third most cited family value is less community-related but may lead to the high self-esteem we must have to be able to care for others well. For the 20 percent of Americans who say "being able to provide emotional support to the family" was the most important family value in their households when growing up, about two-thirds learned this through examples set by parents and family members. And about one-fifth cited a profound life experience:

> I guess it would be listening. I'd be there for them. I didn't receive any of this growing up in an alcoholic home.
>
> *Michigan janitor, single man in his forties*

In this same survey, eight out of ten respondents said that the best way today to teach children the top three family values—respect, responsibility, emotional support—is by modeling: providing good examples, stating positive expectations.

The community needs to help too. According to a 1993 Gallup poll, 90 percent of American parents agree that the public schools should teach core values—like the golden rule, moral courage, caring, tolerance of people from different racial and ethnic backgrounds, democracy, and honesty. Despite agreeing upon this stance, we and our politicians become mired down in oppositional thinking when we try actually to accomplish this. For example, liberals fear the inclusion of religion; conservatives fear political correctness and undermining of parental authority. As a result, many of the national and local attempts to incorporate core values into school curricula become political wrangles, so that our communities cannot reach consensus on what to teach and hence do nothing. "Yet an unwritten community consensus about the behavior and the goals that young people should be guided towards is a far stronger predictor of wholesome youth behavior than affluence, ethnicity, geography, family structure, or social status," according to experts in child development.

# *Action*

Since our communities are already in trouble and in many places this decline in the quality of community life is getting worse each year, we must act effectively to re-create the community we all need.

## Understanding Ourselves and Others

Let's begin by giving some thought to our own needs, thoughts, and potential contributions, since mutual understanding among people in a community qualifies as effective community action.

### *Identify Your Thoughts and Feelings*

What do you like and dislike about your community as a place to live? As always, try to be as *specific* as you can. Declare "I dislike that garbage is collected only every other week" rather than "City services stink." If groups within your community irritate you, or worse, acknowledge these negative feelings—this is addressed in the exercises at the end of the chapter.

### *Evaluate Negative Thoughts and Feelings:* I AM WORTH IT*!*

Given your list of complaints, you may want to consider becoming involved with at least one of these issues—choosing carefully, to prevent burnout and maximize gains.

Determine first if the best use of time spent serving your community is in being involved in any particular project or issue (the largest net gain). You will need to know *exactly* what project or issues you are talking about.

Then ask variations on the standard questions to evaluate your feelings:

I    *Is this matter important to me and/or my community?*

A    *Given the objective facts of the situation, is my position (involvement) reasonable? (Otherwise put: Is what I am contemplating appropriate?)*

M    *Regarding this issue or project, is progress possible? Is the status quo modifiable?*

WORTH IT    *Will my involvement result in a net gain for myself and others?*

These last two questions can be tough ones. To help you formulate your answers, social activist Katrina Shields suggests these considerations:

> The things I feel really concerned about are . . .
> If I were feeling strong and powerful, what I'd like to speak out about is . . .
> The person or people I'd really like to address this to is/are . . .
> The things that will help me speak up are . . .
> The circumstances that would assist my concerns being listened to are . . .
> The ways I avoid or stop myself from doing this are . . .
> My worst fantasy about what might happen if I spoke up is . . .
> What I am willing to do about speaking up in the next week is . . .

Interesting questions, with potentially important answers!

© 1996 Piet Beerends. A.D. Productions, Franktown, Va.

## Acting Effectively

The application of Lifeskills is expanding, but the focus is still on your personal actions. If each of us can act effectively within our community, there will be peace between neighbors and peace in the cities.

### Communicate Better

In community affairs, to communicate better in ways that help to resolve differences not only is a prerequisite for successful action, but actually directly achieves successful action. If your choice for community involvement involves you in controversy, stay especially committed to the Lifeskills you are learning. Goals are not separate from acts, but conditioned by them. Deeds shape the doer.

When you become involved in controversial issues, you are going to experience differences of perspectives, which can lead to real, heartfelt disagreements. Issues relating to social class, property rights, or race are likely to be especially touchy. Should city and county school districts be merged? Should students be bussed? In 1992 in Durham County, North Carolina, the merged city-county school board successfully negotiated these tricky waters and then in 1996 irreconcilably split along racial lines over choosing a new superintendent of schools.

Environmental issues also frequently are charged. Often interested citizens fall into two camps: the Chicken Little crowd, who believe that the end is near and it is all our fault; and those who essentially say we should stop whining about problems not as dire as either the loss of jobs or the costs associated with what they deem excessively stringent standards. Debates can be divisive. Should the nearby valley be flooded, with a dam installed to supply the city's future water needs? Should a new bypass be constructed? Should an expensive sewer treatment plant be built, or should sewage be flushed into the river?

A book reviewer for *The New York Times,* writing on the twenty-fifth anniversary of Earth Day, wants "city people and ranchers, ecologists and economists, tree huggers and loggers, as well as those who cherish the sublimely sterile notion that our country's biological diversity doesn't concern them one way or the other" to engage in "a civil discourse about what we have, what we want, what we need, and how we should proceed."

That reviewer is right on! Since participants in community controversy will continue to live in the same community after resolution of any particular conflict, the most practical goal is to cooperate as often as possible and to feel all right about any decision reached or action taken.

How can this spirit of cooperation be accomplished, when real differences exist? How can all of us keep ever in focus our need to remain a community working together to solve common problems? In short, means must be consistent with ends, if the achievement is to have lasting benefits.

~

The population of three adjacent counties in central Tennessee continues to increase rapidly. Twenty-five years ago, the only center of population was a mid-size town, but it's become a small city in the last fifteen years. Soon existing water sources will be inadequate.

The local water and sewer commission has begun to look into how to meet the area's future water needs. One solution would be to dam the river that flows through a local valley. From an engineering point of view, one location could easily be flooded to create a large reservoir, but a number of homes are located within the proposed boundaries of the reservoir. Building a dam at other, less populated locations would cost more, but is possible. Another solution would be to buy and pipe in water from a neighboring area. Still another alternative would be to take measures that would limit future growth. At the moment, the commission favors creating a large reservoir by damming the river at the cheapest location.

In accordance with national law, all water and sewer authorities must apply for and receive regulatory approval from the United States Army Corps of Engineers early on, before large amounts of public monies have been invested doing extensive background research on a proposed specific project. This evening, the Corps is holding a public hearing on the reservoir solution as part of its permit and environmental review process. All of the members of the water and sewer commission are in attendance. A number of irate taxpayers have shown up. So have some citizens who want to improve the quality of the water.

Calvin Holcomb and his neighbors live in the area the water and sewer commission is proposing to flood. All the residents of this settlement have other jobs, but they supplement their incomes with their large gardens. Some even farm a bit, as the soil around there is especially fertile. One neighbor has a small orchard. In the opinion of some of these landowners, the government has no right to take their land away from them. In most cases, the land has been in families for generations. What kind of democracy would try to kick honest citizens off their land!

This whole issue is going to be unavoidably controversial. The best hope is that the first few speakers establish a tone that is not divisive and helps everyone to look for possible compromises.

**Listen**    The chair of this hearing calls for order, only partially successfully. He lays down the ground rules. People for and against flooding the valley at the suggested location are to take turns speaking for up to two minutes. No decision about whether to issue a permit will be made tonight or even necessarily soon, but the Corps does want to hear what citizens think. The gathered crowd is impossible to quiet completely, though the chair bangs his gavel several times. By lot, those for flooding the valley at this location are chosen to speak first.

Calvin takes several deep breaths to calm himself. He resolves to focus his attention on what is said, pulling out a yellow legal pad to take notes. He then listens carefully until the first speaker has finished his initial remarks.

*Speak*   Calvin has been chosen to speak first for the people of the valley. He takes a few more breaths, uncrossing his arms and remembering to unknit his brow. He begins by summarizing what he heard the other spokesperson say: that she is concerned about costs. Calvin admits that costs are an important consideration.

> "My perspective is as a homeowner and farmer. My granddaddy eked out a living on what is now my and my brothers' land. My father worked for the mill, but he farmed on the side, too. I know every tree and every stone on those eight acres. Losing them would be like losing part of myself.
> "There's no longer a living in that land, but the corn, tomatoes, and green beans I grow feed me and my wife and kids all summer and part of the winter too, since we can and freeze part of the crop."

Calvin has used "I" statements, specifically addressed the issue at hand, and avoided blaming. He has used positive body language and a positive tone of voice. Some of the dam advocates heard what he said and some weren't truly listening, but he had given it his best shot.

*Listen Again*   Fortunately the next speaker for the dam was among those listening. He summarizes what Calvin said, adding, "The people who live in this valley seem to feel a deep attachment to their land." When heckling begins, he reminds people that he has tried to listen respectfully. He requests that others do the same, and that this request not come out of his two minutes! "My major concern is the deterioration in the quality of the drinking water. To me, our water has developed in the last few years a bitter aftertaste. I find myself drinking less and less of it. I don't want my children either to give up drinking much water because it tastes so bad or to have to purchase bottled water."

### Empathize and Consider Acceptance
The first speakers had avoided seeing the other speakers as adversaries. Later speakers became a little more heated. The meeting is drawing to a close, with each side choosing two final spokespersons. Is there any way to return the hearings to the initial cooperative tone?

Calvin plans to give it a last shot:

> "What I would like to have come out of this meeting is that interested citizens begin to work together to see if we can find any solutions that we can all live with. Toward that goal, I think it would be a good idea if each of us talked about how we may have contributed to misunderstanding. Let me start. I have my own well, so I hadn't appreciated how bad your water tastes. I can understand how that would be important to many of you.
>
> "My land is important to me too. It's a connection to my father and grandfather, and it helps me to feed my family. I want to work toward a solution which also honors that."

The other three closing speakers are similarly conciliatory.

### Solve Problems Together
Even if the Army Corps of Engineers were to approve the possibility of the flooding of their land, Calvin and his neighbors would have a number of legal recourses. The resulting litigation could delay dam construction for years. Everyone's interests—the water and sewer commission, the irate taxpayers, citizens concerned about water purity, and Calvin and his neighbors—will be better served if all parties can agree on a compromise early on.

After the meeting is over, some of the participants from the two sides shake hands. Several persons observe that it would be a good idea for them to come to a solution everyone could live with, if the Corps grants a federal permit for the construction of a reservoir. Before the water and sewer commission members are out of the door, someone has suggested that representatives from all points of view meet at the local mediation center, to see if a satisfactory compromise can be found. With this suggestion, potential opponents begin acting almost as partners rather than adversaries. These people are off to a good start in solving their water problems—and in building community.

### Consider Assertion

Most communities offer more health and social services, such as job training, than ever are used by most citizens. Do you need to request some of these services, either for yourself or someone you speak on behalf of?

### Emphasize the Positive

Communities need direct involvement. The Communitarians—a group of ethicists, social philosophers, social scientists, and concerned citizens trying to convince Americans to reinvest in one another—recommend as a minimum:

- being informed
- voting
- practicing nonpolitical community involvement
- paying taxes and encouraging others to pay a fair share also
- serving on juries
- working to see that the amount of private money in public life, such as contributions by lobbying special interest groups to legislators, be reduced as much as possible, and that all political candidates receive some public support to defray campaign expenses, so they remain beholden only to us, the voters

Your unique interests and talents may help you use imagination to figure out additional ways to become positively involved in your community. Our list in *Anger Kills* has thirty-seven categories of potential involvement, from "Abuse of Spouse or Child" (Child Advocacy Commission, Child and Parent Support Services, Coalition for Battered Women, Rape Crisis Center, Women's Center) to "Youth Programs/Recreation/Camps" (Boy Scouts, Boys Club, community centers, 4-H programs, Girl Scouts, Girls Club, Salvation Army Boys and Girls Club, YMCA, YWCA).

You could also contact United Way or a local religious group compatible with your values, whether you belong or not. Also consider the PTA, or service organizations such as the Kiwanis and Junior League.

Another approach is to connect with a volunteer center or government-related initiative.

To learn about volunteer centers and sixty-six corporate volunteer councils across the country, contact:

Points of Light Foundation
1736 H Street, NW
Washington, DC 20006-3912
Phone: 202-223-9186

City Cares organizations connect busy working people in direct-service, team volunteer projects with a variety of schedules and time commitments. Groups exist in Atlanta, Baltimore, Boston, Charlotte, Chicago, Detroit, Greenville (South Carolina), Kansas City (Missouri), Los Angeles, Memphis, Miami, Nashville, New York, northern New Jersey, Phoenix, Philadelphia, Pittsburgh, San Diego, San Francisco, San Francisco Bay Area, Seattle, and Washington, D.C.

City Cares of America
116 East 16th Street, 6th floor
New York, NY 10003-2112
Phone: 212-533-4734

Federal domestic volunteer programs fall into three divisions: AmeriCorps, for paid and full-time helpers; Learn and Serve, for school- and college-based service learning; and Senior Service Corps, for retired seniors. For information contact:

The Corporation for National Service
1201 New York Ave, NW
Washington, DC 29525
Phone: 800-942-2677
Web address: www.nationalservice.org

*Fifty Ways to Help Your Community* by Steve and Sharon Fiffer provides you with the address and telephone number to contact for further information on each project mentioned, should you want to pursue the possibility of adapting one for your community.

## Getting Real

Our community relationships need improving. Certain aspects of community life happen naturally. Church provides friendly contacts. By being on committees and participating in activities there, we stay involved. Being part of the medical center at Duke is a major source of support for Redford. Even helping in the soup kitchen seems easy for Virginia. (She took a leave of absence from the soup kitchen until the first draft of this book was finished and is now evaluating whether to return there or work in an area that taps more of her skills.) But how can we remain invested in the day-to-day happenings of the small city of Durham, North Carolina, when we have chosen to remove ourselves to the beautiful countryside of rural Orange County? It's an ongoing, project-by-project struggle.

We had planned to try to develop some materials for use in public classrooms, based on this book, but then discovered that master teacher Naomi Drew had already developed a similar, splendid curriculum for grammar schools. Other educators as well are developing programs to teach life skills and foster social support. We've chosen therefore to publicize the work of others and to concentrate here on getting all of you interested in this issue. Our dream is that identifying and evaluating feelings, communicating, empathy, acceptance, assertion, problem solving, and five affirmations for each negation (or some variants of this list) become standard in grammar, middle, and high school social studies curricula, just as child development and couples skills become part of the home economics or psychology course, required of students for graduation. At the moment, we ourselves have developed workshops adapting Lifeskills for couples and for African Americans and European Americans trying to improve racial relations. We also give workshops for general groups aimed at encouraging community involvement, but that is only a beginning.

The behaviors we all need to get along well with people in our community are the same as in intimate relationships. The hard part is acting that way with people beyond our normal reach. Yet intuitively we know we need to do this, as each of us has anecdotal evidence that caring people invested in their communities are better off. Virginia likes to remember one of her favorite cousins, Mildred Evans Barnes, who a few years ago was diagnosed at age eighty-four with advanced ovarian cancer and given a half year to live. During the next eight months—Milly outlasted the doctor's predictions—Virginia went on long day trips six times to see her cousin, getting to know Milly better and meeting many visitors.

Cousin Milly made good company. Her comments on politics, religion, conservation, and child-rearing were original and on target. She easily laughed at the foibles of herself and the world around her. Also, she didn't always steer conversation back to herself; Milly didn't seem to need to impress.

Some might say that Mildred Evans Barnes didn't set the world on fire. She lived all her life in Deltaville, a village on the western shore of the Chesapeake Bay, except for four years away at college. Her first job—as a high school history teacher—she held until retirement forty-five years later. Milly had enough to eat and a comfortable home but certainly wasn't rich. Her husband was ninety years old at the time of her death, and they had no children, having married late in life.

Despite being childless and living in a small town, Milly was in most ways average. She did have one exceptional characteristic: She was happy. She liked her parents, even appeared to like her husband, who had the habit of repeating what he already had said a short while before. Hard work didn't seem to bother her. She got excited about inconsequential matters, like family feasts and projects at church. She taught an adult Sunday school class once she retired, a project she took seriously. She became the first female deacon in her church. (Her minister confided that her prayers were a little long for the tastes of many in the congregation, but they were willing to put up with that, out of respect to "Miss Mildred.")

Seeming to be able to get along with most anybody, beginning with herself, at Middlesex County High School, she taught the bright and the not-so-bright with gentleness, three generations of students. She complained a little about one neighbor, who had let his vacant lot harbor snakes, but kept her sense of humor about even that. Virginia never heard her speak unfavorably about anyone else.

No children. A ninety-year-old husband who repeated the same comments over and over. When Virginia first began to visit her cousin, she went in part because she feared Mildred might die a lonely death.

Not a chance. Once people heard Milly was sick, they visited in droves. She had rented out her parents' house for practically no money to a waitress. That woman did the grocery shopping and frequently brought dinner.

Every member of her Sunday school class visited, bringing such presents as a pie made with cherries from a special tree. Most callers returned a number of times.

During the final three weeks of her illness, Milly, in pain, didn't feel well enough to get out of bed. Acquaintances helped, so Milly could stay at home, where she wanted to be.

For her funeral, the Deltaville community packed her little church. Neighbors, a number of former students, and the members of her church were there. Six whole pews at the front were filled with relatives, though many lived several hours away. Virginia observed that everyone seemed sad, but no one seemed conflicted or bitter. She muses that is because they had no regrets or feelings of guilt: everyone must have treated Milly well.

On one of her last visits to the doctor, Milly learned that a nearby bridge spanning the Rappahanock River had been closed for repairs. Milly had thought about that bridge during the night, when she couldn't sleep. She had concluded that what was most important about a bridge were the pillars that hold it up. She told her minister that he should preach a sermon on pillars. They never got around to talking again about that.

After Milly died, a cousin who lived nearby was cleaning up in her bedroom. On the bedside table lay an index card entitled "Bridges." Just five words appeared beneath that title:

HONESTY
KINDNESS
COMPASSION
TOLERANCE
PATIENCE

Despite the heartwarming feelings we get contemplating Milly, her example probably only has limited application to our own lives, as few of us are fortunate and unfortunate enough to live in a place like Deltaville. An example from a heterogeneous community probably has greater relevance, and we originally had planned to choose one such example from Steve and Sharon Fiffer's fifty separate accounts of individuals or groups who have introduced innovative, yet simple ways to make their community a little better. In the end, we dared not choose. What impressed us most was how each person or group had matched interests to local needs. The overarching message in this important book is heartening: each of us can make an extraordinary difference. The people profiled are ordinary men and women, not philanthropists or politicians, social engineers or social workers:

Among them are a teenager in California who fosters racial understanding by pairing pen pals from different ethnic backgrounds; a grandmother in San Antonio who enlists senior citizens to teach and nurture latchkey kids after school; a group of professional women in Chicago who provide suitable clothing to women who are ready to find jobs; a group of African-American men in North Carolina who serve as mentors to teens in need; members of a public school district in Washington who match needy students and business-people as lunch-time buddies; a group of employees in Tennessee who spend their lunch hours delivering meals to the elderly; and a modern-day Johnny Appleseed in Salt Lake City who organizes tree plantings and other environmental activities in urban areas.

And then there's the rarefied example of Mohandas Gandhi and his followers. They began by forging a community of social activists. Then they gradually expanded this community until many fellow Indians on the huge subcontinent of India joined them. Many members of this new community were poor and illiterate, yet they helped lead India out of the British empire and into independence at the end of World War II, though the empire remained vastly more powerful. Most impressive about the early phases of the independence movement in the 1920s and 1930s was the extent to which participants also tried to include the British in a sense of community.

Gandhi conducted his part of the struggle with a strong allegiance to *ahimsa,* which is often translated as "nonviolence" but also includes the ideas of non-coercion, as opposed to coercion, and constructiveness, as opposed to destructiveness. The goal was to eliminate antagonisms rather than the antagonists, and inner mental activity shared importance with interpersonal conduct in achieving this goal. Today, Gandhi's approach to achieving social change is widely admired and copied. For example, the American civil rights movement under the leadership of Martin Luther King, Jr., was modeled in part after the early phase of the Indian struggle. In South Africa, Afrikaners and black Africans transferred the reins of government peaceably in part because their leaders on occasion exercised moral courage as well as political skill.

## *Exercises*

1. For the next month, avoid categorizing—as "them" versus "us"—people with political opinions contrary to your own or people of a different age, sex, skin color, religion, ethnic or national group, sexual orientation, speech, or income. You may want to focus especially on those groups you already have identified as irritating you. Observe how this depolarization affects your attitudes and behaviors.
2. For the next month, avoid letting yourself think in either-or sound bites: family values and the religious right versus tolerance and government intervention; multiculturalism versus Eurocentrism; traditional values versus feminism; pro-life versus pro-

choice; liberalism versus conservatism. Instead, simply observe any differences between your and another position and focus on the question, "How can we find common ground?" Observe how this re-creation of the vision of a communicating circle engaged in building community affects your attitudes and behaviors.

3. Try to participate in one activity within your community that brings you in contact with people in need. Stretch a little but stay within your comfort zone.

4. Review the list on page 253 of minimum political participation recommended by Communitarians. Is this a list you are comfortable with?

# Part V

# *Distant Others*

"It's refreshing to find someone today who's _not_ angry."

© The New Yorker Collection 1995 Bernard Schoenbaum
from cartoonbank.com. All Rights Reserved

# 14. Other Americans

People, I just want to say, you know, can we all get along? Can we get along? Can we stop making it horrible for the older people and the kids? . . .Please, we've got to get along here.

*Rodney King, during the 1992 Los Angeles riots, which were occasioned by the acquittal from an all-white jury of four white policemen charged with striking King fifty-six times in eighty-one seconds as he lay on the ground, an event recorded on videotape. According to the testimony of these policemen, just before that, King had attacked them as he resisted arrest.*

"You really don't believe in political solutions, do you?"
"I believe in political solutions to political problems. But man's primary problems aren't political; they're philosophical. Until humans can solve their philosophical problems, they're condemned to solve their political problems over and over and over again. It's a cruel, repetitious bore."

*Tom Robbins,*
Even Cowgirls Get the Blues

The psychology of the individual is reflected in the psychology of the nation. Only a change in attitude of the individual can initiate a change in the psychology of the nation.

*Carl Jung*

The first major problem in America today: As citizens, we have stopped caring about the decline of what Americans traditionally have valued. In the early 1830s, French aristocrat Alexis de Tocqueville traveled to America to study our democracy. He observed extreme individualism exceeding that of any other nation. Citizens felt disconnected from their ancestors *and* descendants. They felt separated from contemporaries, too. Countering this focus on the self were Americans' involvements in minor public affairs and in protection of the rights and interests of all citizens, as well as the presence of institutions like voluntary political and industrial associations, the press, and the judiciary. Tocqueville also observed—for that era—Americans' relative economic and social equality, which today is giving way to increasing inequalities. Where are we headed, as economic and social equality seem ever more distant goals and unbridled individualism is so celebrated? Can we find our way back to a sense of mutual commitment to one another? Can we renew our institutions?

The second major problem in America today: We care, but we express that caring in ways that lead to mutual alienation. Any *collective* sense of a shared moral quest is crumbling beside an extreme enchantment by each person with a self-righteous personal perspective—*my* values, *my* political perspective, *my* religious insights.

Can we instead retain our values, yet develop a new respect for Americans who have a perspective different from our own?

Cynical, angry, aggressive people are on average less healthy, compared to nonhostile counterparts. When distribution of wealth becomes too inequitable, the health of the entire nation declines. The current state of affairs in America may be affecting not only our quality of life, but even how long we live.

## Vision

A positive sense of purpose once again imbues our citizens and politics. Caring about each other, Americans commit to the welfare of every citizen, actively involving themselves in others' well-being.

Almost everyone listens with an open mind not only to yea-sayers, but to those opposed to the listener's point of view. Skills at listening, empathy, and (occasionally) acceptance of differences help us manage our diversity and become a model for the future integrated culture of the developed world in the twenty-second century.

## Do You Recognize Aspects of Yourself?

Agreeing not to discuss politics and religion is one of the reasons Andrew Kowalski Sr. and Andrew Kowalski Jr. get along so well.

Andy fought in Korea in a unit of brave men. He still keeps a picture of them on the wall in his den, to remind him of those heroes.

> "People today aren't building on that heritage. Teenagers, bumping into passersby, loll around the malls—smoking cigarettes, and doing I'd-rather-not-think-about-what else. Even the girls talk like guttersnipes. The girls behave as badly as the boys—

I can't tell the difference anymore. If I'd ever used words like that in front of my father, I wouldn't have said them a second time. But many of these kids don't have fathers. Or jobs either. Welfare is a big part of the problem. So are their lazy, no-good parents. And what's happened to the concept of volunteering for community service? I'm doing my part, but precious few others are, despite incessant whining about how bad things are and that the *government*—not them, mind you, but bureaucrats—should do something! This country is going to hell, that is clear."

Back in the days of Vietnam, Andrew Jr. dropped out of college for a semester so he could devote himself full-time to the anti-war movement—now there was a cause worth sacrificing for!

"Today, people don't seem to be willing to put that kind of energy into righting wrongs, even though this country wallows in deep trouble. The poor lose ground, the wealthy pile up riches, yet help for the poor is what keeps getting cut in government budgets. While people vote *themselves* tax cuts. Selfishness is what it is. Nobody today is standing up for the little guy—look at the high school dropout rate, the teenage pregnancies, the attitude of a lot of people toward African Americans, immigrants, or even toward women. Instead, they're blaming the victims and trying to return to a past that wasn't all that hot for anyone who wasn't a white middle-class male. Whine, whine, whine, blame someone else, blame someone else. This country is going to hell, that is clear."

## Knowledge

Witness the title of a 1996 popular treatise written by political scientist Susan Tolchin: *The Angry American: How Voter Rage Is Changing the Nation.*

As Walt Kelly, the cartoonist of Pogo, once put it, "We are all responsible one way or the other for our myriad pollutions, public, private, and political." But before specific political problems can even be addressed, we first need to confront our negativism.

## The Current Situation

The evidence that we are a troubled nation is everywhere. One manifestation of our lack of commitment to our collective well-being is our refusal to confront the changed economic situation: Young people will inherit a number of financial problems occasioned by our failure to live within our newly reduced income. Social security and pension systems have paid out funds to current beneficiaries at rates that cannot be sustained in the future. By 1993, our national deficit was over $4.5 trillion. Annual interest on this debt was $292 billion, and the average American family's share of the national obligation stood at $58,098.

Thirty-seven million Americans (15 percent of the population) *lack* health insurance coverage, while many doctors, patients, insurance companies, hospitals, attorneys, and assorted others bilk the insurance and Medicare and Medicaid systems.

At least some Americans are anxious about the groups other Americans are joining. For example, after the Oklahoma bombing, the Senate held hearings on the 224 militias now operating in thirty-nine states, to explore whether these militias present a threat.

Most disturbing of all is what loosely could be called our attitudes. A Times Mirror Center study of September 1994 concluded that America had become an increasingly bitter, frustrated, cynical, and selfish place over the seven years the center had been conducting polls.

- Americans were increasingly indifferent toward the problems of African Americans and other minorities and resentful toward immigrants.
- Fewer Americans thought government should take care of needy people.
- Public disgust with Washington was significantly worse than in 1992. More voters wanted traditional politicians replaced with a fresh, new batch. In some states, term limits were being voted in.
- More than 70 percent of Americans thought the media, especially television news shows, hurt the country more than they help.
- Only 33 percent of the public thought that elected officials cared about their beliefs, down from 36 percent in 1992 and 47 percent in 1987.
- Only 42 percent believed government was run for the benefit of all people, compared to 57 percent in 1987.

Other evidence of the surly national mood abounds:

- Think of the facial expression and body language of fashion models.
- Someday when you are driving alone, flip your radio dial at random, stopping whenever you hit a talk show.

- Monitor letters to the editor in local newspapers.
- Ask acquaintances at random what they think of Congress and the president.
- Observe generations' comments about each other in the media.

Specific documentation of the growing incivility in America comes from a poll of one thousand residents of the Dallas–Fort Worth metropolitan area commissioned by *The Dallas Morning News* in August 1995. Sixty-nine percent of those polled agreed that "People today appear to be more angry than they were a few years ago." Interestingly, only 22 percent agreed with the statement "*I* am generally more angry today than I was a few years ago." Similarly high percentages agreed that today compared to a few years ago, people are more inclined to be impolite, express their anger in a violent way, get angrier faster, and be unable to control their anger.

Television reflects—maybe even exacerbates—America's current emphasis on the negative. In March 1995, a CNN report found that over the past few years, local TV news devoted an increasing proportion of each newscast to violent crimes. During this same period in the same cities, police statistics showed rates of violent crime had actually declined!

To keep these reports of newly negative or uncaring attitudes in perspective, it's important also to note the basic satisfaction most Americans feel. An international Gallup poll of residents in eighteen countries, conducted in April 1995, found Americans among the most satisfied people in the world. United States residents ranked second to Canada in satisfaction with housing, income, health, education, jobs, leisure time, electronic equipment, food, clothing, and furniture. Eighty-three percent of Americans are satisfied with their personal lives, and 64 percent with the way democracy works. Just 11 percent say they want to move permanently to another country.

## Present Wisdom

For fifty years after the beginning of World War II, Americans consumed half of the world's goods. Today, Americans find themselves in relative political and economic decline. Less affluent Americans are especially affected, as the middle class erodes and the lowest 40 percent of our population earns as much income after taxes as the top one percent after taxes. (This inequality may grow as more and more jobs involve the application of knowledge—not physical strength—to work.) Other national problems abound: crime;

random violence; the deterioration of our public schools; the wide distribution of firearms.

Some Americans have retired from being concerned about these matters. Among those who still care, some citizens long for a return to traditional values and ways, both to solve our problems and to address our negativism and malaise. Other citizens, including many working women and minorities—rejecting this approach—call for widespread additional changes. Polarized issues include the federal budget, flag burning, abortion, English versus bilingualism, and affirmative action. These several groups rarely communicate with one another and rarely work together to resolve differences. Our country gyrates from election to election. This new "tribalism" sometimes correlates with differences in educational level and social class, with *both* sides disliking and distrusting the other, without practicing listening! It's "us" versus "them" for many, many Americans.

## Effects on Health and Well-Being

We have reported extensively in this book the research demonstrating the efficacy of social support in face-to-face encounters. While perhaps impossible to document, surely support of all Americans for one another must follow the pattern of face-to-face relationships and also be good for health.

The widening gap since 1980 between rich and poor may itself contribute to deteriorating health in many segments of the United States population. Researchers have long known that those with lower education levels, lower income, or lower job status are far more likely to develop serious illnesses or die at an earlier age than those higher on the socioeconomic ladder (Chapter 4). Now British epidemiologist Richard Wilkinson has brought to light a new risk: How the income is distributed within a country is an important factor in the *overall* health of that country, as measured by average life expectancy. In a comparison of income and life expectancy levels in a sample of industrialized nations, Wilkinson found that the lower the percentage of each country's total income and post-tax benefits received by the bottom 70 percent of the population, the lower was the average life expectancy in that country. Indeed, the size of the income gap between rich and poor was a far stronger predictor than was the level of average income.

Two research teams, one led by University of California epidemiologist George Kaplan and the other by Harvard public health researcher Bruce Kennedy, recently found a similarly strong linkage between income distribution and mortality rates across all fifty states in this country. In those states where the least well-off 50 percent of the population received over 21 percent of the total household income for the state—places like Utah, Hawaii, Wisconsin, Minnesota, and Washington—the average death rate was around 725 per 100,000 per year. In states where the least well-off half of the population received less than 19 percent of the total household income— places like Louisiana, Mississippi, New York, Kentucky, and Alabama—an average of over 925 persons died per 100,000 each year. These higher death rates in the states with larger inequalities in distribution of wealth could not be explained by differences in the states' average income levels or proportion of African Americans in the population. Those states in which the least well-off 10 percent showed the largest decline in share of the total income from 1980 to 1990 also showed the largest increase in death rates over the same period.

What might account for the higher death rates in those states with a larger gap between rich and poor? Such states had higher rates of violence, more people without health insurance, less investment in education and literacy, and larger proportions of people on various forms of welfare. In addition to the obvious hazards, these indicators all point to greater life difficulties experienced by those living in the states with larger income inequalities. This situation could boost levels of depression, hostility and anger, or social isolation, all of which put persons at higher risk of disease and death, as we learned in Chapter 3. These psychosocial risk factors increase the likelihood a person will engage in harmful health behaviors like smoking and drinking. They also increase activation of the fight-or-flight response.

More may be involved than just that. In trying to understand how larger gaps between rich and poor might lead to poorer health, Harvard researcher Bruce Kennedy points to "the pervasive sense of anger and frustration among the working middle class, a distrust of others, distrust of government and other institutions, and intense feeling about inequities in how they are compensated for their efforts" as potential pathways.

Such negative feelings can only have increased in the United States over the past decade. Statistics on our growing inequities are worth repeating. From 1983 to 1989, 66 percent of the total gain in net financial wealth was received by the top 1 percent, and 37 percent by the next 19 percent of the population, while the bottom 80 percent lost 3 percent.

As we learned in earlier chapters, when relationships with those close to us are bad, everyone's health suffers. The studies just reviewed show that the health of entire populations—nations and states—also can suffer when societal relationships deteriorate; as is the case, for example, in the widening of the gap between the haves and have-nots.

## *Crossover*

Lack of collective well-being spills over into personal lives. Our collective cynicism, malaise, mutual rancor, and lack of pulling together to solve national problems affect our children, jobs, and neighborhoods.

## *Action*

If America is to change, individual citizens have to become more positively proactive and less negatively reactive. Practicing your Lifeskills can help you to do this.

## Understanding Yourself and Others

For many of us, the hardest step will be the first one, where we switch from inaction to involvement.

### *Identify Your Thoughts and Feelings*

One danger of chronicling national problems is that you may conclude that the situation is hopeless, so first let's put America's problems into perspective. For the first time since the end of World War II, we no longer fear nuclear catastrophe. While we are not as prosperous as before and no longer have the highest average income, we Americans still possess the most wealth of any nation.

Have we developed an anger habit, inherited from the days when assertive anger brought about needed, positive changes in national policy in Vietnam and civil rights? While the disadvantaged and disempowered are very much with us, much of our rage doesn't seem to be on behalf of these groups. So let's begin acting deliberately by identifying the problem as in part one of perception.

Once you have recovered your perspective, try on an ongoing basis as you get information from newspapers, news magazines, TV, and radio to identify feelings around *specific* national issues or situations, like primaries or elections, pending national legislation, ongoing political issues that will be on the agenda year after year, or national policies concerning big issues, like welfare, taxes, conservation, peace, or war.

### Evaluate Negative Thoughts and Feelings: I AM WORTH IT!

Mark is aware that the present congressman for the fifth district probably will be retiring next year. While this district is heavily weighted toward one party, that party contains a rather wide spectrum of political opinions, which means the party nomination will be up for grabs. One potential candidate is known to favor reforming the present system of lobbying and campaign contributions to give a louder voice to ordinary citizens, positions she has fought for in the state legislature. Mark is concerned about this issue. Should he call this potential candidate to see if any campaign efforts are under way to secure her the nomination? Mark is aware of experiencing a mixture of feelings of hopefulness and cynicism, energy and lethargy.

**I** *Is this matter important to me?*
"My wife and kids, even my job, are more important to me. But hey, this indirectly affects all of that, so yes."

**A** *Are my thoughts and feelings appropriate, given the facts?*
"All of my thoughts and feelings are on the mark. On the one hand, she might not get the nomination. Even if she did, she might not win the election. And even if she won, she'd only have one vote. But she's good enough that she probably would get re-elected. And we need to do something about lobbying reform, that's for sure!"

**M** *Is the situation modifiable?*
"I don't know."

**WORTH IT** *Balancing the needs of myself and the public good, is taking action worth it?*
"She might ask me for money. She might want me to promise some time helping. But hey, I still can put whatever limits I want on both of those. And if we could turn the present political situation around, the whole country would benefit—we'd all win! What the heck—at least I'll call her."

### Communicate Better
Remember the speaking guidelines:

• Just do it.
• Make "I" statements.

- Report your feelings.
- Speak out of your personal experience.
- Be specific.
- Send positive nonverbal messages.

"Ms. Smith, this is Mark Carrington calling. I live in Bowie's Creek and have been following in the newspaper for several years how you have fought for lobbying and campaign contribution reform in our legislature. My guess is that next year the fifth district seat will be open, and I've heard your name mentioned as a possible candidate. This pleases me because of your record on giving the government back to ordinary people. I have a full-time job and a young family and also not much money. Still, I might like to help a little bit if you do run. What's your situation? Are you considering making a run for it?"

"That's an interesting question you ask. And one I've heard a lot recently. And pondered. But it takes a lot of resources to run. Money. Volunteers. The backing of my colleagues."

"What I hear you saying is that you have thought about it, but you don't know if there's enough support out there to give you a realistic shot at winning. Have I understood you?"

"Yes."

"If I and nine others each promised five hours of time campaigning on your behalf, would that make a difference?"

"Yes. It would be a start. That—and some similar lists from citizens in other towns—would strengthen my hand with colleagues inside the party."

"So you would need a list of those ten names, with a promise of five hours of time each, to have in hand when you approach party officials over the next few months. I'll see if I can come up with those names and promises, and I'll get back to you within three weeks to let you know what I come up with."

## Acting Effectively

We suggest that all of us need to shift responsibility for our national well-being back onto ourselves.

### Consider Assertion, and Emphasize the Positive

In public opinion surveys, readers, listeners, and viewers complain about negative news. But surveys—and television ratings—also show that people seem more interested in negative news, sensational news, news about crime and violence and corruption than in what we customarily think of as "positive" news. As *Los Angeles Times* staff writer David Shaw observes in his probing analysis of the epidemic of cynicism in the media, "To remain in business, the news media must—to some extent—give people what they want."

As an exercise over the next month, whenever you are about to blame some "them" or other for America's problems, stop yourself. Ask the question, "What could *I* do to improve the situation?" For example, you begin one evening by blaming your local radio or TV evening news channel for focusing almost exclusively on negative events. Catching yourself, you ask your I AM WORTH IT questions, get four yeses, and then call the station to request that they balance their presentations.

### Practice Listening, Empathy, and Acceptance, and Emphasize the Positive

If we as a nation are to rediscover a set of uplifting national principles to which we can all pledge allegiance, we must try to develop a shared vision of the true, the just, and the good or, barring that ambitious goal, at least enough respect for each other that we can address differences civilly and fruitfully. Such goals become reachable when citizens practice listening, empathy, acceptances of differences, and the five-affirmations-for-each-negation ratio. An approach that arrives at national policies by building consensus will be more widely embraced long-term than any dictated by one group of the religious, political, or traditional-versus-post-traditional spectrum besting another—around a particular issue, a national election, or even a Supreme Court decision. Such consensus may not always be possible, or even morally desirable, but it is surely possible sometimes—for example, in an agreed focus on the national need to nurture children and to give their needs national priority.

Can we proceed beyond even that, to include other Americans as part of the family we care about? We think that's possible. As a thorny example, let's together try to adopt such an attitude around the particularly sensitive and volatile issue of abortion. Imagine yourself back at the time this event was widely reported in the press.

On July 29, 1994, seventeen months after a similar shooting, also in Pensacola, Florida, Dr. John Britton and his escorts, James Barrett and June Barrett, were shot with a 12-gauge shotgun fired by Paul Hill as they approached an abortion clinic. Dr. Britton and Mr. Barrett died instantly from head wounds. Mrs. Barrett was wounded in the arm. Police soon made an arrest, as Mr. Hill did not try to flee.

Paul Hill, a former minister of two conservative Presbyterian denominations and a self-employed auto detailer and restorer, had long advocated violence against abortion doctors. He was married and the father of three young children. After his arrest, Mr. Hill said, "I know one thing. No innocent babies are going to be killed in that clinic today."

In providing services to the clinic, Dr. John Britton, a general practitioner, seems to have had mixed motives. Married and the father of five children, he personally thought abortion was wrong, but he did believe in a woman's right to choose. Earlier he had been on medical probation for "unprofessional conduct" and for once prescribing large amounts of drugs.

James Barrett, a retired Air Force lieutenant colonel, probably did not believe in abortion himself but also was committed to a woman's right to choose. He had volunteered to be an escort through his church, in response to a wave of antiabortion demonstrations and violent protests.

June Barrett, a retired nurse, had motivations like her husband's. After the shootings, she said she planned to continue escorting doctors and patients into the clinic.

Those are the facts. Now try to imagine yourself at the time having reacted with respect and empathy for everyone, at the same time that you retained commitment to your personal beliefs.

For all the embryos ever aborted at Pensacola, their chances for life have been snuffed out. Adopting that perspective, try to be aware of the pain of these losses of life.

What a terrible decision the pregnant women had to make. Try to share the heartbreak and trauma each woman felt. Try to understand her decision from her perspective. Can you extend compassion to her? Can you hope for help for her and all other women with similar dilemmas in the future?

Try to empathize with the commitment Paul Hill felt. Try to understand the depth of his convictions. Can you hope that he will experience comfort from his family and friends? that he will come to experience compassion for those he slew?

Try to hope that June Barrett will be comforted in her sorrow by her family and friends. Can you hope that she may again know peace? Can you hope that she too can empathize and understand, can extend her compassion to Paul Hill and to all embryos ever aborted at that clinic?

Can you bless the soul of James Barrett? Can you hope that all his friends and family will be sustained by his memory, able to feel compassion to all involved in this tragedy?

Can you bless the soul of John Britton? Can you hope that his friends and family will be sustained by his memory and able to feel compassion toward all involved in this tragedy?

Can you practice empathy toward the picketers at the Pensacola clinic and those who support them?

Can you practice empathy toward all the workers connected with the clinic?

Don't forget the abortion protesters who decry violent methods of opposition and are saddened by this tragedy!

Or the pro-choice advocates also saddened by this tragedy!

At the same time you are trying to practice empathy, do not forget your own beliefs in this matter. You may want to work toward what you think is right. If you have been successful in the above exercise, you will be ready to engage in dialogues with those of contrary beliefs. This will increase the likelihood that you—and they—will find some common ground and be able to effect some changes, such as decreasing unwanted pregnancies; providing pregnant women with balanced information, perhaps from all participants in the dialogue; shoring up support systems for women who decide to have the child; shoring up support systems for women who decide to abort; establishing guidelines for future dialogues.

## Getting Real

Admittedly, we have an added layer of motivation that probably affects how we treat other Americans. Devoting a good portion of our lives to the advocacy of Lifeskills, think how bad we'd feel if in fact these behaviors turned out not to be a sufficient guide for successfully living together with fellow countrymen, as well as with our own consciences. Having observed that, let us also report that listening, empathizing (especially important!), and sometimes practicing acceptance toward individuals and groups with religious, political, and social views different from our own has made a difference in how we feel about these people and how we treat them. Let us also say that this posture does not make us less involved in public matters.

Just last week, we were asked to sign a petition with local, regional, and perhaps national ramifications. This document requests that our governor oppose locating a thruway around Durham near existing parklands. The proposed road has been on planning maps for decades and funds for this project were allocated by the state in 1989. At present, our local transportation advisory committee has asked that the state department of transportation negotiate on the design and location of the road, incorporating suggestions that all interested parties have put forth.

As presently envisioned, this proposed multilane closed-access road would follow the river that winds around the city until it could connect up with the interstate. The road would cross several creeks that feed into the Eno River. The land along the banks of the Eno is now almost all part of a more than three-thousand-acre park that forms a twenty-mile-long forested buffer protecting the river. This property was acquired over the last couple of decades, thanks to the concerted efforts of many involved citizens. Most of this stretch borders the proposed thruway. Opponents say that the new road would block access to trails in two locations and create noise that would be audible along the entire length of land where the river and road would parallel. Silt from road construction, followed by continuous run-off of grease, oil, and other contaminants from pavement, would degrade the high quality of the river's water.

Our first inclination was to sign the petition immediately. The park is a wonderful local resource that respects our earth and the diversity of life on it. Animals need a safe home somewhere in our community—roadkill will inevitably happen more often if the highway is built near the park. Human needs are involved too— future generations living in this area will need to have a place for communing with nature. Furthermore, the creation of the park is an excellent example of citizens working together in a positive way to improve our community and respect our land. Every year, the volunteers of the Eno River Association hold a major festival, with proceeds going to purchase more land, so the park can continue to expand. And many of the people in our community we most respect and admire agree with the petition.

But wait a minute. What are the arguments supporting the proposed location for the thruway? The ones we initially heard concern how clogged major arteries in the city have become at rush hour. We don't travel these routes then, so we are unaware of the extent of that problem for commuters. Public transportation and carpooling, obviously desirable, are advocated by some park supporters as the necessary alternatives to the thruway. We don't know how likely it is that these solutions would ever happen. What plans are afoot to couple relocating the proposed thruway with improving public transportation or encouraging carpooling, and how do commuters feel about that? We seem to recall an earlier proposed thruway that actually crossed the river—is this proposal an attempt to compromise, yet still stay close to the city? If the proposed location is successfully nixed, will there soon be another alternate route proposed? Is the department of transportation mainly trying to save money? Do present alternatives close to the city already exist? Are they being rejected by government officials because they would cross more properties where houses have already been built, requiring costly out-of-court settlements or condemnation settlements in court?

If construction delays would result, what would be the implications of that for an area increasing so rapidly in population? Will any next alternate route be much farther out? What would that do to commutes, in terms of the amount of time the average citizen spends on the road and the amount of gas consumed? What would be the environmental impact and construction costs for the additional miles of concrete required for a bigger circle? After considering all of these perspectives, we concluded that we lacked enough information to evaluate that petition just yet.

Empathizing with different perspectives on a particular topic is easier than mustering the effort required to become better informed. We have already invested a couple of phone calls in finding out which government departments to write to for information. Once we get that, we'll need to decide whether it's desirable that the thruway be built at all. Then, there's the issue of alternate routes. Next is to ask how much effort we want to put into defending whatever position we've come to, when other personal, professional, and public issues also cry out for our time and attention.

## Exercises

1. During the next month, each time you are about to dislike a "them," engage in the exercise of trying to imagine what the world looks like from that perspective. Then ask yourself how you, and others like yourself, may be contributing to any rigidity "they" may have, by how you look down upon, caricature, or avoid truly listening to the heartfelt concerns of this group. Conclude by brainstorming about ways to build bridges.

2. Continue the exercise from Chapter 13 of avoiding letting yourself think in either-or sound bites: family values and the religious right versus tolerance and government intervention; multiculturalism versus Eurocentrism; traditional values versus feminism; pro-life versus pro-choice; liberalism versus conservatism. Instead, simply observe any differences between your position and another's position and focus on the question "How can we find common ground?" Observe how this re-creation of the vision of a communicating circle engaged in building community affects your attitudes and behaviors.

# 15. All Children in America

And what about the young men who committed acts of brutality on that day? Was there no one to teach them? When they were growing into the monsters that we have labeled them, were there no heroes to save them from themselves? I am grateful to have been there for my friend, Tak Hirata, but perhaps we all should have been at that intersection long before that tragic day in April. If I had been there then, how many might have been spared a coarse and bitter fate? How many might have been rescued or can yet be rescued, if there were only a gathering of heroes?

*Gregory Alan-Williams, who rescued*
*a motorist during the Los Angeles riots*
*of 1992 from an angry mob armed*
*with bottles and metal rods.*

- About 98 percent of U.S. homes have television sets, more than have indoor toilets or telephones.
- Videocassette recorders and cable are in half or more U.S. homes and schools.
- Children begin watching TV before their first birthday and have favorite programs by their second or third birthday.
- Children watch television 2–4 hours a day, spending more time viewing than any one other thing except sleeping. (A child may engage in another activity at the same time. Often, family members are viewing the same program.)
- Most of what children watch on television is either programming designed to entertain or commercial advertising designed to sell products and services.
- Children have learned facts, become less prejudiced, and increased their interpersonal skills by viewing particular television programs at home.
- The more hours of "regular television" children watch, the more they hold traditional sex-role attitudes, behave aggressively, and want advertised products.

*Aimée Dorr and Beth E. Rabin,*
*experts in the effects of television*
*on children*

"I'M BACK, MR. WILSON. I THOUGHT I'D GIVE YOU ANOTHER CHANCE TO BE *NICE*."

DENNIS THE MENACE® used by permission of Hank Ketcham and © North America Syndicate.

How a child is treated from conception to age three, more than any other period of life, affects his or her subsequent intelligence and sociability, as well as adaptability to change and opportunities. Intense and prolonged fight-or-flight responses associated with early abuse, deprivation, and even mild neglect are likely to persist into adulthood, compromising not only a person's emotional well-being but also the person's physical health. Extremely important to a child's healthy development, not only in this early period but also through adolescence, is frequent attention from caregivers and a strong, supportive community involved with children—to affirm and encourage, to set limits. Today many young persons lack this.

In communities, never have citizens been less involved with other people's children. Numerous Americans say that they care about the many poor, often fatherless children in our country *and* indict the welfare system as currently structured. They ponder what, if anything, they can reasonably do, yet often take no action. Meanwhile, many of America's children are growing up under terrible conditions, which may be getting worse, and *most* of America's children are growing up in suboptimal situations.

# What Will Be Our Vision?

Conservatives and liberals agree that young Americans are at risk for present and future mental and physical health problems. While this is especially true for poor and minority children, many affluent young suburbanites also seem lost. This situation must be changed, all agree—we are talking about at least a quarter, and in milder form most, of our children. While all around the country, a number of hopeful little projects are afoot, at the moment they represent only a small drop into a big bucket, though we are encouraged by the efforts of former chairman of the Joint Chiefs of Staff Colin Powell and others to call us to action.

Conservatives and liberals alike are beginning to agree that involvement of every American in local action to help children would ameliorate some problems. This might assume a number of forms:

- providing direct care out of spiritual or ethical commitment
- experiencing enough anger on behalf of children to demand change in institutions (child care centers, schools, police departments, social services, churches, housing, community centers, drug rehab programs)
- designing governmental or corporate policies that restructure career paths so parents could work less or one parent could stay at home when children were young, without sacrificing life-long vocational opportunities
- using political involvement ("You want my vote? How are you making children a priority?")
- visiting child care centers
- tutoring in the public schools
- working with kids in community centers or on the playing fields
- working with at-risk parents
- demanding programs that work with at-risk parents
- working to reduce the frequency of teenage pregnancy
- providing after-school alternatives to a steady diet of cartoons and sit-coms
- developing enough vision and hope ourselves that we could pass these on

The list continues. The final list and the forms these actions take would depend on the talents, dreams, resources, and *cooperation* with one another we bring.

We cannot see yet what this tomorrow would be like. Let's first try to envision turning around the fate of our children by extending ourselves to see them as they currently are and to care about what we learn, with all Americans working cooperatively to ensure the welfare of all young people.

## Do You Recognize Aspects of Yourself?

Mary is the busy mother of three active youngsters, each of whom needs a lot of attention. In addition, she wants to spend time with her husband, her parents, her husband's parents, and her friends. Mary also has a part-time job. She knows current conditions for many children in America are bad, sometimes even terrible. How can she juggle time for her own children, the rest of her family and her friends, her job, and helping children less fortunate than her own?

## Knowledge

### The Current Situation

Giving the United States the worst ranking among eighteen Western industrialized nations, a recent study states that one child in four in America lives below the poverty line. Currently, more children in our country are poor than at any time since 1965.

More than a quarter of all households with children have just one parent. By age eighteen, at least 50 percent of Americans will have spent some time in a single-parent household. This constitutes an enormous burden for the resident caregiver and a significant loss for the child.

An estimated 25 percent of American teenage girls become pregnant at least once before age twenty. Largely as a result of teenage pregnancies, almost one-third of all babies born in the United States have unmarried mothers. The percentage of teenage first-time mothers in America nearly equals the percentages in Jordan, the Philippines, and Thailand; is twice as high as in England, France, and Canada; and is nine times as high as in the Netherlands and Japan. But the birthrate for teenagers is dropping—2 percent lower in 1992 and another 2 percent in 1993.

In *When the Bough Breaks,* liberal economist Sylvia Ann Hewlett argues that this neglect of America's children costs money in the long run. Every dollar spent on enriched preschool programs saves from five to six dollars in remedial education, welfare, and crime control. On average, every dollar spent on prenatal care for high-risk women saves more than three dollars in medical costs during the baby's first year of life. Nationwide, teen births cost 19.8 billion dollars in 1988.

Hewlett cites a study that concludes that investing money in family supports also saves money for employers. She suggests adding additional societal price tags to represent the fear of many Americans for the safety of themselves and their property and the threat posed by an inadequately trained labor force to America's international economic eminence.

When first written, this chapter included quite a broad range of problems confronting children in America. Soon, the chapter threatened to expand into a book itself, so we have dropped most of the doleful details. In another area we could be looking at, David Hamburg, president of the Carnegie Corporation, sees early adolescence, along with early childhood, as an especially vulnerable life stage, when many children become set on a course that leads them to drop out of school, commit violence or other criminal acts, become pregnant, become mentally ill, abuse drugs or alcohol, attempt suicide, die, or become disabled from injuries. Also dropped from the original version of this chapter is the desperate, crack-infested environments of ghetto children, who daily witness poverty and mass unemployment, who fear random or purposeful violence against them, and who at times perpetrate violence themselves. We also don't describe the problems of inferior education and a tax structure unfavorable to families.

Instead, to illustrate the problems American children face, this chapter focuses on child care and television. Think of these as symptomatic of a much broader lack of practical caring among America's citizens for all of America's children.

Child care does highlight a major national problem. (This chapter is not a criticism of paid child care per se. A survey of studies of its effects on young children leads to ambiguous conclusions, as a broad range of researchers report quite disparate findings—some find paid child care harmful, some don't. Nor are we ready to offer specific suggestions for improving the lot of our children. At present, liberal and conservative experts are offering quite different solutions to the problem.)

Though over half of infants are born into two-job households, fewer than 40 percent of America's forty-nine million working women have job-protected *paid* maternity leave of at least six weeks' duration. In contrast, many other countries grant cash payments to mothers to compensate for time lost from work because of pregnancy or childbirth. The length of paid maternity leave ranges from nine to twenty-nine weeks in the ten most developed European countries.

Seventy-five percent of children are brought up in two-job households. Few American parents work flexible hours; the average workweek lasts longer than a generation ago. Because of how busy they are—along with the high aspirations of the present generation of parents for a close and warm relationship with their children—40 percent of parents across the country believe that they are not devoting enough time to educating their children.

Many working parents worry about daytime care. By the early 1990s, a relatively lucky one-third of three- and four-year-olds attended preschools or child care centers. These situations unfortunately are no guarantee of quality. By the late 1990s, of the ninety-seven thousand child care centers, only five thousand were accredited by the National Association for the Education of Young Children, with another ten thousand seeking accreditation. Of the eighty-two thousand nonaccredited centers, only 10 percent were rated as good, 84 percent were rated mediocre, and 6 percent were rated poor. Children not in centers are often casually kept by almost anybody, frequently penned up in small rooms, sometimes watching television nonstop. Nationwide, 15 percent of care for children ages two and a half to five and at least 30 percent of care for infants is considered by experts to be actually harmful. Providers are not addressing health and safety needs, providing support, or encouraging learning.

Standards of child care are low. In many states, one caretaker may watch up to eight children, including infants. In 1987, more than half of child care workers earned less than five dollars per hour. Personnel usually leave within a year. Twenty-three states lack regulations requiring pre-service training for child care teachers. Even among child care providers working in centers, only 60 percent have *any* training in child development and a much lower percentage have training in infant and toddler development. In home-based day care, percentages are lower still.

School-age children also face suboptimal conditions of care. During snow days, teacher workdays, or when the child is ill, many working parents must cobble together makeshift arrangements. School days are shorter than workdays, school vacations longer than work vacations. During late afternoons, summers, and school vacations, most working parents have a day-to-day struggle to provide adequate supervision and transportation.

Part of this slack is taken up by TV, radios, VCRs, computer games, magazines, and old and new breeds of comic books. Young children spend more hours before the TV than engaged in any other single activity except sleep. The typical two- to five-year-old spends *thirty hours a week* in front of the tube, nearly a third of waking hours. Six- to eleven-year-olds cut back to twenty-five hours a week. Over half of this time, parents are watching the same shows. Twenty-nine percent of children aged eight to twelve report their families "usually" watch television during dinner, while an additional 19 percent stated that television is on sometimes during dinner.

A good portion of American TV time will be spent watching advertisements designed to encourage purchases. On average, children watch over *twenty thousand* TV commercials every year. According to the consensus of many child development experts, perhaps half of the direct influence of television is through these commercials.

Research shows that children who watch a great deal of television overestimate the degree of danger and crime in the world, and underestimate the helpfulness and trustworthiness of people. They see too much physical violence and sexuality emphasizing physical beauty and conquest.

Compare this to *Sesame Street,* which originated in the United States in 1969. This children's public television program for three- to five-year-olds appears today in one hundred countries, adapted to the language, culture, and traditions of each nation. In the Canadian version, English- and French-speaking children play together, while Dutch, Moroccan, Turkish, and Surinamese children in Holland can watch children like themselves getting along with the other children. Today, *Sesame Street* has been joined by a number of other worthwhile television programs for children. But these are not yet the norm.

## Present Wisdom

The younger the child, the more pernicious the negative effect of most commercial television. More important than all the influences already mentioned is what the child is not doing while watching TV. Children work by playing—the primary means whereby they develop intellectually, socially, and physically. While a child watches television, she is not engaged in self-initiated play. Primarily for this reason, the American Academy of Pediatrics recommends an upper limit of one and a half hours per day of television-watching for young children.

The TV is probably successfully competing with the child for the adult's attention, unless the child misbehaves dramatically. While current programming discourages much interaction among viewers, some experts believe that programs could be developed which would set the stage for subsequent child-caregiver interaction.

An electronic "V" chip can now block out violent programs from a particular television set, and a new system of ratings informs the public about the suitability of any particular program for children. With these tools in place, will most parents now monitor the quantity and quality of television their children are watching? In addition, television executives have voluntarily pledged three hours of children's educational programs each week. Is it possible that *everyone* will continue along these pathways, with the goal of children's well-being ever in mind?

## Effects on Health and Well-Being

Today's youth are less hearty than previous generations. Compared to counterparts even ten years ago, young people today perform less well on tests of strength, endurance, and general muscle tone. Obesity among children and youth has increased 50 percent over the past twenty years. What accounts for this? Increased TV time? Junk food? Or in combination, TV advertisements for junk food? Parents too busy to prepare healthful meals? Elimination of recess in many schools? Replacement of school kitchens with trucked-in processed food?

Additionally, children's mental health is deteriorating. Developmental psychologist William Damon points to a widely cited study of parents' and teachers' observations conducted between 1976 and 1989:

> The results showed behavioral declines for children of all ages and both sexes during the study's thirteen-year period. In 1989, according to parents and teachers, children were far more likely to "destroy things belonging to others," to "hang around with others who get into trouble," to do poorly on their schoolwork, to be "underactive," "whining," "sullen," "stubborn," and "irritable." More children were lying and stealing; more were being held back a year at school; more were friendless; and more had chronic though minor physical problems such as frequent stomachaches. Fewer children were participating in sports or other healthy outdoor activities, and fewer had found any activity that truly engaged them, including their education.

While this is a United States study, this crisis exists throughout much of the world today.

Current deep emotional troubles of young people include compulsive gambling, sleep and eating disorders, the rising teenage suicide rate, and alcohol-related accidents. As already observed in Chapter 9, in contrast to the general national decline, drug abuse is on the rise among teens.

## *Crossover*

How will we as a nation support this present generation of understimulated and undernurtured children? If all of us care deeply enough—parents, other relatives, and everyone else in each community—what a generation of responsible and committed adults we would bequeath the world! In her study of those who had risked their own lives to rescue Jews from the Nazi Holocaust, psychologist Eva Fogelman found these heroes' upbringing decisive:

> Usually, they came from loving, warm, nurturing homes, where they developed a sense of confidence about their abilities and a sense of independence. As children, when they did something wrong, their parents didn't punish them physically or take away their love but rather explained to them what they had done wrong. Through this kind of discipline, they were able to begin to think for themselves. Also, as children, many of them had role models—either their own parents or another parental figure or siblings—who were involved in helping activities in daily life. And of the rescuers I interviewed, ninety percent grew up in families where they were encouraged to accept people who were different from them. For this reason, they could see the Jews as human beings, despite Nazi propaganda.

## *Actions*

Given how busy most of us are and that most of us want to spend a good portion of our free time with our own family and friends, we need to stay very focused when we consider the needs of all children. We also need to use efficiently any time we devote to their well-being.

# Understanding Ourselves and Others

We hope and believe that most of us, whatever our political and religious beliefs, can commit to wanting to improve the lot of all children. To reach our collective goal, each of us must stay aware of present problems and appreciate the perspectives of others also interested in the well-being of America's children.

### Identify and Evaluate Your Thoughts and Feelings

Margaret Fischer reads in her newspaper that a national foundation is considering funding child care centers in some areas with large numbers of families on welfare. One of the areas being considered for funding is located in her hometown, Denver. While infants, toddlers, and preschoolers would spend their days at the center, their parents would first go back to school and, after completing training, get a job, probably at minimum wage.

Margaret works hard herself as a hairdresser, standing on her feet all day, breathing in chemicals, doing head after head, six days a week. She really gets riled up at the idea that some families get a free ride. She's quite in touch with her angry feelings on this matter! She knows a few single-parent families who are on welfare, and are most of those mothers lazy! But Margaret has to admit that they also don't seem to know how to go about improving themselves. And she knows they lack job skills.

Margaret has recently been reading about how important the first three years are for the entire rest of a child's life. She isn't sure the parents she knows will ever be able to make it in the working world. But she knows their present situation—and the present situation of their children—needs changing. A few demonstration projects, free of federal bureaucracy, seem to her a good investment.

She knows that if only "bleeding-heart liberals"—people who make four times as much money as she does and who aren't aware of what it takes for the average person to get ahead—get involved the project won't be its best. Those liberals don't know what these kids need, that's for sure. They probably won't want any rules. They may not even make the kids pick up their own toys. They may not even try to teach them honesty and other basic values. And it's a cinch they won't appreciate how tired these mothers will be after a day of real work.

Perhaps she could contact the foundation to tell them of her thoughts. Maybe she could even get a little involved if her community were selected as one of the project sights. (The idea of working with those mothers doesn't appeal, she has to admit. But maybe.)

First she has to decide if she wants to invest even *some* time in finding out about the project.

I  *Is this matter important to me?*
"Not personally. Well, maybe. If I consider this as an efficient way to change a situation I don't approve of, maybe. And there are the kids."

A  *Are my thoughts and feelings appropriate, given the facts?*
"What do I feel? Angry at the mothers. Maybe a little bit sorry for them, too. And I definitely pity the kids. Sure, that feels right."

M  *Is the situation modifiable?*
"Is there *anything* I can do to change the situation? Frankly, I don't know. All I have done to date is complain. That hasn't changed anything, except to make me and my friends madder."

WORTH IT  *Balancing the needs of myself and the children involved, is taking action worth it?*
"That depends. To answer that question, I need to know about the foundation, what areas are being chosen, and what the project, once started, will be like."

### Communicate Better and Empathize

For many Americans to decide to make the welfare of children a priority would be an important first step, but in itself, not enough. To achieve this shared goal, Americans need to listen to one another's ideas and speak up at town and city meetings, at meetings in the workplace, and in national elections. Empathy with other spokespersons (and children at risk) will be necessary, as perspectives are going to be in contrast, debates potentially rancorous. Here are some potential topics that might come up for discussion:

- What, if anything, can be done to improve the availability of child care?
- What, if anything, can be done to improve the quality of child care?
- Does children's television programming—and/or all television programming—need regulating by the government for quality control?
- Should paid parental leave be national policy, and if so, how much leave?
- What should be our tax policies toward children?
- What should be our public spending policies toward children?

- Is employment opportunity for parents a children's issue?
- What, if anything, should be done to discourage teenage pregnancies?
- How could we make the workplace family-friendly, yet realistically profitable?
- Is the workweek the right number of hours?
- Is job-sharing desirable?
- Can people who work part-time have a career, as opposed to a job?
- Are alternative work schedules feasible?
- Should decisions about job policies be made by individual companies or government mandates?
- Does telecommuting have a role to play?
- Do satellite work locations have a role to play?
- How can our schools be made safer?
- How can spiritual values be kindled among our citizens?
- How can parental responsibility be encouraged?

## Acting Effectively

As in other matters concerned with our collective well-being, the means we choose to achieve our goals cannot be separated from the goals themselves.

### Consider Acceptance and Assertion

Of all the relationships in this book, the one with America's children requires the most delicate balancing act between (sometimes) conflicting impulses toward acceptance and assertion. Experts agree that committed, trained parents are each child's best hope—even child-abuse programs often focus on supporting the parents in their own efforts to change—so you must work well with parents and uphold children in ways that do not threaten parental autonomy. And if you are to help children, you must work within existing communities (acceptance). Yet you must keep the real focus on the unmet needs of the children (assertion).

### Emphasize the Positive

Teachers rank strengthening parents' roles in their children's schooling as the issue that should receive the highest priority in public education policy. Assisting with homework is one way we parents could do this. If each parent of a child aged one through nine spent one hour five days a week reading or working on school-work with the child, American parents would annually devote at least 8.7 billion hours to improving their children's scholarship. In money terms, if the child's teacher spent the same one-on-one time, the cost to the American taxpayer would be around $230 billion— about the same as what the American public pays yearly for the entire American K-12 public education enterprise.

Maybe you can even see yourself spending some time on a regular basis with one or several children outside your family—as tutor, surrogate big brother or sister, surrogate aunt or uncle, surrogate grandparent.

Wider community involvement in children's issues is critical if we are to address our collective problems. If we citizens practiced Lifeskills, think what we could accomplish together as we tried to improve the lot of children!

## *Getting Real*

A number of years ago, Virginia volunteered at Child and Parent Support Services (CAPSS), whose mission was preventing child abuse. In addition to other programs, CAPSS coupled volunteers with troubled parents, the logic being that the best way to protect a child was by supporting his or her parents. After initial training, Virginia was assigned to a young woman we'll call Pat, a ward of the state. The social worker told Virginia that Pat had been removed from her own home as a toddler, after being abused and neglected. The foster parents she went to live with reputedly locked her in a closet to discipline her, and there was also some suspicion of sexual abuse, never proven. By the time Pat was taken out of this foster home at age five, she was recalcitrant, devious, and prone to setting fires. Pat then moved through a series of foster settings, though one social worker took a special interest in her, contributing to her support from her own income and giving her extra attention. At age thirteen, Pat fell in with a wild crowd, soon becoming pregnant. She gave up that child when he was a few months old, after a social worker found evidence of bites inflicted on the infant's body.

By age sixteen, while still a ward of the state, Pat became pregnant again, this time moving in with the father, a young man devoted to her and the baby son. But life was hard. When Virginia first met Pat, there was again suspicion of child abuse, never proven. The little family was struggling financially. The father held a menial job, but Pat could not manage to keep one. (She would pick arguments, not show up, and otherwise create problems before getting fired or quitting.) Pat and her husband, though together less than a year, had begun to quarrel.

Once a week, Virginia would take Pat out for an afternoon on the town, perhaps lunch and a trip to the library—occasionally a trip to the laundromat. Or the motor vehicles office for an identification card. Or to pick up a job application. Most evenings, Virginia would call Pat, or go over to her place if there was a problem. She remembered Pat at Christmas, though the record player she gave her was soon broken.

Virginia was becoming worked into the general fabric of Pat's life, spending more and more time and energy. Pat still couldn't get it together. And Virginia was feeling overextended, as she still had young children herself. Pat spent grocery money on cigarettes and beer. She watched TV all day. One time Virginia discovered that the baby, howling, had had only Kool-Aid for the last two days. After purchasing formula and dried milk for backup, she talked to Pat about her situation. Virginia next conferred with social services, once again to inform them of what she was observing and to get advice. After several long conversations between Pat and Virginia, with Virginia mainly listening, Pat decided that she was not ready to be a mother—it was just too hard. Adoptive parents were found for the nine-month-old baby.

Several weeks later, Pat left her husband—taking off with a group of Hell's Angels. Within three months, she was reported to be pregnant again. Virginia made some feeble and unsuccessful efforts to reconnect with Pat, but she's never seen her again. Looking back, Virginia realizes that she had taken on a situation that exceeded her resources. She feels good that she was helpful in monitoring the care the baby was receiving and getting the baby out when the situation became untenable—she hopes that damage to him had been minimal. She feels bad that she couldn't enable Pat to become an adequate mother and be at peace with herself. She thinks she did help Pat some.

Virginia now knows that she needs to volunteer for projects that are a better match for her abilities and resources. Her experience with Pat, while initially discouraging—who doesn't want to be the white knight for someone in distress—has only convinced her more deeply of the need for more volunteerism.

As has happened recently in West Virginia, children themselves can also be actively involved in their own nurture. Each year, the West Virginia Department of Education sponsors a Social Studies Fair for school districts throughout the state, to judge student solutions to community problems. One recent winner was the twenty-five students in Diana Stender's seventh grade geography class at Ellsworth Middle School in Middlebourne, a town of nine hundred:

"We collected toys and baby supplies for an orphanage in Ecuador."

"We wrote letters to State officials and helped obtain funding for a local senior citizens center. We studied the effects of what might happen if our school consolidated with other schools and our county superintendent of schools took our results with her, when she attended state meetings to get funds for consolidation." (Funding for a new $15 million middle school–high school has since been approved.)

"We each 'adopted' a grandparent and sent them cards, called them on the phone, and did small helping jobs for them. We collected scrap metal and gave the proceeds from its sale— several hundred dollars—to a boy named Johnny Hollingshead, in Wheeling, West Virginia, who has leukemia. We each donated fifty cents to buy Johnny a sweatshirt to remember us by. We planted flowers at our school. Our class sponsored a Patriotic Essay Contest."

The student co-leader of the school consolidation project observed: "More important than all the awards is what we accomplished. We learned we can really make a difference, and even though we were only thirteen years old, we helped our school, our community, and our superintendent. And we gained confidence in ourselves."

Another student said: "I want everyone to understand that this project was a class project. We all worked together." He also applauded the teacher's time and effort. "She scheduled field trips, pointed us in the right directions for our research, and helped us learn how important each of our project ideas was."

At the beginning of the project, Mrs. Stender asked her students about their plans after high school graduation. Most had no plans; a few had doubts about completing high school. Afterward, all students in her class could name at least one career they might consider, ranging from lawyer to veterinarian, to Air Force officer, to professional baseball player. Every student planned to complete high school.

This single project drew a wide circle of caring individuals. Kudos to:

- "grandparents" who let themselves be adopted
- parents who supported these projects
- whoever arranged the details of the Ecuador connection
- whoever bought the scrap metal
- officials who harnessed student interest to strengthen arguments for school consolidation and the senior center
- Mrs. Stender
- state educators who sponsored the West Virginia Social Studies Fair
- West Virginia taxpayers who let public monies be invested in this way
- student leaders
- each student in Ellsworth Middle School class 7-3

## *Exercises*

1. If your schedule permits, try to arrange to visit a child care center or school located in one of the less-affluent areas of your community.
2. Watch a few minutes of Saturday morning children's TV programs by yourself or with your kids. If you have children, talk to them about the programs and commercials.
3. The next time you encounter a child you don't know well, but with whom you have a chance to talk, listen carefully to whatever the child has to say. It may be enough to remain attentively silent, or you may need to ask some leading questions.
4. Are there dual-career parents of young children in your neighborhood? Can you think of ways, within the limits of time and interest, to support them?
5. Resolve to pay closer attention during the next year to issues affecting children. When you discover an issue where your involvement would help—from volunteering to community discussions to writing a government official—consider participating, with active use of Lifeskills. In choosing projects, stay within your comfort zone, though you may want to stretch a bit, if you need to.

# 16. All Human Beings

Never do to others what you would not like them to do to you.

*K'ung-Fu-tzu, known in*
*the West as Confucius*

Compassionate of others' welfare will we abide, of kindly heart without resentment.

*Siddhartha Gautama,*
*known as the Buddha*

That which is hateful unto thee, do it not unto thy fellow.

*Hillel,*
*Jewish sage*

Love your neighbor as yourself.

*Jesus Christ*

Those who have faith and do righteous deeds, they are the best of creatures.

*Muhammad, founder of Islam*

The Vietnamese are our brothers, the Russians are our brothers, the Chinese are our brothers: and one day we've got to sit down together at the table of brotherhood.

*Martin Luther King, Jr.*

Our global borders are dissolving. The popularity of the Internet continues to increase worldwide. Nuclear weapons can be secretly placed—in any corner of the globe. Environmental degradation in one area of the earth can destroy other areas as well. The evidence is ubiquitous—overwhelming, as never before—that we are interconnected with everyone on this planet.

Technological advances within developed nations so far dominate

BIZARRO © 1995 by Dan Piraro. Reprinted by permission of UNIVERSAL PRESS SYNDICATE. All rights reserved.

the new interconnections. Two-thirds of all the people on earth have never used a telephone! If they suddenly acquired one, along with the ability to speak in any language, what might they say to those individuals accustomed to E-mail and the Internet?

Like it or not, the fate of our children and children's children intertwine with the fate of all other children now and in the future. Our global society must support everyone, or all will languish. Maybe perish as well. In the future, there will only be one possible positive answer to "Who is your neighbor?"

## Vision

"Which of the following comes closest to your definition of family?" Look at recent survey results of twelve hundred Americans asked this question:

A group of people related by blood, marriage, or adoption: 22 percent

A group of people living in the same household: 3 percent

A group of people who love and care for each other: 74 percent

What would happen to our world if we made everybody family?

## *Do You Recognize Aspects of Yourself?*

"First CNN shows footage from Ethiopia of squatting toddlers with distended bellies and hair falling out. I send money. I walk in the CROP walk the next year to raise funds for programs to reduce worldwide hunger. Then CNN shows me footage from Rwanda. I send money again. But combatants blow up the food trucks, and the grain rots in storage bins, while kids starve. And what was I to do about the Bosnians and the Serbs? It wasn't my idea to break up Yugoslavia. And *I* certainly don't go around killing people because they have a different religion from mine.

"Now our preacher is focusing on a Central America kick. Liberation theology is what it's all about. What would Jesus be doing? What am I supposed to do—leave my family and go live there?

"I want to care, I truly do. But how?"

## *Knowledge*

By 1975, four billion people inhabited the earth. By 1993 human beings numbered 5.6 billion. By 2025, this will increase to probably eight to nine billion, with almost all the increase in the less-wealthy developing countries.

## The Current Situation

Feeding more people will require cultivating marginal lands not now farmed, which will increase operating costs, leaving even fewer resources for agricultural practices that encourage land conservation.

As the contentious 1994 United Nations population conference in Cairo, Egypt, demonstrated, cultural differences affect national perspectives on the problem. Spokespersons of many countries advocate educating women, since educated, employed, financially independent women on average have fewer children; some Middle

Eastern representatives fear this may imperil the future of their highly structured, sexually differentiated societies. Delegates from underdeveloped countries prefer to emphasize raising standards of living—since low living standards lead parents to have many children in order to ensure the survival of some offspring who will support them in old age; developed countries prefer direct focus on birth control. Birth control advocacy—to further complicate the issue—arouses objections by some religious leaders.

Wealth is already quite unevenly distributed. In 1991, the per capita gross domestic product of Japan was $36,300, of Sweden $32,600, of the United States $23,100. By contrast, India's per capita GDP was $360, Nigeria's $278. After nearly five decades of unprecedented economic growth globally, over a billion people each live on less than $370 a year. Put in terms of geography, the fifth of the world's population who live in Europe, North America, and Japan are well-to-do. The other four-fifths fall further behind.

Perhaps one last issue relates to all the others. In 1986, Rushworth Kidder of *The Christian Science Monitor* interviewed twenty-two leading global citizens, to discover the half-dozen major, first-intensity, make-it-or-break-it issues on the twenty-first century's agenda. He had expected to hear about five problems that, in the end, did indeed figure strongly on the list: the nuclear threat; environmental degradation; the population crisis; the gap between haves and have-nots; and the need for education reform. But he was unprepared for the force with which another issue came up: the pervasive concern about a global breakdown in ethics and morality.

## Present Wisdom

In a book entitled *The Need to Have Enemies and Allies,* Vamik Volkan, a psychoanalyst and past president of the International Society of Political Psychology, maintains that members of an ethnic or national group usually identify as enemies those belonging to another group. According to Volkan, most human beings acting as individuals—and societies acting together—project onto other people their own unresolved personal conflicts, attributing to the enemy or "other" those parts of themselves they reject. Volkan maintains that by attributing to our enemies those characteristics about ourselves we can't acknowledge, we comfort ourselves that "we" are distinct from—and better than—"them." The consequences range from denigrating ethnic jokes to war and genocide.

When people dehumanize others, small differences are accentuated. (After all, one otherwise wouldn't hate people enough to want

© O.G.P.I. 1996

to denigrate or even kill them.) This tendency of people to set themselves apart can be seen the world over, Volkan argues. From our outside perspective, the people on the island of Cyprus seem much alike. Not to the people living there! The Turks prefer cigarettes in red and white packages; the Greeks, those in blue and white. Want to know who's who in Northern Ireland? Catholics paint their front doors and gates green; Protestants paint theirs blue. On the west coast of India, Garati women wear the shoulder section of their saris on the right—Marathi women wear it on the left.

Until antagonisms between the United States and the Soviet Union diminished with the breakup of the Soviet Union, American cartoonists often depicted Russia in terms of a menacing long-clawed bear—far from the image of a teddy! Most issues of the Soviet humor magazine *Krokodil* ("Crocodile") were full of drawings of the American eagle portrayed in similarly menacing caricatures.

Since Volkan completed his study, the Russians have been transformed from an enemy who wanted to bury us to people who suffered greatly in World War II and have trouble finding adequate housing and food—that now being of greater concern than burying us. Can these changed descriptions be of the same people? Were they always the way we see them now? (This image may change again, as internal Russian politics shift.)

If Volkan's theories that our human nature makes us prone to creating enemies are correct, can human beings outgrow—or at least control the harmful effects of—this tendency?

Another related question: Four-fifths of the world's population consists of people of color; can we get beyond skin color as a factor in judging people? Genetically, even the most sophisticated molecular biologists cannot tell whether cells come from a white, black, yellow, or brown member of Homo sapiens.

## Effects on Health and Well-Being

In *The Immune Power Personality,* Henry Dreher reports on an unpublished study by Joel Weinberger of medical patients who learn present-mindedness at Jon Kabat-Zinn's famous University of Massachusetts Stress Reduction Clinic. Before their eight sessions at the clinic, a group of twenty-seven patients, who suffered from headaches, chronic pain, autoimmune disorders, heart problems, or high blood pressure, took projective tests, in which they interpreted vague pictures of people interacting with each other. After their training, all experienced relief of their physical symptoms. In addition, when they were given new projective tests, again asked to interpret vague pictures, they demonstrated by their interpretations that they also had achieved a greater sense of affiliative trust and a sense of belonging to someone or something bigger than themselves. They typically described the characters in the pictures as having a close emotional bond, with overtones of love or empathy; they saw them as belonging to something larger than themselves—a family, organization, spiritual force, and so on. The greater these patients' sense of oneness with others, the more likely they were to have sustained physical benefits when retested two years later. In other words, connectedness is healing.

## *Crossover*

The world as we know it may outlast our lifetimes. But for the generations who follow, no number of Lifeskills practiced toward themselves, their families, and their communities will suffice to ensure a safe and stable existence, if the rest of the earth's inhabitants do not achieve relatively good health and well-being. What better way to raise our own self-esteem than to contribute toward that worthy goal!

## Action

Peace in the world begins with each of us.

## Understanding Ourselves and Others

You will recall from Chapter 13 that misunderstandings become more likely once people divide the world into all-encompassing categories of "us" and "them." One way we can avoid these simplistic lumpings is to learn more about others and then to try to develop an appreciation of one another.

### Identify Your Thoughts and Feelings

Do you dislike certain cultures? If you can identify enemies or at least groups against whom you have antipathies, try to keep these groups in mind as you read the rest of this chapter.

Your other important task is to become aware that people elsewhere are influenced by policies here. When you gain such awareness around a specific issue, like national trade and military policies, ask yourself how you feel about what is happening.

### Evaluate Your Negative Thoughts and Feelings: I AM WORTH IT!

Cameron reads in a news magazine that certain Chinese nurseries have extremely high death rates and that the children there are living under appalling conditions. Many of the children in these nurseries have been abandoned by their parents, especially little girls whose parents longed for a son under the one-child-per-couple policy of the Chinese government. Cameron initially reacts with anger and sadness.

Cameron lacks many facts. The article he read was based on a documentary by two filmmakers with hidden cameras, who journeyed across southern and central China seeking out the worst nurseries, filming some orphans living and often dying under horrifying conditions. Are these cases typical or just the most sensational? How widespread are such conditions? And is the high death rate in these orphanages the result of a governmental policy of deliberate starvation to try to get rid of these rejected children or a reflection of the poor health of these abandoned children when found? Are these orphanages receiving less funding than other government agencies, or in this poor country, are all government facilities suffering the same from the lack of funds? Why does the Chinese government have a one-child policy? If it's because of poverty and over-crowding, why are the Chinese so poor and so crowded? If upon examination, Chinese policies toward orphanages or birth control seem terribly wrongheaded, what are the options of an outside gov-ernment? an outside individual? Since he can't yet answer these questions, Cameron is not yet in a position to evaluate his thoughts and feelings. He needs information first.

### Communicate Better and Empathize

You may have misconceptions about cultures you dislike. You'll learn more about what people in the other culture think and feel by reading; current junior high texts are easily digested and offer quick overviews. To get past cultural stereotypes, try to meet someone from any group or country you think you dislike. Listen, then empathize. Cameron is going to learn a lot as he reads up on the Chinese.

After listening and empathizing, you may have the opportunity to set aside the misconceptions foreigners have about us, which you can correct by sharing what you are like—your interests, priorities, concerns, and habits.

Unfortunately, though Cameron knows some Chinese Ameri-cans, he has little opportunity to talk with native Chinese.

## Acting Effectively

What will be the outcome of our collective future? What will the future of our great-grandchildren and their great-grandchildren be like?

### Consider Acceptance

Unless a person has lived in another culture, his or her native way of doing things will probably seem the only reasonable option. Someone in the United States may think: "What responsible person could lie in the sun while his children run around in rags? Who wouldn't want to limit the size of her family?" Yet once you under-stand the options—as well as the "ground rules"—in another cul-ture, that cultural perspective may become understandable. You still can work to change opportunities in that part of the world, to

increase resources so others have additional options. But can you
couple this work for future change with a degree of present acceptance, so that these peoples receive your respect as they are right
now?

### Consider Assertion

Have the policies of your country, and other countries, affected
opportunities elsewhere? Should you and your country assume some
responsibility for the unmet legitimate economic needs not being
met? Are certain changes in our governmental policies called for,
and if so, can you influence that? You might consider examining
family planning, trade, or conditions attached to economic and military aid.

On the other hand, are policies in other countries putting you
and other Americans at an unfair disadvantage? If so, should you
attempt to influence those policies?

Have international attempts to improve conditions in poor sec-
tions of the globe made matters better or worse? Do you need to be
involved in this issue? You don't need to be on a Senate subcom-
mittee to make a difference. Consider sending letters to the editor of
your newspaper, writing your congressman or our president, or
trying to interest the world outreach committee at your church,
synagogue, or temple.

### Emphasize the Positive

What are *you* doing to increase mutual respect and commitment
between people in your country and those in other parts of the
world? Some easy options:

- Contact government officials, along the lines suggested under
  "Consider Assertion."
- Insist that public schools teach about other cultures.
- Ask that public libraries stock juvenile and adult books on other
  cultures.
- Contribute to international helping organizations, like UNICEF.
- Speak up when someone is misinformed.
- Write your newspaper when coverage seems unbalanced.
- Contact your TV station when their perspective is skewed.
- Within whatever spiritual tradition you practice, ask for the well-
  being of foreigners in your prayers or centering-times.

This list only gets you started. How can you develop a level of
caring deep enough to sustain you in helping people you may never

meet in person? Vaclav Havel, the former president of the Czech Republic, suggests the best route is to focus on what he calls "the miracle of Being, the miracle of the universe, the miracle of nature, the miracle of our own existence."

The universe is awe-inspiring. Consider its size. Our good friend, University of North Carolina astronomer Morris Davis, who helped us write most of this section, points to a comparison in a college text: if everything in the universe were reduced in size by a *trillion,* our sun would be the size of a mustard seed and the nearest star beyond the sun 6 miles away. That star, Proxima Centauri in our Milky Way galaxy, is actually 4 light-years away—light from this star, traveling at the rate of 186,000 *miles per second,* takes four years to reach us. At greater and greater distances, individual stars cannot be discerned in galaxies; only the combined light of all the stars can be seen. This is like looking at a city at night from an airplane at 30,000 feet: we perceive the light as one lit-up blob. The farthest galaxy recently discovered is 14 billion light-years away!

Since it takes time for light to reach us from any astronomical source, whenever we gaze at the sky, we are looking back into history. Thus we see Proxima Centauri not as it is just now, but as it was four years ago. And the most distant galaxy is visible—but only as it was fourteen billion years ago, close to the Big Bang, believed by astronomers to be the origin of the entire universe.

Our galaxy, the Milky Way galaxy, contains approximately 100 billion stars similar to our sun. Astronomers are mostly convinced that as many as 10 percent of them, in all likelihood, have planetary systems similar to our own solar system. In addition, our galaxy contains all kinds of star clusters, black holes (remains of super-giant stars), white dwarfs (end products of stars like our sun), large clouds of gas, and dust called nebulae. Millions of galaxies have shown up on celestial photographs—Morris Davis estimates such galaxies may number in the billions as our telescopes increase in power. Galaxies vary in size, the largest ones containing a trillion stars. Some astronomers refer to our universe as the "galaxian zoo." Its inhabitants are a variety of spiral types of galaxies like our Milky Way, dwarf elliptical galaxies, giant elliptical galaxies, irregular galaxies, Seyfert galaxies, quasars, and radio galaxies.

And Morris has reported only what astronomers know or can reasonably speculate about. We wonder if perhaps some anti-matter galaxies exist that human beings can't yet observe.

Perhaps contemplations on this scale will help you transcend yourself. For Vaclav Havel, such transcendence is a key step toward good relationships with all:

It logically follows that, in today's multicultural world, the truly reliable path to coexistence, to peaceful coexistence and creative cooperation, must start from what is at the root of all cultures and what lies infinitely deeper in human hearts and minds than political opinion, convictions, antipathies, or sympathies: It must be rooted in self-transcendence. Transcendence as a hand reached out to those close to us, to foreigners, to the human community, to all living creatures, to nature, to the universe; transcendence as a deeply and joyously experienced need to be in harmony even with what we ourselves are not, what we do not understand, what seems distant from us in time and space, but with which we are nevertheless mysteriously linked because, together with us, all this constitutes a single world.

In Havel's opinion, such transcendence is "the only real alternative to extinction."

## Getting Real

Let's face it: frequent international scientific contacts give the two of us advantages not available to many. Our success in being citizens of the world reflects less on our openness than on our opportunities and the absence of any required personal sacrifices involved in this internationalism. A larger challenge has been to remain empathetic with traditional patriots who still identify exclusively with their own country. We have worked hard on this and been on a small crusade about it in some liberal circles.

Virginia was active for years in the movement to reverse the arms race. The pressure seems off that issue, so now she focuses on Lifeskills.

Reaching out to others need not be a chore. Sometimes the connections come from unexpected opportunities. In 1987, as part of a scientific exchange sponsored by the National Heart, Lung, and Blood Institute, Redford and his colleague Peter Kaufmann visited the Soviet Union, ending up at the Cardiology Research Institute in Tbilisi, capital of the Soviet Republic of Georgia. Entertainment there was lavish, with delicious food and drink in generous quantities and heartfelt toasts. Redford's final invitation was to a wedding reception held in a village located high up in the Caucasus Mountains.

The large wedding reception, with its inspired banquet and

expansive toasts, surpassed even the best efforts of the previous three nights in Tbilisi.

Suddenly, the professional toastmaster, called the *tamehda,* began effusively to toast Peter and Redford, along with Georgian-American and Soviet-American friendship. The translator whispered to Peter and Redford that they must respond, which Redford did.

> Dear friends! Your words do us great honor, and we thank you for such a warm welcome here tonight. During the past few days, it has been our privilege to visit with our Georgian colleagues at the Cardiology Institute in Tbilisi.
>
> During this time, we have learned many things from them that will help to make our science better when we return to the United States. We hope that we have been able to share with them some of our knowledge, and if you permit, let me repeat just one thing our research has taught us: Hostility is bad for the health of individual persons. If one has a cynical mistrust of others, if one experiences anger frequently toward others, and if one frequently expresses that anger in aggressive behavior toward others, then, our research has taught us, such persons are too often destined for an early grave.
>
> Surely it must be true that what is bad for the health of individuals is bad for the health of nations! So let me raise my glass and share my wish for the health of our nations; let there be between us more trust, less anger, and no aggression!
>
> But our purpose here tonight is not to speak of relationships between nations, but to honor the newly married couple. For among all human relationships, it is in marriage that the highest levels of trust are achieved.
>
> Therefore, let me conclude by raising my glass to the bride and groom to wish them a lifetime of trust, joy, and kindness!

Everyone rose as one and shouted their agreement with these sentiments. Redford was much in demand the rest of the night, for everyone—men and women alike—wanted to dance with him.

Let's all dance.

## *Exercises*

1. Thought for one day: Redwoods are the oldest, biggest trees on earth, despite their shallow roots. How do they manage for

thousands of years not to topple over? By connecting up to the roots of other trees.

2. Ponder why we don't have an earth flag and pledge of allegiance. Create such a flag and pledge; then share what you have drawn and written with at least two other people.

3. Imagine it's the year 3000 and you have been assigned the task of writing a world history, to cover the last one thousand years. If you could wish an ideal future, what would that history say?

4. Look into the face of another person you encounter (family member, friend, or stranger, adult or child). Observe. Then think about the uniqueness of this person, unlike any other in the past or future, unlike any other manifestation anywhere else in the universe.

5. Remember from Chapter 6 the exercise to keep composing and, if necessary, revising your list of priorities for your life. Complete your latest ranking and post your list in a prominent place, perhaps your mirror or refrigerator door.

6. Set aside a half-hour. Locate a place where you will not be disturbed. After thinking about how you want to spend your remaining time on earth, compose your ideal future—and inevitable—obituary.

# Epilogue:
# The Caring Family

*I*magine that for the rest of your life, you try to live skillfully, in all of your relationships. You grow old, and one day near your end, you look back over the time since you began to practice Lifeskills.

Envision yourself first alone at home. With ever-increasing frequency over the years, you identified and evaluated feelings and thoughts, accepted yourself. You usually gave yourself positive messages. You asserted yourself when necessary, solved problems when possible. When solitary, you kept good company.

Building on this solid base, you valued others, too. So invite in your partner, now older and cherished by you. Look deeply into your partner's eyes. Report some of your innermost feelings and thoughts. Listen with interest, empathy, and acceptance, in affirmation.

If you have children, picture them as they arrive, their faces, their voices, their special smell. Your children's roots in you sustained them. In your company, young children were affirmed and guided, teenagers headed off in positive directions, sometimes beyond your longings or imagination. Adult children received unconditional love and respect.

In turn, you remain rooted in your parents. Recall them. Like a green and budded plant, you sent sustenance back through listening, speaking, empathy, acceptance, and affirmation.

Warmly invite in friends, then neighbors.

Next envision yourself at work. The amount of time and energy devoted to work was in right balance with the rest of your life. Also, you helped yourself and others usually to plan together, share ideas, work in concert.

Picture culturally diverse groups in your community, seeing now individual faces. In community forums, you got your points across *and* were sometimes changed by what you learned.

Envision children outside your immediate circle whom you helped, their particular faces relaxed, inquisitive.

Could you include everybody? Could you treat your own

family with care, yet expand your circle this far, without feeling overextended?

If not, comfort yourself. Realize that in most relationships, you are imagining yourself extended beyond what was ever before required. Yet know that if you apply them consistently, your Life-skills will enable you to succeed much of the time.

When ready, imagine gently holding your partner's and children's hands. Your children reach out toward friends, who in turn clasp other hands, until a chain reaches across the oceans. Outermost voices, unfamiliar sounds in Mandarin, Spanish, Swahili, and many other tongues, once again speak faintly. Somehow understanding the foreign words, through the years you listened attentively. You empathized, accepted. You affirmed your fellow human beings by words and deeds. You do so again.

Within the past few weeks, the atoms you just breathed in have been exhaled by everyone else on earth—including the impoverished people your imagination can keep out, if you repress all caring. Instead, envision having acknowledged your shared humanity. You listened. Empathized. Accepted. Proceeding beyond acceptance, you shared. You encouraged elected officials to make this national policy.

You learned to identify and evaluate your thoughts and feelings, to communicate well, to act effectively, and to emphasize the positive. Imagine having received similar treatment from others who reciprocated.

You sense inner peace, power, a connection with All.

You and distant others managed occasionally to communicate, in a caring fashion. Eventually, earth's inhabitants in their singular bodies will share genes from you and them. When you contemplate this shared fate, you still feel fearful, but also now hopeful.

Some acquaintances returned your interest and commitment to getting along well. You managed to discover some common ground.

Your intimates usually gave back respect and caring. Some came to cherish you.

Being alone became increasingly pleasurable. Sometimes reaching out to others nurtured them deeply, which in turn helped you feel good about yourself. You are reconnected to others, healthy, whole.

You are part of a caring family.

# Notes

## Introduction

xix When a large survey sample of Americans: Massachusetts Mutual Life Insurance Company, *1991 American Family Values Study: A Return to Family Values,* Springfield, Mass.: Mass Mutual, 1991, p. 44.

## 1. The Best of Times, the Worst of Times

4 During the last two to four million years. . . . nothing less than a death sentence: Lionel Tiger, *The Pursuit of Pleasure,* Boston: Little, Brown, 1992, pp. 23, 54–55, 63.

4 In *The Evolving Self:* Mihalyi Csikszentmihalyi, *The Evolving Self: A Psychology for the Third Millennium,* New York: HarperCollins, 1993.

5 The old order Amish. . . . New Guinea do not experience depression: Robert Wright, "The Evolution of Despair," *Time* (28 August 1995): pp. 52–53.

6 In 1940, only 15 percent of young people. . . . We have more money: Arlene Skolnick, *Embattled Paradise: The American Family in an Age of Uncertainty,* New York: Basic Books, 1991, pp. 1–18.

6 Another big shift marked the postwar period. . . . and whether they ever felt inadequate as parents: Joseph Veroff, Elizabeth Douvan, and Richard A. Kulka, *The Inner American: A Self-Portrait from 1957–1976,* New York: Basic Books, 1981, p. 23.

7 From her study of working parents, sociologist Arlie Hochschild. . . . work seems like "home": Arlie Russell Hochschild, "There's No Place Like Work," *New York Times Magazine* (20 April 1997): p. 52.

7 Between 1985 and 1990: *Statistical Abstracts 1993,* Landham, Md.: Berhan Press, 1993, p. 27.

7 Recent figures show less mobility: *New York Times* (12 September 1995): p. 1.

## 2. First, Know Thyself

10 Questions to assess depression: Lenore Sawyer Radloff, "The CES-D Scale: A Self-Report Depression Scale for Research in the General Population," *Applied Psychological Measurement* 1, no. 3 (summer 1977): pp. 385–401.

## 3. Relationships Matter!
### The Scientific Evidence for Effects on Our Health

26 When you can measure: William Thomson, Lord Kelvin, *Popular Lectures and Addresses, 1891–1894.*

28 To determine this, researchers have measured . . . recipients' perceptions of that support and their satisfaction with it: Barbara R. Sarason, Gregory R. Pierce, and Irwin G. Sarason, "Social Support: The Sense of

Acceptance and the Role of Relationships," in *Social Support: An Interactional View,* ed. Barbara R. Sarason, Irwin G. Sarason, and Gregory R. Pierce, New York: John Wiley, 1990, pp. 118–121.

29  A twenty-nine-year study: J. S. House, K. R. Landis, and D. Umberson, "Social Relationships and Health," *Science* 241 (1988): pp. 540–545.

29  In one study of heart attack victims: R. B. Case et al., "Living Alone After Myocardial Infarction: Impact on Prognosis," *Journal of the American Medical Association* 267 (1991): pp. 515–519.

29  In a follow-up study of patients with coronary disease: R. B. Williams et al., "Prognostic Importance of Social and Economic Resources Among Medically Treated Patients with Angiographically Documented Coronary Artery Disease," *Journal of the American Medical Association* 267 (1992): pp. 520–524.

29  Duke psychologist John Barefoot surveyed doctors: J. C. Barefoot, W. G. Dahlstrom, and R. B. Williams, "Hostility, CHD Incidence and Total Mortality: A 25-Year Follow-up Study of 255 Physicians," *Psychosomatic Medicine* 45 (1983): pp. 59–63.

29  Numerous other studies . . . impact of hostility: T. W. Smith, "Hostility and Health: Current Status of a Psychosomatic Hypothesis," *Health Psychology* 11 (1992): pp. 139–150.

30  Evidence suggests that from young adulthood hostile people are isolated: Ibid.

30  Their marriages can be rancorous: Ibid.

30  The authoritarian style . . . top bosses: Meyer Friedman and Diane Ulmer, *Treating Type A Behavior and Your Heart,* New York: Knopf, 1984, pp. 81–82.

30  Studies of healthy persons in both the United States and Denmark . . . these depressive tendencies: R. Anda et al., "Depressed Affect, Hopelessness, and the Risk of Ischemic Heart Disease in a Cohort of U.S. Adults," *Epidemiology* 4 (1993): pp. 285–294. J. C. Barefoot and M. Schroll, "Symptoms of Depression, Acute Myocardial Infarction, and Total Mortality in a Community Sample," *Circulation* 93: pp. 1976–1980.

30  Psychologist Nancy Frasure-Smith and her colleagues: N. Frasure-Smith, F. Lesperance, and M. Talajic, "Depression Following Myocardial Infarction: Impact on 6-Month Survival," *Journal of the American Medical Association* 270 (1993): pp. 1819–1825.

30  My colleague John Barefoot also has found: J. C. Barefoot et al., "Depression and Long-Term Mortality Risk in Patients with Coronary Artery Disease," *American Journal of Cardiology* 78 (1996): pp. 613–617.

31  Industrial psychologist Robert Karasek and his colleagues. . . . no latitude in setting work pace: R. A. Karasek and T. Theorell, *Healthy Work: Stress, Productivity, and the Reconstruction of Working Life,* New York: Basic Books, 1990.

31  In a study of women workers at a large corporation. . . . likely to be socially isolated: R. B. Williams et al., "Psychosocial Correlates of Job Strain in a Sample of Working Women," *Archives of General Psychiatry,* 54 (1997): pp. 543–48.

31  Other researchers . . . stress on the job: J. V. Johnson, E. M. Hall, and T. Theorell, "Combined Effects of Job Strain and Social Isolation on Cardiovascular Disease Morbidity and Mortality in a Random Sample of

the Swedish Male Working Population," *Scandinavian Journal of Work, Environment, and Health* 15 (1989): pp. 271–279.

31  As with depression . . . studies at both Duke and Cornell . . . five years after a heart attack: R. B. Williams et al., "Prognostic Importance of Social and Economic Resources Among Medically Treated Patients with Angiographically Documented Coronary Artery Disease," *Journal of the American Medical Association* 267 (1992): pp. 520–524. W. Ruberman et al., "Psychosocial Influences on Myocardial Infarction," *New England Journal of Medicine* 311 (1984): pp. 552–559. W. Ruberman et al., "Education, Psychosocial Stress, and Sudden Cardiac Death," *Journal of Chronic Disease* 36 (1983): pp. 151–160.

31  For example, lower-grade government civil servants. . . . high cholesterol levels: M. G. Marmot et al., "Employment Grade and Coronary Heart Disease in British Civil Servants," *Journal of Epidemiology and Community Health* 3 (1978): pp. 244–249.

32  For example, my colleagues and I found in a recent study of working women. . . . high strain jobs: R. B. Williams et al., "Psychosocial Correlates of Job Strain in a Sample of Working Women," *Archives of General Psychiatry* 54 (1997): pp. 543–548. T. Pincus and L. F. Callahen, "What Explains the Association Between Socioeconomic Status and Health: Primarily Access to Medical Care or Mind-Body Variables?" *Advances* 11 (1995): pp. 4–36.

32  My Duke colleague John Barefoot found: J. C. Barefoot et al., "Depressive Affect, Hostility, and Socioeconomic Status (SES): Interrelationships and Joint Effects on Health" (paper presented at the Annual Meeting of the American Psychosomatic Society, New Orleans, March 1995).

32  In his study of Alameda County residents. . . . residents of Kuopio, Finland: G. A. Kaplan, "Where Do Shared Pathways Lead? Some Reflections on a Research Agenda," *Psychosomatic Medicine* 57 (1993): pp. 208–212.

32  In a study of elderly residents in Glostrup, Denmark: J. C. Barefoot et al., "Depressive Affect, Hostility, and Socioeconomic Status (SES): Interrelationships and Joint Effects on Health" (paper presented at the Annual Meeting of the American Psychosomatic Society, New Orleans, March 1995).

36  My Duke colleague Edward Suarez has been: E. C. Suarez and R. B. Williams, "Situational Determinants of Cardiovascular and Emotional Reactivity in High and Low Hostile Men," *Psychosomatic Medicine* 51 (1989): pp. 404–418.

36  During daily life as well: E. C. Suarez et al., "Hostility-Related Differences in Urinary Excretion Rates of Catecholamines" (paper presented at the Annual Meeting of the Society for Psychophysiological Research, Chicago, 1991). M. K. Pope and T. W. Smith, "Cortisol Excretion in High and Low Cynically Hostile Men," *Psychosomatic Medicine* 53 (1991): pp. 386–392.

36  One example: John M. Gottman, *Why Marriages Succeed or Fail: What You Can Learn from the Breakthrough Research to Make Your Marriage Last*, New York: Simon and Schuster, 1994. John M. Gottman, *What Predicts Divorce? The Relationship Between Marital Processes and Marital Outcomes*, Hillsdale, N.J.: Lawrence Erlbaum, 1994.

36 University of Utah psychologist Timothy Smith has found: T. W. Smith and K. D. Allred, "Blood Pressure Reactivity During Social Interaction in High and Low Cynical Hostile Men," *Journal of Behavioral Medicine* 11 (1989): pp. 135–143.

36 In a parallel to the findings ... weaker parasympathetic calming effects ... led to anger: S. Fukudo et al., "Accentuated Vagal Antagonism of Beta Adrenergic Effects on Ventricular Repolarization: Differential Responses Between Type A and Type B Men," *Circulation* 85 (1992): pp. 2045–2053. R. P. Sloan et al., "Cardiovascular Autonomic Control and Hostility in Healthy Subjects," *American Journal of Cardiology* 74 (1994): pp. 298–300.

36 Thus, increased sympathetic function: R. C. Vieth et al., "Sympathetic Nervous System Activity in Major Depression: Basal and Desipramine-Induced Alterations in Plasma Norepinephrine Kinetics," *Archives of General Psychiatry* 51 (1994): pp. 411–422. R. M. Carney et al., "The Relationship Between Heart Rate, Heart Rate Variability, and Depression in Patients with Coronary Artery Disease," *Journal of Psychosomatic Research* 32 (1988): pp. 159–164. F. Holsboer et al., "Blunted Corticotrophin and Normal Response to Human Corticotrophin-Releasing Factor in Depression," *New England Journal of Medicine* 311 (1984): p. 1127.

37 Persons who report low social support ... high levels of social support: R. Fleming et al., "Mediating Influences of Social Support on Stress at Three Mile Island," *Journal of Human Stress* 8 (1982): pp. 14–22.

37 The latter possibility: T. W. Kamarck, S. B. Manuck, and J. R. Jennings, "Social Support Reduces Cardiovascular Reactivity to Psychological Challenge: A Laboratory Model," *Psychosomatic Medicine* 52 (1990): pp. 42–58.

37 Working women with young children: L. J. Luecken et al., "Stress in Employed Women: Impact of Marital Status and Children at Home on Neurohormone Output and Home Strain," *Psychosomatic Medicine* 59 (1997): pp. 352–359.

37 Large-scale studies ... Ilene Siegler ... increased heart attack risk: I. C. Siegler et al., "Hostility in Late Adolescence Predicts Coronary Risk Factors at Mid-Life," *American Journal of Epidemiology* 136 (1992): pp. 146–156. K. W. Scherwitz et al., "Hostility and Health Behaviors in Young Adults: The CARDIA (Coronary Artery Risk Development in Young Adults) Study," *American Journal of Epidemiology* 136 (1992): pp. 136–145.

39 The high adrenaline levels in hostile persons: A. D. Shiller et al., "Hostility Is Associated with Lymphocyte Beta-2 Adrenergic Receptor/Adenylate Cyclase Activity," *Psychosomatic Medicine* 56 (1994): p. 174.

39 Thus, our preliminary findings point: E. C. Suarez et al., "Anger Increases Expression of Interleukin-1 on Monocytes in Hostile Women" (paper presented at the Annual Meeting of the American Psychsomatic Society, Williamsburg, Va., March 1996).

41 Psychiatrist Emil Coccaro and colleagues: E. F. Coccaro et al., "Serotonergic Studies in Patients with Affective and Personality Disorders," *Archives of General Psychiatry* 46 (1989): pp. 587–599.

41 Bowman-Gray researcher Jay Kaplan: M. B. Botchin et al., "Low Versus High Prolactin Responders to Fenfluramine Challenge: Marker of Behavioral Differences in Adult Male Cynomolgus Macaques," *Neuropsychopharmacology* 9 (1993): pp. 93–99.

41 National Institutes of Health researcher Dee Higley: J. D. Higley et al., "Cerebrospinal Fluid Monoamine and Adrenal Correlates of Aggression in Free-ranging Rhesus Monkeys," *Archives of General Psychiatry* 49 (1992): pp. 436–441.

41 In one study, monkeys given. . . . close proximity to other monkeys: M. J. Raleigh et al., "Serotonergic Mechanisms Promote Dominance Acquisition in Adult Male Vervet Monkeys," *Brain Research* 559 (1991): pp. 181–190.

41 In a study of patients with borderline personality disorder: C. Salzman et al., "Effect of Fluoxetine on Anger in Symptomatic Volunteers with Borderline Personality Disorder," *Journal of Clinical Psychopharmacology* 15 (1995): pp. 23–29.

42 Harvard physiologist Richard Verrier has shown: R. L. Verrier, "Neurochemical Approaches to the Prevention of Ventricular Fibrillation," *Federation Proceedings* 45 (1996): pp. 2191–2196.

42 Other research shows that stimulation of the same serotonin receptors: P. R. Saxena and C. M. Villalon, "Cardiovascular Effects of Serotonin Agonists and Antagonists," *Journal of Cardiovascular Pharmacology* 7 (1990): pp. S17–S34.

42 Favoring the most parsimonious explanation: R. B. Williams, "Neurobiology, Cellular and Molecular Biology, and Psychosomatic Medicine," *Psychosomatic Medicine* 56 (1994): pp. 308–315.

43 For example, psychologist Nancy Frasure-Smith and her colleagues: N. Frasure-Smith and R. Prince, "The Ischemic Heart Disease Life Stress Monitoring Program: Impact on Mortality," *Psychosomatic Medicine* 47 (1985): pp. 431–445.

43 A similar 50 percent reduction: M. Friedman, C. E. Thoresen, and J. J. Gill, "Alteration of Type A Behavior and Its Effect on Cardiac Recurrences in Post Myocardial Infarction Patients: Summary Results of the Recurrent Coronary Prevention Project," *American Heart Journal* 112 (1986): pp. 653–665.

43 Instead of reduced recurrence rates: D. M. Ornish et al., "Can Lifestyle Changes Reverse Coronary Heart Disease? The Lifestyle Heart Trial," *Lancet* 2 (1990): pp. 129–133.

44 Stanford psychiatrist David Spiegel and his colleagues: D. Spiegel et al., "Effect of Psychosocial Treatment on Survival of Patients with Metastatic Breast Cancer," *Lancet* 2 (1989): pp. 888–890.

44 In another study, UCLA psychiatrist Fawzy Fawzy and his colleagues: F. I. Fawzy et al., "Malignant Melanoma: Effects of an Early Structured Psychiatric Intervention, Coping, and Affective State on Recurrence and Survival 6 Years Later," *Archives of General Psychiatry* 50 (1993): pp. 681–689.

45 University of Pittsburgh psychologist Thomas Kamarck has shown: T. W. Kamarck, S. B. Manuck, and J. R. Jennings, "Social Support Reduces Cardiovascular Reactivity to Psychological Challenge: A Laboratory Model," *Psychosomatic Medicine* 52 (1990): pp. 42–58.

45  And Southern Methodist University psychologist James Pennebaker has
    found: J. W. Pennebaker, *Opening Up: The Healing Power of Confiding in
    Others*, New York: William Morrow, 1990.

45  Taking a different tack: C. K. Ewart et al., "Reducing Blood Pressure
    Reactivity During Interpersonal Conflict: Effects of Marital Communica-
    tion Training," *Behavior Therapy* 15 (1984): pp. 475–484.

45  And finally, I and my colleagues at Duke have shown: R. B. Williams
    et al., "Stress Management Training Boosts Social Support in Married
    Working Mothers" (paper presented at the Fourth International Congress
    of Behavioral Medicine, Washington, D.C., March 1996).

## 4. Relationships Matter!
### The Scientific Evidence for Effects on Others' Health

47  . . . the magnitude of children's accomplishments . . .: Betty Hart and
    Todd Risley, *Meaningful Differences in the Everyday Experience of Young
    American Children*, Baltimore: Paul H. Brookes, 1995, p. 210.

47  . . . a prevention agenda for children: Rune J. Simeonsson, *Risk,
    Resilience, and Prevention: Promoting the Well-Being of All Children*, Balti-
    more: Paul H. Brookes, 1994, p. xi.

59  Over 80 percent of all violent offenders: D. A. Hamburg, *Today's Chil-
    dren: Creating a Future for a Generation in Crisis*, New York: Times Books,
    1992.

60  During World War II: R. Spitz, *The First Year of Life*, New York: Inter-
    national Universities Press, 1965.

60  At the University of Wisconsin, psychologist Harry Harlow: H. R.
    Harlow and M. K. Harlow, "The Young Monkeys," in *Readings in Psy-
    chology Today*, 2d. ed., New York: Delmar, 1972.

60  In research conducted at the National Institutes of Health: J. D. Higley
    et al., "Paternal and Maternal Genetic and Environmental Contributions
    to Cerebrospinal Fluid Monoamine Metabolites in Rhesus Monkeys
    (Macaca mulatta)," *Archives of General Psychiatry* 50 (1993): pp. 615–623.
    J. D. Higley, S. J. Suomi, and M. Linnoila, "A Longitudinal Assessment
    of CSF Monoamine Metabolites and Plasma Cortisol Concentrations in
    Young Rhesus Monkeys," *Biological Psychiatry* 32 (1992): pp. 127–145.
    J. D. Higley et al., "A Nonhuman Primate Model of Type I and II
    Excessive Alcohol Consumption" (paper presented at the Annual
    Meeting of the American College of Neuropsychopharmacology, San
    Juan, P.R., December 1995).

61  Another line of research: M. Boccia, "Availability of Attachment Figures
    and Infant Distress Following Maternal Separation" (paper presented at
    the Annual Meeting of the Society of Behavioral Medicine, Washington,
    D.C., March 1996).

62  In an elegant research program conducted at McGill University: M. J.
    Meaney et al., "Molecular Basis for the Development of Individual Dif-
    ferences in the Hypothalamic-Pituitary-Adrenal Stress Response," *Cel-
    lular and Molecular Neurobiology* 13 (1993): pp. 321–347.

65  Psychologists Betty Hart and Todd Risley have conducted: T. Hart and
    T. R. Risley, *Meaningful Differences in the Everyday Experience of Young
    American Children*, Baltimore: Paul H. Brookes, 1995.

66  Further indirect evidence: I. Lissau-Lund-Sorensen and T. I. A. Sorensen, "Prospective Study of the Influence of Social Factors in Childhood on the Risk of Overweight in Young Adulthood," *International Journal of Obesity* 16 (1992): pp. 169–175. I. Lissau-Lund-Sorenson and T. I. A. Sorensen, "Parental Neglect During Childhood and Increased Risk of Obesity in Young Adulthood," *Lancet* 343 (1994): pp. 324–327.

66  Studies by University of Pittsburgh psychologist Karen Matthews: K. A. Matthews, K. L. Woodall, and T. Jacob, "Negative Family Environment as a Predictor of Boys' Future Status on Measures of Hostile Attitudes, Interview Behavior, and Anger Expression," *Health Psychology* 15 (1996): pp. 30–37.

66  At the National Institutes of Health: M. J. P. Kruesi et al., "A 2-Year Prospective Follow-Up Study of Children and Adolescents with Disruptive Behavior Disorders: Prediction by Cerebrospinal Fluid 5-hydroxyindoleacetic Acid, Homovanillic Acid, and Autonomic Measures?" *Archives of General Psychiatry* 49 (1992): pp. 429–435.

## 5. Lifeskills

73  When researchers interrupt people at random: Ed Diener and Randy J. Larsen, "The Experience of Emotional Well-being," in *Handbook of Emotions,* ed. Michael Lewis and Jeannette Haviland, New York: Guilford Press, 1993, pp. 405.

83  *Meditate.* It is good for everyone to be able to focus attention at will: Lawrence LeShan, *How to Meditate: A Guide to Self-Discovery,* New York: Bantam, 1974, still in print, provides a good overview of meditation, though his primary focus is on spiritual benefits.

85  Psychologist John Barefoot, a colleague at Duke . . . dumb question, if ever I heard one!: John Barefoot, "Developments in the Measurement of Hostility," in *Hostility, Coping, and Health,* ed. Howard S. Friedman, Washington, D.C.: APA, 1992, pp. 13–31.

91  Empathize to Understand Others' Behavior: The best overall examination of empathy is Nancy Eisenberg and Janet Strayer, eds., *Empathy and Its Development,* Cambridge, England: Cambridge Univ. Press, 1987. *Counseling Psychologist* devoted volume 5 (1975) to empathy.

91  Empathy may be a natural behavior: Leslie Brothers, "A Biological Perspective on Empathy," *American Journal of Psychiatry* 146, no. 1 (January 1989): pp. 10–19. Martin L. Hoffman, "The Contribution of Empathy to Justice and Moral Judgment," in *Empathy and Its Development,* ed. Nancy Eisenberg and Janet Strayer, Cambridge, England: Cambridge Univ. Press, 1987, p. 51. Ross A. Thompson, "Empathy and Emotional Understanding: The Early Development of Empathy," in *Empathy and Its Development,* chap. 6 (pp. 119–145). Nancy Eisenberg, "Empathy and Sympathy," in *Child Development Today and Tomorrow,* ed. William Damon, San Francisco: Jossey-Bass, 1989, chap. 7.

91  Children a year and older: Marian Radke-Yarrow and Carolyn Zahn-Waxler, "Roots, Motives, and Patterns in Children's Prosocial Behavior," in *Development and Maintenance of Prosocial Behavior,* ed. Edwin Staub et al., New York: Plenum, 1984, pp. 81–99. Randy Lennon and Nancy Eisenberg, "Gender and Age Differences in Empathy and Sympathy," in *Empathy and Its Development,* pp. 195–217.

92   In his excellent book, *Sound Mind, Sound Body:* American Association for the Advancement of Science annual meeting (February 1993) as quoted by Kenneth Pelletier, *Sound Mind, Sound Body: A New Model for Lifelong Health,* New York: Simon and Schuster, 1994, pp. 41–42.

92   Mirja Kalliopuska, a University of Helsinki psychologist: Mirja Kalliopuska, "Attitudes Towards Health, Health Behavior, and Personality Factors Among School Students Very High on Empathy," *Psychological Reports* 70 (June 1992): pp. 1119–1122.

92   Further, Dr. Kalliopuska has successfully trained: Kenneth Pelletier, *Sound Mind, Sound Body: A New Model for Lifelong Health,* New York: Simon and Schuster, 1994, p. 42. Mirja Kalliopuska and Unito Tiitinen, "Influence of Two Developmental Programmes on the Empathy and Prosociability of Preschool Children," *Perceptual and Motor Skills* 72 (February 1991): pp. 323–328.

96   Practice Assertion and Acceptance: In his review of the literature, Richard F. Rakos, *Assertive Behavior: Theory, Research, and Training,* New York: Routledge, 1991, stresses cultural variability and the importance of context.

96   In a small study comparing extremes: John M. Williams and John K. Stout, "The Effect of High and Low Assertiveness on Locus of Control and Health Problems," *Journal of Psychology* 119 (March 1985): pp. 169–173.

96   Only when relationships are positive: James C. Coyne and Anita DeLongis, "Going Beyond Social Support: The Role of Social Relationships in Adaptation," *Journal of Consulting and Clinical Psychology* 54 (1986): pp. 454–460. Many of the chapters in *Social Support: An Interactional View,* New York: John Wiley, 1990, the excellent volume edited by Barbara R. Sarason, Irwin G. Sarason, and Gregory R. Pierce, address the subtle and complex trade-offs sometimes involved in giving or receiving social support. For example, a spouse who is too protective following a heart attack may interfere with the patient's regaining a sense of autonomy and personal efficacy.

99   Our Duke group: I. M. Lipkus et al., "The Structure of the Cook-Medley Hostility Scale as Assessed by Multidimensional Scaling" (paper presented at the meeting of the Society of Behavioral Medicine, San Francisco, March 1993).

100  Using volunteer subjects: John Gottman, *Why Marriages Succeed or Fail: What You Can Learn from the Breakthrough Research to Make Your Marriage Last,* New York: Simon and Schuster, 1994, is the popular presentation of this information. John M. Gottman, *What Predicts Divorce? The Relationship Between Marital Processes and Marital Outcomes,* Hillsdale, N.J.: Lawrence Erlbaum, 1994, covers the same general subject in a more scholarly approach. Both books are treated more extensively in Chapter 7.

101  Researchers report that: Ed Diener and Randy J. Larsen, "The Experience of Emotional Well-being," in *Handbook of Emotions,* ed. Michael Lewis and Jeannette Haviland, New York: Guilford Press, 1993, pp. 405–415. Ed Diener, "Subjective Well-Being," *Psychological Bulletin* 95 (1984): pp. 542–575.

## 6. Begin with a Good Relationship with Yourself

107 Being a socially competitive species . . . even more dissatisfied with ourselves. Randolph Nesse and George Williams, *Why We Get Sick: The New Science of Darwinian Medicine,* New York: Times Books, 1994, p. 138 f. Cf. Holly Brubach, "Heroine Worship: The Age of the Female Icon," *New York Times Magazine* (24 November 1996): pp. 55–57. She focuses on how women call on various aspects of public personalities to reconfigure their own lives.

107 In an article in *American Psychologist:* Philip Cushman, "Why the Self is Empty: Toward a Historically Situated Psychology," *American Psychologist* (May 1990): pp. 559–610.

110 During one of their early weekly sessions: "Coronary/Cancer Prevention Project: Year I Curriculum," unpublished syllabus, p. 4.

110 Dr. Friedman and his associates: Virginia A. Price et al., "Relation Between Insecurity and Type A Behavior," *American Heart Journal* 129 (March 1995): pp. 488–491.

110 During the first half of this century: Arne Naess, *Gandhi and Group Conflict: An Exploration of Satyagraha: Theoretical Background,* Oslo: Universitetsforlaget, 1974, pp. 107–112.

110 Several systematic surveys: Ed Diener, "Subjective Well-being," *Psychological Bulletin* 95 (1984): pp. 542–575.

111 In a twist on this: J. Michael McGinnis and William H. Foege, "Actual Causes of Death in the United States," *Journal of the American Medical Association* 270 (10 November 1993): pp. 2207–2212.

111 In a 1993 study: Ed Diener and Randy J. Larsen, "The Experience of Emotional Well-being," in *Handbook of Emotions,* ed. Michael Lewis and Jeannette Haviland, New York: Guilford Press, 1993, p. 409.

111 Maybe "emotional blind spots" also can register: S. J. Mann, J. P. Henry, G. E. Schwartz, D. A. Weinberger, "The Unconscious and Psychosomatic Illness: Time for a Revival" (paper presented at the 1996 meeting of the American Somatic Society, Williamsburg, Va., 8 March 1996).

112 In Antwerp, Belgium: Johan Denollet and D. L. Brutsaert, "Personality and Mortality After Coronary Heart Disease," *Psychosomatic Medicine* 57 (1995): pp. 582–589.

112 In a study of university students: Kenneth L. Dion and Karen K. Dion, "Romantic Love: Individual and Cultural Perspectives," in *The Psychology of Love,* ed. Robert J. Sternberg and Michael L. Barnes, New Haven, Conn.: Yale Univ. Press, 1988, pp. 264–289.

112 One conclusion from the overall research picture: Keith Crnic and Marcela Acevedo, "Everyday Stresses and Parenting," in *Handbook of Parenting,* vol. 4, *Applied and Practical Parenting,* ed. Marc H. Bornstein, Mahwah, N.J.: Lawrence Erlbaum, 1995, p. 283.

112 In a 1979 study: Catherine S. Chilman, "Parent Satisfactions-Dissatisfactions and Their Correlates," *Social Service Review* (June 1979): pp. 195–213.

113 Several studies indicate: William B. Swann, Jr., and Jonathon D. Brown, "From Self to Health: Self-Verification and Identity Disruption," in *Social Support: An Interactional View,* ed. Barbara R. Sarason, Irwin G. Sarason, and Gregory R. Pierce, New York: John Wiley, 1990, chap. 6, pp. 150–172.

114  Happiness, sadness, fear: Paul Ekman and Wallace V. Friesen, *Unmasking the Face: A Guide to Recognizing Emotions from Facial Clues,* Englewood Cliffs, N.J.: Prentice-Hall, 1975. Paul Ekman, "Facial Expression and Emotion: 1992 Award Address," *American Psychologist* 48 (April 1993): pp. 384–392.

## 7. Your Partner

129  Today, most of us expect: Steven Mintz and Susan Kellogg, *Domestic Revolutions: A Social History of American Family Life,* New York: Free Press, 1988. John Demos, *Past, Present, and Personal: The Family and the Life Course in American History,* New York: Oxford Univ. Press, 1986, Chapter 1 stresses the variability of these general trends.

129  Of currently existing marriages: *Satistical Abstract of the United States,* Landham, Md.: Berhan Press, 1993, p. 100.

129  By the time American youth reach age eighteen: *The Family Under Siege,* Washington, D.C.: American Research Council, 1989, as quoted in David Elkind, *Ties That Stress: The New Family Imbalance,* Cambridge, Mass.: Harvard Univ. Press, 1994, p. 77.

129  By 1995, 4.6 million couples a year: *Time* (27 February 1995): pp. 51–52.

130  Marital therapists maintain: Sonya Rhodes with Josleen Wilson, *Surviving Family Life: The Seven Crises of Living Together,* New York: G. P. Putnam, 1981.

130  As noted in Chapter 5: John Gottman, *Why Marriages Succeed or Fail: What You Can Learn from the Breakthrough Research to Make Your Marriage Last,* New York: Simon and Schuster, 1994, is the popular presentation of this information. John M. Gottman, *What Predicts Divorce? The Relationship Between Marital Processes and Marital Outcomes,* Hillsdale, N.J.: Lawrence Erlbaum, 1994, covers the same general subject in a more scholarly approach. Both books are used here.

132  For example, a large random sample: Lisa F. Beckman and S. Leonard Syme, "Social Networks, Host Resistance, and Mortality: A Nine-Year Follow-up of Alameda County Residents," *American Journal of Epidemiology* 109 (1979): pp. 186–204.

133  Unmarried men and women: James Goodwin, "The Effect of Marital Status on Stage, Treatment, and Survival of Cancer Patients," *Journal of the American Medical Association* 258, no. 21 (4 December 1984): pp. 3125–3130.

133  Divorced people are twice as likely to develop lung cancer. . . . higher rates of tuberculosis: Kenneth Pelletier, *Sound Mind, Sound Body: A New Model for Lifelong Health,* New York: Simon and Schuster, 1994, p. 152.

133  Experts report that in the small universe of a couple . . . *and* physical well-being: T. W. Smith, "Interactions, Transactions, and the Type A Pattern: Additional Avenues in the Search for Coronary-Prone Behavior," in A. W. Siegman and T. M. Dembrowski, eds., *In Search of Coronary-Prone Behavior,* Hillsdale: N.J.: Lawrence Erlbaum, 1989, pp. 91–116. James C. Coyne and Anita DeLongis, "Going Beyond Social Support: The Role of Social Relationships in Adaptions," *Journal of Consulting and Clinical Psychology* 54 (1986): p. 455.

133  Compared to happily married counterparts: Janice K. Kiecolt-Glaser et

al., "Marital Quality, Marital Disruption, and Immune Function," *Psycho-somatic Medicine* 49 (January-February 1987): pp. 13–34.

133 In another study of Illinois Bell Telephone middle- and upper-level executives: Cited in Henry Dreher, *The Immune Power Personality: 7 Traits You Can Develop to Stay Healthy*, New York: Dutton, 1995, chap. 4, pp. 133–137. Ouellette's earlier publication surname was Kobasa.

134 Disagreements where partners behave badly: Janice K. Kiecolt-Glaser et al., "Negative Behavior During Marital Conflict Is Associated with Immunological Down-Regulation," *Psychosomatic Medicine* 55 (1993): pp. 395–409.

134 Since this study, the Glasers have extended.... harmful to health: Janice K. Kiecolt-Glaser et al., "Marital Conflict in Older Adults: Endocrinological and Immunological Correlates," *Psychosomatic Medicine* 59 (1997): pp. 339–349.

134 The damage continues: Ronald Glaser, "Psychoneuroimmunology: Can Psychological Interventions Modulate Immunity?" *Journal of Consulting and Clinical Psychology* 60 (1992): pp. 569–575.

134 A marital problem is more likely: S. R. Beach, E. E. Sandeen, and K. D. O'Leary, *Depression in Marriage*, New York: Guilford Press, 1990, as cited by Wayne M. Sotile, *Psychosocial Interventions for Cardiopulmonary Patients: A Guide for Health Professionals*, Human Kinetics, 1996, p. 140.

135 In one study, participants were initially chosen: K. D. Alfred and T. W. Smith, "Social Cognition in Cynical Hostility," *Cognitive Therapy and Research* 15 (1991): pp. 399–412.

135 Experimenters have also concluded: Leonard Berkowitz, "Experimental Investigations of Hostility Catharsis," *Journal of Consulting and Clinical Psychology* 35 (1970): pp. 1–7.

135 University of Utah psychologist Tim Smith: T. W. Smith and P. W. Brown, "Cynical Hostility, Attempts to Exert Social Control, and Cardiovascular Reactivity in Married Couples," *Journal of Behavioral Medicine*, in press.

135 Primate studies among monogamous species: B. A. Lapin and G. M. Cherkovich, "Environmental Changes Causing the Development of Neuroses and Corticovisceral Pathology in Monkeys," in *Society, Stress, and Disease: The Psychosocial Environment and Psychosomatic Diseases*, ed. L. Levi, London: Oxford Univ. Press, 1971, vol. 1, pp. 266–279.

135 Fortunately, statistically only 15 percent: National Opinion Research Center at the University of Chicago, as reported in *The New York Times* (9 October 1994), sec. 4, p. 3. Compare the much larger numbers in an earlier review article by Anthony P. Thompson, "Extramarital Sex: A Review of the Research Literature," *The Journal of Sex Research* 19 (February 1983): pp. 1–22. The Research Center survey was a large study and also seems more reliable.

135 A Johns Hopkins study found: C. K. Ewart et al., "Reducing Blood Pressure Reactivity During Interpersonal Conflict: Effects of Marital Communication Training," *Behavioral Therapy* 15 (1984): pp. 473–484.

136 In a study of young couples together over a year: Mark H. Davis and H. Alan Oathout, "Maintenance of Satisfaction in Romantic Relationships: Empathy and Relational Competence," *Journal of Personality and Social Psychology* 53 (1987): pp. 397–410.

136 When marriage and divorce counselor Judith Wallerstein examined: Judith Wallerstein and Sandra Blakeslee, *The Good Marriage: How and Why Love Lasts,* Boston: Houghton Mifflin, 1995, p. 91.

136 Researchers who studied women reared in institutions: Michael Rutter, "Resilience in the Face of Adversity: Protective Factors and Resistance to Psychiatric Disorder," *British Journal of Psychiatry* 147 (1985): pp. 601, 604.

136 Not surprisingly, parents who agree about child-rearing: Jeanne H. Block, Jack Block, and Andrea Morrison, "Parental Agreement-Disagreement on Child-Rearing Orientations and Gender-Related Personality Correlates in Children," *Child Development* 52 (1981): pp. 965–974.

136 Long-term follow-up studies of children of divorce: Judith Wallerstein and Sandra Blakeslee, *Second Chances: Men, Women, and Children a Decade After Divorce,* New York: Ticknor and Fields, 1989. M. E. J. Wadsworth, *The Imprint of Time: Childhood, History, and Adult Life,* Oxford: Clarendon, 1991, pp. 116, 141.

136 A number of research studies suggest that divorce: Robert E. Emery, "Interparental Conflict and the Children of Discord and Divorce," *Psychological Bulletin* 92 (1982): pp. 310–330. Also see John H. Grynch and Frank D. Fincham, "Marital Conflict and Children's Adjustment: A Cognitive-Contextual Framework," *Psychological Bulletin* 108 (1990): pp. 267–290.

136 In some troubled marriages: Maggie Scarf, *Intimate Worlds: Life Inside the Family,* New York: Random House, 1995, pp. 319–328.

140 (During their week-long engagement, Leo Tolstoy: Martine de Courcel, *Tolstoy: The Ultimate Reconciliation,* trans. Peter Levi, New York: Charles Scribner's Sons, 1988, pp. 75, 81, 214, 242.

140 Suppose your partner: Shakespeare, *Anthony and Cleopatra,* act II, scene ii, lines 240–241.

143 One parent is in charge: Maggie Scarf, *Intimate Worlds: Life Inside the Family,* New York: Random House, 1995, pp. 319–328.

145 Emphasize the positive: The destructive role of negative attributions in marriage is a hot topic right now. See T. N. Bradbury and F. D. Fincham, "Attributions in Marriage: Review and Critique," *Psychological Bulletin* 107 (1990): pp. 3–33.

145 Judith Wallerstein's study of fifty: Judith S. Wallerstein and Sandra Blakeslee, *The Good Marriage: How and Why Love Lasts,* Boston: Houghton Mifflin, 1995, p. 190.

147 In our earlier book: Redford Williams and Virginia Williams, *Anger Kills: Seventeen Strategies for Controlling the Hostility That Can Harm Your Health,* New York: Harper/Perennial, 1994, p. 201 f.

152 In *No Exit*: Jean-Paul Sartre, *No Exit and Three Other Plays,* trans. S. Gilbert, New York: Vintage, 1989, pp. 17, 45.

## 8. Your Young Child

155 Family life not only educates: At Abbott House in Westchester County, New York, October 1965, as quoted in Daniel Patrick Moynihan, *Family and Nation: The Godian Lectures, Harvard University,* San Diego, Calif.: Harcourt Brace Jovanovich, 1986, p. 38.

155 Fortunately—and unfortunately: Barbara J. Tinsley, "The Influence of Familial and Interpersonal Factors on Children's Development and Associated Cardiovascular Risk," in *Hostility, Coping, and Health,* ed. Howard S. Friedman, Washington D.C.: APA, 1992, p. 192.

155 Yogesh Gandhi tells the story: Yogesh Gandhi, foreword to *Learning the Skills of Peacemaking: An Activity Guide for Elementary-Age Children on Communicating, Cooperating, Resolving Conflict,* by Naomi Drew, Rolling Hills Estates, Calif.: Jalmar, 1987, no page number.

157 According to the editor of the state-of-the-science handbook on parenting: Marc H. Bornstein, preface to *Handbook of Parenting,* vol. 4, *Applied and Practical Parenting,* ed. Marc H. Bornstein, Mahwah, N.J.: Lawrence Erlbaum, 1995, p. xvii.

157 In these difficult times: *U.S. News and World Report* (27 February 1995): pp. 47–48.

157 Yet in one large survey: Massachusetts Mutual Life Insurance Company and *Family Fun Magazine, The American Family Time Satisfaction Study,* Springfield, Mass.: Mass Mutual and *Family Fun,* 1993, pp. 6, 10–12.

157 Another estimate: U.S. Department of Education, *Strong Families, Strong Schools: Building Community Partnerships for Learning,* Washington, D.C.: U.S. Dept. of Ed., Sept. 1994, p. iv. For copies of this publication, call 1-800-USA-LEARN.

158 In a 1994 national survey: Massachusetts Mutual Life Insurance Company, *America's Children Talk About Family Time, Values, and Chores,* Springfield, Mass.: Mass Mutual, 1994, pp. 53–57.

159 In this same survey: Ibid., pp. 20–21.

159 The third most frequently cited category: Ibid., chap. 5.

159 In psychologist Kenneth Pelletier's study: Kenneth Pelletier, *Sound Mind, Sound Body: Personal Strategies for Optimal Health,* New York: Simon and Schuster, 1994, chap. 2.

159 On the other side of the coin, mothers of troublemakers: Theodore Dix and John E. Lochman, "Social Cognition and Negative Reactions to Children: A Comparison of Mothers of Aggressive and Nonaggressive Boys," *Journal of Social and Clinical Psychology* 9 (1990): pp. 418–438. John Lochman, "Self- and Peer Perceptions and Attributional Biases of Aggressive and Nonaggressive Boys in Dyadic Interactions," *Journal of Consulting and Clinical Psychology* 55 (1987): pp. 404–410. John Coie et al., "Predicting Early Adolescent Disorders from Childhood Aggression and Peer Rejection," *Journal of Consulting and Clinical Psychology* 60 (1992): pp. 783–792.

160 When researching her book on families: Maggie Scarf, *Intimate Worlds: Life Inside the Family,* New York: Random House, 1995, introduction. Also see Michael Rutter, "Protective Factors in Children's Responses to Stress and Disadvantage," in *Primary Prevention of Psychopathology,* vol. 3, *Social Competence in Children,* ed. M. W. Kent and J. E. Rolf, Hanover, N.H.: Univ. Press of New England, 1979, pp. 65–66, for another

account of the buffering effects of a good relationship with at least one parent.

160 A British study has followed: M. E. J. Wadsworth, *The Imprint of Time: Childhood, History, and Adult Life,* Oxford: Clarendon, 1991, pp. 71–77, 98.

160 The same conclusion has been reached: U.S. Department of Education, *Strong Families, Strong Schools: Building Community Partnerships for Learning,* Washington, D.C.: U.S. Dept. of Ed., Sept. 1994, p. 2.

160 Berkeley child psychologist: Diana Baumrind, "Rearing Competent Children," in *Child Development Today and Tomorrow,* ed. W. Damon, San Francisco: Jossey-Bass, 1989, pp. 349–378. Diana Baumrind, "Current Patterns of Parental Authority," *Developmental Psychology Monograph,* Washington, D.C.: APA, January 1971, vol. 4, pp. 1–103. Diana Baumrind, "Parental Disciplinary Patterns and Social Competence in Children," *Youth and Society* 9, no. 3 (1978).

161 In 1981 some members of the National Association of School Psychologists: As reported by William A. Galston, "A Liberal-Democratic Case for the Two-Parent Family," in *Rights and the Common Good: The Communitarian Perspective,* ed. Amitai Etzioni, New York: St. Martin's Press, 1995, p. 142.

161 In earlier times, families often were disrupted: Michael Walzer, "The Communitarian Critique of Liberalism," in *New Communitarian Thinking: Persons, Virtues, Institutions, and Communities,* ed. Amitai Etzioni, Charlottesville: Univ. of Virginia Press, 1995, pp. 58–59. John Demos, *Past, Present, and Personal: The Family and the Life Course in American History,* New York: Oxford Univ. Press, 1986.

161 Studies of identical twins reared apart: Thomas J. Bouchard, Jr., et al. "Sources of Human Psychological Differences: The Minnesota Study of Twins Reared Apart," *Science* 250 (12 October 1990): pp. 223–228.

161 One child in ten: P. A. Klaczynski and E. M. Cummings, "Responding to Anger in Aggressive and Nonaggressive Boys: A Research Note," *Journal of Child Psychology and Psychiatry* 30 (1989): pp. 309–314.

161 She stresses easily: Doris E. Durrell, *The Critical Years: A Guide for Dedicated Parents,* Oakland, Calif.: New Harbinger, 1984, pp. 24–28.

161 Here is a similar, this time historical, example: Robert M. Sapolsky, *Why Zebras Don't Get Ulcers: A Guide to Stress, Stress-Related Diseases, and Coping,* New York: W. H. Freeman, 1994, pp. 89–90.

162 In another study, this time in Oklahoma: Richard D. Clover et al., "Family Functioning and Stress as Predictors of Influenza B Infection," *The Journal of Family Practice* 28 (May 1989): pp. 535–539.

162 A representative sample of Harvard undergraduates: Linda G. Russek and Gary E. Schwartz, "Perceptions of Parental Caring Predict Health Status in Midlife: A 35-Year Follow-up of the Harvard Mastery of Stress Study," *Psychosomatic Medicine* 59 (March/April 1997): pp. 144–149.

162 You will recall from Chapter 4 the Kansas study: Betty Hart and Todd Risley, *Meaningful Differences in the Everyday Experience of Young Children,* Baltimore: Paul H. Brookes, 1995.

163 Children in the Los Angeles school system: Reginald M. Clark, "Why Disadvantaged Students Succeed: What Happens Outside School Is Critical," *Public Welfare* (spring 1990): p. 22.

163 As mentioned in Chapter 4, psychologist Karen Matthews and her colleagues: K. L. Matthews et al., "Negative Family Environment as a Predictor of Boys' Future Status on Measures of Hostile Attitudes, Interview Behavior, and Anger Expression," *Health Psychology* 15 (1996): pp. 30–37.

163 Over the past twenty years: Michael Rutter, "Resilience in the Face of Adversity: Protective Factors and Resistance to Psychiatric Disorder," *British Journal of Psychiatry* 147 (1985): p. 602.

164 Social scientists can even predict: Beverly J. Wilson and John M. Gottman, "Marital Interaction and Parenting," in *Handbook of Parenting*, vol. 4, *Applied and Practical Parenting*, ed. Marc H. Bornstein, Mahwah, N.J.: Lawrence Erlbaum, 1995, chap. 2, pp. 33–55. John M. Gottman, *What Predicts Divorce? The Relationship Between Marital Processes and Marital Outcomes*, Hillsdale, N.J.: Lawrence Erlbaum, 1994, pp. 296–298.

164 Marital Satisfaction: Keith Crnic and Marcela Acevedo, "Everyday Stresses and Parenting," in *Handbook of Parenting*, vol. 4, *Applied and Practical Parenting*, ed. Marc H. Bornstein, Mahwah, N.J.: Lawrence Erlbaum, 1995, p. 288.

164 In a study of two middle-class suburbs of Milwaukee: Catherine S. Chilman, "Parent Satisfactions-Dissatisfactions and Their Correlates," *Social Service Review* (June 1979): pp. 195–213.

165 Even infants require this: Maggie Scarf, *Intimate Worlds: Life Inside the Family*, New York: Random House, 1995, pp. 179–182.

166 We suggest you read: John Gottman with Joan DeClaire, *The Heart of Parenting: Raising an Emotionally Intelligent Child*, New York: Simon and Schuster, 1997.

166 When observers on site: C. L. Fawl, "Disturbances Experienced by Children in their Natural Habitats," in *The Stream of Behavior*, ed. R. G. Barker, New York: Appleton-Century-Crofts, 1963. R. Forehand et al., "Mother-Child Interactions: Comparison of the Noncompliant Clinic Group and a Nonclinic Group," *Behavior Research and Therapy* 13 (1975): pp. 79–84. C. Minton, J. Kagan, and J. A. Levine, "Maternal Control and Obedience in the Two-Year-Old Child," *Child Development* 42 (1971): pp. 1973–1974. J. B. Reid, ed., *A Social Learning Approach to Family Interventions: Observations in Home Settings*, vol. 2, Eugene, Ore.: Castalia, 1978, as reported by John B. Reid and K. Kavanagh, "A Social Interactional Approach to Child Abuse: Risk, Prevention, and Treatment," in *Anger and Hostility in Behavioral Disorders*, ed. Margaret Chesney and Ray Rosenman, Washington, D.C.: Hemisphere, 1985, p. 243.

166 In a study of eighty-five "problem free": P. Chamberlain, "Standardization of a Parent Report Measure," (Ph.D. diss., Univ. of Oregon, 1980), as reported by John B. Reid and K. Kavanagh, "A Social Interactional Approach to Child Abuse: Risk, Prevention, and Treatment," in *Anger and Hostility in Cardiovascular and Behavioral Disorders*, ed. Margaret Chesney and Ray Rosenman, Washington, D.C.: Hemisphere, 1985, p. 243.

169 Forty percent of parents: Massachusetts Mutual Life Insurance Company, *The American Family Time Satisfaction Study*, Springfield, Mass.: Mass Mutual, 1993, p. 28.

169 In surveys, both parents and children: Massachusetts Mutual Life Insur-

ance Company, *America's Children Talk About Family Time, Values, and Chores,* Springfield, Mass.: Mass Mutual, 1993, pp. 20–22. Massachusetts Mutual Life Insurance Company, *America's Children Talk About Family Time, Values, and Chores,* Springfield, Mass.: Mass Mutual, 1994, pp. 32–39.

169 Listening carefully: Betty Hart and Todd Risley, *Meaningful Differences in the Everyday Experience of Young Children,* Baltimore: Paul H. Brookes, 1995, p. 79.

170 A prominent Yale child psychologist: Robert J. Sternberg and Wendy M. Williams, "Parenting Toward Cognitive Competence," in *Handbook of Parenting,* vol. 4, *Applied and Practical Parenting,* ed. Marc H. Bornstein, Mahwah, N.J.: Lawrence Erlbaum, 1995, pp. 259–275.

170 After an acrimonious hearing in a divorce case: Abigail Van Buren, "Transcript of a Divorce Proceeding," *The (Durham, N.C.) Herald Sun* (9 October 1994).

## 9. Your Teenager

175 In colonial times, children worked: Joseph F. Kett, *Rites of Passage: Adolescence in America 1790 to the Present,* New York: Basic Books, 1977. Our summary is much less nuanced than Kett's well-researched tome, which differentiates among different time periods and different social classes.

175 In the last decade or so, a growing number of experts: David Elkind, *Ties That Stress: The New Family Imbalance,* Cambridge, Mass.: Harvard Univ. Press, 1994. John Demos, *Past, Present, and Personal: The Family and the Life Course in American History,* New York: Oxford Univ. Press, 1986, chap. 5. David A. Hamburg, *Today's Children: Creating a Future for a Generation in Crisis,* New York: Times Books, 1992, pp. 169–275.

175 In the future, jobs with high social status: Charles Murray, lecture given at Duke University, spring 1995. Jerry Adler, "The Rise of the Overclass," *Newsweek* (31 July 1995): pp. 35–46.

176 Many teenage girls still feel evaluated: "Mission Impossible," *People* (3 June 1996): pp. 67, 73.

176 Teenage girls, maybe even more than boys: Mary Pipher, *Reviving Ophelia: Saving the Selves of Adolescent Girls,* New York: Ballantine, 1994.

176 Twenty-eight percent of high school seniors: National Institute on Drug Abuse, *National Survey Results on Drug Use from the Monitoring the Future Study, 1975–1993,* Washington, D.C.: NIH, publication no. 94-3809, 1994, chap. 4.

176 In the present-day United States: J. Snyder and Patterson, "Family Interaction and Delinquent Behavior," in *Handbook of Juvenile Delinquency,* ed. H. C. Quay, New York: John Wiley, 1987, as quoted by Eva L. Feindler, "Adolescent Anger Control: Review and Critique," in *Progress in Behavior Modification,* ed. Michel Hersen, Richard M. Eisler, and Peter M. Miller, vol. 26, Newbury Park, Calif.: Sage, 1990, p. 12.

177 More than 50 percent of adolescents: A. E. Kazdin, "Treatment of Antisocial Behavior in Children: Current Status and Future Directions," *Psychological Bulletin* v 102, no. 2 (1987): pp. 187–203, as quoted in Eva Feindler, "Adolescent Anger Control: Review and Critique," in *Progress*

*in Behavior Modification,* ed. Michel Hersen, Richard M. Eisler, and Peter M. Miller, Newbury Park, Calif.: Sage, 1990, p. 12.

177 By the time young people with the highest hostility scores: T. W. Smith et al., "Cynical Hostility at Home and Work: Psychosocial Vulnerability Across Domains," *Journal of Research in Personality* 22 (1988): pp. 525–548. Also see T. W. Smith and K. D. Frohm, "What's So Unhealthy About Hostility? Construct Validity and Psychosocial Correlates of the Cook and Medley HO Scale," *Health Psychology* 4 (1985): pp. 503–520.

177 In *Greater Expectations:* William Damon, *Greater Expectations: Overcoming the Culture of Indulgence In America's Homes and Schools,* New York: Free Press, 1995, pp. 18, 45, 102, 85, 89–90. Also see Robert Coles, *The Moral Life of Children,* Boston: Atlantic Monthly Press, 1986. Cole stresses the great integrity of some children, despite their difficult circumstances.

178 Among students aged ten to thirteen: National Commission on Children 1991, as quoted in U.S. Department of Education, *Strong Families, Strong Schools: Building Community Partnerships for Learning,* Washington, D.C.: U.S. Dept. of Ed., Sept. 1994, p. 3.

178 In one study, for example, family members: Janet C. Meininger and Laura L. Hayman, "Similarity Between Parents and Adolescent Offspring in Anger and Hostility" (paper presented at the Fourth International Congress of Behavioral Medicine, Washington, D.C., March 1996).

178 It should come as no surprise: W. A. Greene, S. Goldstein, and A.J. Moss, "Psychological and Social Variables Associated with Sudden Death from Apparent Coronary Heart Disease," *Psychosomatic Medicine* 35 (1973): pp. 458–459.

182 In an article: Florence Littauer, "You've got Yourself a Deal," in *Chicken Soup for the Soul: 101 Stories to Open the Heart and Rekindle the Spirit,* written and compiled by Jack Canfield and Mark Victor Hansen, Deerfield Beach, Fla.: Health Communications, 1993, pp. 281–282.

183 Helen Mrosla, a Franciscan nun: Helen P. Mrosla, "All the Good Things," *New Age Journal: Source Book, 1994,* p. 39. This was originally published in *Proteus: A Journal of Ideas* (spring 1991) and also is reprinted in *Chicken Soup for the Soul,* written and compiled by Jack Canfield and Mark Victor Hansen, Deerfield Beach, Fla.: Health Communications, 1993.

## 10. Your Parents

194 Only about 5 percent: Steven Mintz and Susan Kellogg, *Domestic Revolutions: A Social History of American Family Life,* New York: Free Press, 1988, p. 218.

194 In a 1994 national survey of one thousand children: Massachusetts Mutual Life Insurance Company, *America's Children Talk About Family Time, Values, and Chores,* Springfield, Mass.: Mass Mutual, 1994, pp. 15–16. Massachusetts Mutual Life Insurance Company and *Family Fun Magazine, The American Family Time Satisfaction Study,* Springfield, Mass.: Mass Mutual and *Family Fun,* 1993, p. 10.

194 Forty-seven percent of Americans: Massachusetts Mutual Life Insurance

Company, *1991 American Family Values Study: A Return to Family Values,*
Springfield, Mass.: Mass Mutual, 1991, p. 10.

195   Your parents will probably enjoy: Mark A. Edinberg, *Talking with Your
Aging Parents,* Boston: Shambhala, 1987, pp. 18–22.

195   When parents become extremely ill: Janice Kiecolt-Glaser, et al.,
"Chronic Stress and Immunity in Family Caregivers of Alzheimer's Disease Victims," *Psychosomatic Medicine* 49 (1987): pp. 523–535.

198   In his helpful book: Harold Bloomfield, *Making Peace with Your Parents:
The Key to Enriching Your Life and All Your Relationships,* New York:
Ballantine, 1983, pp. 31–41.

## 11. Your Friends

207   As families and communities deteriorate: James C. Coyne and Anita De
Longis, in "Going Beyond Social Support: The Role of Social Relationships in Adaptation," *Journal of Consulting and Clinical Psychology* 54
(1986), cite a literature which suggests this, p. 454, but they themselves
propose that often only a supportive spouse will do, p. 456.

207   Numerous studies document: Lisa F. Berkman and S. Leonard Syme,
"Social Networks, Host Resistance, and Mortality: A Nine-Year Follow-
up Study of Alameda County Residents," *American Journal of Epidemiology*
109 (1979): pp. 186–204.

207   Recall the study of Duke heart patients: Redford B. Williams et al.,
"Prognostic Importance of Social and Economic Resources Among
Medically Treated Patients with Angiographically Documented Coronary
Artery Disease," *Journal of the American Medical Association* 267 (1992): pp.
520–524.

208   Building on the initial work: Joshua M. Smyth, "Written Emotional
Expression: A Meta-Analytic Review" (paper presented at General Poster
Session 1 of the American Psychosomatic Society meeting, 7–9 March
1996, Williamsburg, Va).

## 12. Your Coworkers

221   Americans are working longer hours . . . while women add on twenty-
seven more hours: *State of Working America, 1994–1995,* Biennial, 1994,
pp. 72–73. Arlie Russell Hochschild, "There's No Place like Work."
*New York Times Magazine* (20 April 1997), p. 52. Robert Karasek and
Tores Theorell, *Healthy work: Stress, Productivity and the Reconstruction of
Working Life,* New York: Basic Books, 1990. Hours at work include
commuting and overtime.

221   In better-paying, more prestigious jobs . . . incomes over $50,000 a year
spend 52.4 hours a week: Sylvia Ann Hewlett, *When the Bough Breaks:
The Cost of Neglecting Our Children.* New York: Harper/Collins, 1991, p.
79, citing a Harris Poll. She cites magazine and newspaper sources for the
work week for executives.

221   (Almost 50 percent more children live in poverty today compared to fifteen years ago.) *Statistical Abstract of the United States: 1996,* p. 472.

221   Sixty-four percent of workers: "Working in Dilbert's World," *Newsweek*
(12 August 1996): pp. 55–56.

222 The summary study of *New York Times* reporter: Daniel Goleman, *Emotional Intelligence: Why It Can Matter More Than I.Q.*, New York: Bantam, 1995, chap. 10.

223 A Chicago Study: Leonard I. Pearlin and Morton A. Lieberman, "Social Sources of Emotional Stress," in *Research in Community and Mental Health*, ed. R. Simmons, Greenwich, Conn.: JAI Press, 1979, pp. 217–248.

223 Two pioneers in workplace health: Robert Karasek and Tores Theorell, *Healthy Work: Stress, Productivity, and the Reconstruction of Working Life*, New York: Basic Books, 1990.

223 The research of Redford: Redford B. Williams et al. "Psychosocial Correlates of Job Strain in a Sample of Working Women," *Archives of General Psychiatry* 54 (1997): pp. 543–548.

224 Suppose your job doesn't use all your skills: Robert Karasek and Tores Theorell, *Healthy Work: Stress, Productivity, and the Reconstruction of Working Life*, New York: Basic Books, 1990, p. 53.

224 Two in three working parents: Massachusetts Mutual Life Insurance Company, *The American Family Time Satisfaction Study*, Springfield, Mass.: Mass Mutual, 1993, p. 39.

225 Research has also demonstrated: Keith Crnic and Marcela Acevedo, "Everyday Stresses and Parenting," in *Handbook of Parenting* vol. 4, *Applied and Practical Parenting*, ed. Marc H. Bornstein, Mahwah, N.J.: Lawrence Erlbaum, 1995, p. 278.

225 Lifeskills do help workers: Redford B. Williams et al., "Stress Management Training Boosts Social Support in Married Working Mothers" (paper presented at the Annual Meeting of the Society of Behavioral Medicine, Washington, D.C., March 1996).

228 A number of investigators have concluded: Robert A. Baron, "Countering the Effects of Destructive Criticism: The Relative Efficacy of Four Interventions," *Journal of Applied Psychology* 75, no. 3, (1990): pp. 235–245.

## 13. Community

238 The traditional American community was relatively homogeneous: While relatively homogeneous, America was scarcely egalitarian. For at least two-thirds of American history, a majority of the domestic adult population was ineligible for full citizenship. African Americans, native Americans, and women set little of the agenda, as they often were excluded from public service (including the military and jury duty), voting and office holding, even mandatory public schooling. Rogers M. Smith, "American Conceptions of Citizenship and National Service," in *New Communitarian Thinking: Persons, Virtues, Institutions, and Communities*, Charlottesville: Univ. of Virginia Press, 1995, pp. 233–243.

241 Choice and entitlement: Lawrence Friedman, *The Republic of Choice: Law, Authority, and Culture*, Cambridge, Mass.: Harvard Univ. Press, 1990. For the sense of entitlement, also see Susan J. Tolchin, *The Angry American: How Voter Rage Is Changing the Nation*, Boulder, Colo.: Westview, 1996, pp. 25–26, 36–39.

241 Since 1974, each General Social Survey: Robert D. Putham, "Bowling

Alone: America's Declining Social Capital," *Journal of Democracy* 6 (1995): pp. 67–70, 73. See also the whole article, pp. 65–78.

242 Tables 13-1 and 13-2: Massachusetts Mutual Life Insurance Company, *Mass Mutual American Family Values Study: Results of Focus Group and Survey Research,* Springfield, Mass.: Mass Mutual, 1991, pp. 42–44.

243 Whenever people are divided: David L. Hamilton and Tina K. Trolier, "Stereotypes and Stereotyping: An Overview of the Cognitive Approach," in *Prejudice, Discrimination, and Racism,* ed. John F. Dovidio and Samuel L. Gaertner, Orlando, Fla.: Academic Press, 1986, pp. 129, 131, 132, 136, 152.

244 Probably the leading basis for grouping people: Compare *Racial Healing,* by Yale legal scholar Harlon Dalton. Dalton sees one solution to racial troubles in admitting our differences. "The trick . . . is for all of us to realize that we too have a point of view, a perspective, a set of experiences through which we view the world." Harlon L. Dalton, *Racial Healing: Confronting the Fear Between Blacks and Whites,* New York: Doubleday, 1995.

244 Where social class is comparable: David A. Hamburg, *Today's Children: Creating a Future for a Generation in Crisis,* New York: Times Books, 1992, p. 40.

244 In numerous studies, small groups: Wendy M. Williams and Robert J. Sternberg, "Group Intelligence: Why Some Groups Are Better Than Others," *Intelligence* 12 (1988): pp. 351–377.

244 Two additional conclusions from the already mentioned Alameda County study: Lisa F. Berkman and S. Leonard Syme, "Social Networks, Host Resistance, and Mortality: A Nine-Year Follow-up Study of Alameda County Residents," *American Journal of Epidemiology* 109 (1979): pp. 186–204.

244 In another study—of 232 patients: Thomas E. Oxman, Daniel H. Freeman, Jr., and Eric D. Manheimer, "Lack of Social Participation or Religious Strength and Comfort as Risk Factors for Death After Cardiac Surgery in the Elderly," *Psychosomatic Medicine* 57 (1995): pp. 5–15.

244 Phyllis Moen, of the Life Course Institute at Cornell: Phyllis Moen, Donna Dempster-McClain, and Robin M. Williams, Jr., "Social Integration and Longevity: An Event History Analysis of Women's Roles and Resilience," *American Sociological Review* 54 (1989): pp. 635–647. P. Moen, D. Dempster-McClain, and R. M. Williams, "Successful Aging: A Life Course Perspective on Women's Multiple Roles and Health," *American Journal of Sociology* 97, no. 6 (1992): pp. 1612–1638. Moen measured mental but not physical health in 1956; she maintains that good mental health correlates with good physical health. We also wonder about the effects of age.

245 Certain religious groups: Lisa F. Berkman, "Assessing Social Networks and Social Support in Epidemiologic Studies," in *Social Networks and Health: Proceedings of the National Symposium on Networks and Health in Copenhagen, November 1994,* ed. Erik Mortensen and Jens Egsgaard, Copenhagen: Sundhedsvaesen, 1995, p. 41.

245 In one study from the early 1980s: Randolph C. Byrd, "Positive Therapeutic Effects of Intercessory Prayer in a Coronary Care Unit Population," *Southern Medical Journal* 81 (1988): pp. 826–829.

246 A 1992 survey: Massachusetts Mutual Life Insurance Company, *National Survey on Communicating Family Values,* Springfield, Mass.: Mass Mutual, 1992, pp. 5–24, Appendix A, pp. 6–7.

247 The community needs to help too: William Damon, *Greater Expectations: Overcoming the Culture of Indulgence in America's Homes and Schools,* New York: Free Press, 1995, pp. 95–100.

248 To help you formulate your answers: Katrina Shields, *In the Tiger's Mouth: An Empowerment Guide for Social Action,* Philadelphia, Pa., New Society, 1994, p. 9.

249 Often interested citizens fall into two camps: Michael Specter, "Not That Hard Being Green," *New York Times Book Review* (23 April 1995): p. 13.

249 A book reviewer for *The New York Times:* David Quammen, "Live and Let Die," *New York Times Book Review* (23 April 1995): p. 16.

253 The Communitarians: The best general introduction to the Communitarians is Amitai Etzioni, *The Spirit of Community: The Reinvention of American Society,* New York: Touchstone, 1993.

253 Our list in *Anger Kills:* Redford Williams and Virginia Williams, *Anger Kills: Seventeen Strategies for Controlling the Hostility That Can Harm Your Health,* New York: Harper/Perennial, 1994, pp. 137–140.

255 We had planned: Naomi Drew, *Learning the Skills of Peacemaking: An Activity Guide for Elementary-Age Children on Communicating, Cooperating, Resolving Conflict,* Rolling Hills Estates, Calif.: Jalmar Press, 1995.

255 Other educators as well are developing programs: David A. Hamburg, "Teaching Life Skills and Fostering Social Support," in *Today's Children: Creating a Future for a Generation in Crisis,* New York: Times Books, 1994, chap. 13. Daniel Goleman, *Emotional Intelligence,* New York: Bantam, 1995, chap. 16. Other programs work successfully with children prone to violence. *New York Times* (28 May 1997): p. A16.

257 Among them are: Steve Fiffer and Sharon Sloan Fiffer, *Fifty Ways to Help Your Community: A Handbook for Change,* New York: Doubleday, 1994, pp. xi, xii.

258 And then there's the rarefied example of Mohandas Gandhi: For a beautiful extrapolation of Gandhi's principles, as well as some original additions based on his own involvement in conservation, see Arne Naess, *Ecology, Community, and Lifestyle: Outline of a Ecosophy,* trans. and ed. David Rothenberg, Cambridge, England: Cambridge Univ. Press, 1989, pp. 148–150. Naess extensively discusses his summary of Gandhi's approach in *Ghandhi and Group Conflict: An Exploration of Satyagraha: Theoretical Background,* Oslo: Universitetsforlaget, 1974.

## 14. Other Americans

263 People, I just want to say: As quoted by Haynes Johnson in *Divided We Fall: Gambling with History in the Nineties,* New York: Norton, 1994, p. 183.

263 "You really don't believe in political solutions, do you?": Tom Robbins, *Even Cowgirls Get the Blues,* New York: Bantam, 1976, p. 332. Robbins offers as an alternative a New Age philosophy very reflective of the 1970s.

263 In the early 1830s: Alexis de Tocqueville, *Democracy in America,* New York: Mentor, 1956.

265   Witness the title: Susan J. Tolchin, *The Angry American: How Voter Rage is Changing the Nation*, Boulder, Colo.: Westview, 1996.

265   The current situation: Many of the ideas in this section come from Russell Baker, "God's Angry Land," *New York Times* (22 October 1994) and Haynes Johnson, *Divided We Fall: Gambling with History in the Nineties*, New York: Norton, 1994.

266   After the Oklahoma bombing: Susan J. Tolchin, *The Angry American: How Voter Rage is Changing the Nation*, Boulder, Colo.: Westview, 1996, p. 117.

266   A Times Mirror Center study: *The (Durham, N.C.) Herald Sun* (21 September 1994): p. A4.

267   Specific documentation of the growing incivility: Jeffry Weiss, "Most in Poll Perceive a Rising Tide of Anger," *Dallas Morning News* (20 August 1995).

267   Television reflects . . . rates of violent crime had actually declined: Lawrie Mifflin, "Crime Falls, but Not on TV," *New York Times* (6 July 1997): section 4, p. 4.

267   An international Gallup poll of residents in eighteen countries: *USA Today* (late June 1995).

267   This inequality may grow: Peter F. Drucker, "The Age of Social Transformation," *Atlantic Monthly* (November 1994): pp. 53–80. Charles Murray (lecture delivered at Duke University, May 1995).

268   Polarized issues include the federal budget: Susan J. Tolchin, *The Angry American: How Voter Rage is Changing the Nation*, Boulder, Colo.: Westview, 1996, pp. 81, 107.

268   Now British epidemiologist: Richard Wilkinson, "Income Distribution and Life Expectancy," *British Medical Journal* 304 (1992): pp. 165–168.

268   Two research teams: G. A. Kaplan et al., "Inequality in Income and Mortality in the United States: Analysis of Mortality and Potential Pathways," *British Medical Journal* 312 (1996): pp. 999–1003. B. P. Kennedy, I. Kawachi, and D. Prothrow-Stith, "Income Distribution and Mortality: Cross-Sectional Ecological Study of the Robin Hood Index in the United States," *British Medical Journal* 312 (1996): pp. 1004–1008.

273   As *Los Angeles Times* staff writer David Shaw observes: *Los Angeles Times* (17 April 1996): pp. 1, 10, 11.

273   On July 29, 1994: *New York Times* (30 and 31 July 1994).

274   After the shootings: "Abortion Clinic Shootings," *Unitarian-Universalist World* (November–December 1994): p. 42.

## 15. All Children in America

278   And what about the young men: Gregory Alan-Williams, *A Gathering of Heroes: Reflections on Rage and Responsibility: A Memoir of the Los Angeles Riots*, Chicago: Academy Chicago Pub., 1994.

278   About 98 percent of U.S. homes: Aimée Dorr and Beth E. Rabin, "Parents, Children, and Television," in *Handbook of Parenting*, vol. 4, *Applied and Practical Parenting*, ed. Marc H. Bornstein, Mahwah, N.J.: Lawrence Erlbaum, 1995, p. 323.

281   The Current Situation: These problems are not new. The original Carnegie Council on Children (1972–1977) concluded that America's

commitment to children lagged behind that of most other industrialized nations. John Demos, *Past, Present, and Personal: The Family and the Life Course in American History,* New York: Oxford Univ. Press, 1986, p. 195. Kenneth Keniston et al., *All Our Children: The American Family Under Pressure,* New York: Harcourt Brace Jovanovich, 1977.

281 Giving the United States: *New York Times Magazine* (8 October 1995): p. 52.

281 Currently, more children in our country: Children's Defense Fund, *The State of America's Children: Yearbook 1994,* Washington, D.C.: CDF, 1994. Children below poverty level: 14.9 in 1970 to 21.2 in 1994. *Statistical Abstract of the U.S.: 1993,* Landham, Md.: Berhan Press, 1993, p. 472.

281 More than a quarter of all households: American Research Council, *The Family Under Siege,* Washington D.C.: ARC, 1989, as quoted in David Elkind, *Ties That Stress: The New Family Imbalance,* Cambridge, Mass.: Harvard Univ. Press, 1994, p. 77.

281 An estimated 25 percent: *New York Times Magazine* (8 October 1995): p. 53. William Damon, *Greater Expectations: Overcoming the Culture of Indulgence in America's Homes and Schools,* New York: Free Press, 1995, pp. 10–11.

281 In *When the Bough Breaks:* Sylvia Ann Hewlett, *When the Bough Breaks: The Cost of Neglecting Our Children,* New York: Basic Books, 1991.

282 In another area we could be looking at: David A. Hamburg, *Today's Children: Creating a Future for a Generation in Crisis,* New York: Times Books, 1992.

282 A survey of studies of its effects on young children: Phyllis Moen, *Women's Two Roles: A Contemporary Dilemma,* New York: Auburn, 1992, pp. 81–91.

282 At present, liberal and conservative experts: Some liberal solutions: David A. Hamburg, *Today's Children: Creating a Future for a Generation in Crisis,* New York: Times Books, 1992, chap. 7. Also see J. Q. Wilson, "What to Do About Crime," *Commentary* 98, no. 3 (1994): pp. 25–34, as quoted in *Strong Families, Strong Schools,* pp. 16–17. Hill M. Walker et al., "First Steps: An Early Intervention Program for Antisocial Kindergartners," in press. Daniel Goleman, *Emotional Intelligence: Why It Can Matter More Than IQ,* New York: Bantam, 1995, pp. 281, 183. Some foreign solutions: Steven Greenhouse, "If the French Can Do It, Why Can't We?" *New York Times Magazine* (14 November 1993): pp. 59–62. Scandinavian countries: David A.Hamburg, *Today's Children: Creating a Future for a Generation in Crisis,* New York: Times Books, 1992, pp. 118–119. Japanese daycare: *New York Times* (1 February 1995): p. A4. Some conservative solutions: Phyllis Moen, *Women's Two Roles: A Contemporary Dilemma,* New York: Auburn, 1992, chap. 6.

282 Though over half of infants: Steven Mintz and Susan Kellogg, *Domestic Revolutions: A Social History of American Family Life,* New York: Free Press, 1988, p. 307, footnote 11 gives figures before the law guaranteeing unpaid leave by large companies was passed.

283 The length of paid maternity leave: W. Dumon, ed., *Family Policy in EEC-Countries: Report Prepared for the Commission of the European Communities, Directorale General for Employment, Social Affairs, and Education,* Luxembourg: Office of Official Publications of the European Community, 1990, and W. Dumon, ed., *National Family Policies in EC-Countries in 1991,* Brussels: Directorale General for Employment, Industrial

Relations, and Social Affairs, 1991, contain general information on all legislation in member states pertaining to families.

283 Because of how busy they are: P. Finney, "The PTA/*Newsweek* National Education Survey," *Newsweek* (17 May 1993) as quoted in U.S. Department of Education, *Strong Families, Strong Schools: Building Community Partnerships for Learning*, Washington, D.C.: U.S. Dept. of Ed., Sept. 1994, p. iv. For copies of this publication, call 1-800-USA-LEARN. While throughout history, parents usually worked long hours, in the period after World War II, many middle-class mothers possessed modern conveniences, yet still stayed home. This is the standard that today's parents are comparing themselves against. William Damon, *Greater Expectations: Overcoming the Culture of Indulgence in Today's Homes and Schools*, New York: Free Press, 1995, pp. 28–29.

283 By the late 1990s: Tony Marcano, "Study Says Accreditation Is No Guarantee on Day Care Centers," *New York Times* (20 April 1997).

283 In 1987: Zero to Three (National Center for Clinical Infant Programs), *Heart Start: The Emotional Foundations of School Readiness*, Arlington, Va.: NCCIP, 1992, p. 22.

284 On average children watch: David Elkind, *The Ties That Stress: The New Family Imbalance*, Cambridge, Mass.: Harvard Univ. Press, 1994, p. 57.

284 Research shows: G. Gerbner et al., "The Mainstreaming of America: Violence," profile no. 11., *Journal of Communications* 30 (1980): pp. 10–29, as cited in David Elkind, *Ties That Stress: The New Family Imbalance*, Cambridge, Mass.: Harvard Univ. Press, 1994, p. 57.

284 Compare this to *Sesame Street:* David Hamburg, "Education for Conflict Resolution: Report of the President/1994," New York: Carnegie Corp., 1994, p. 11.

285 While current programming discourages: Conference sponsored by the Institute for Human Communication Research, spring 1995, Durham, N.C.

285 Additionally, children's mental health is deteriorating: William Damon, *Greater Expectations: Overcoming the Culture of Indulgence in America's Homes and Schools*, New York: Free Press, 1995, p. 13. Thomas Achenbach and Catherine Howell, "Are American Children's Problems Getting Worse? A 13-Year Comparison," *Journal of the American Academy of Child and Adolescent Psychiatry* 32, no. 6 (November 1993): pp. 1145–1154.

286 Current deep emotional troubles: William Damon, *Greater Expectations: Overcoming the Culture of Indulgence in America's Homes and Schools*, New York: Free Press, 1995. David Elkind, *Ties That Stress: The New Family Imbalance*, Cambridge, Mass.: Harvard Univ. Press, 1994, chap. 9. J. David Hawkins, Richard F. Catalano, Jr., and associates, *Communities That Care: Action for Drug Abuse Prevention*, San Francisco: Jossey-Bass, 1992.

286 In her study of those who had risked: Neil Miller, "Who Were the Rescuers? An Interview with Eva Fogelman, Winner of the 1995 UUA Melcher Book Award," *Unitarian-Universalist World* (May/June 1996): p. 25.

289 Teachers rank strengthening parents' roles: Louis Harris and associates, *Metropolitan Life Survey of the American Teacher 1993: Violence in American Public Schools*, New York: Met Life, 1993.

289  If each parent of a child: U.S. Department of Education, *Strong families, Strong schools: Building Community Partnerships for Learning,* Washington, D.C.: U.S. Dept. of Ed., Sept. 1994, p. 7. Calculations based on information from the *1994 Condition of Education,* the *1993 Digest of Education Statistics,* and the *1993 Statistical Abstract of the United States.*

291  Each year, the West Virginia Department of Education: Jim Delisle, *Kid Stories: Biographies of 20 Young People You'd Like to Know,* Minneapolis, Minn.: Free Spirit, 1991, pp. 117–122.

## *16. All Human Beings*

295  In the future: The opposite could happen. Where different peoples have come in close contact with each other, historically the result has been conflict. First the regions within European countries fought each other, then one European nation fought another, more recently regions of the world have aligned against other regions—with conflicts often continuing within whenever no outside enemy existed, as happened recently in the Balkans. In the past, communities generally have been created by excluding those who are different. "Profile of Mark Taylor: Bridging the Gap Between Religion and Technology," (Au), *Education Life, New York Times* (7 January 1996): p. 43.

295  "Which of the following": Massachusetts Mutual Life Insurance Company, *Mass Mutual American Family Values Study: Results of Focus Group and Survey Research,* Springfield, Mass.: Mass Mutual, 1991, p. 11.

296  By 1975, four billion people: Paul Kennedy, *Preparing for the Twenty-First Century,* New York: Random House, 1993, chap. 2. Neil Campbell, *Biology,* 3d ed., Redwood City, Calif.: Benjamin Cummings, 1993, p. 1101. The latest United Nations survey figures now project the earth's population in the year 2025 at closer to 8 billion than the originally estimated 9 billion. The family planning and other aid programs of the 1960s and 1970s, augmented by more recent programs to give women more economic power and social status, account for the lower projections, according to the United Nations officials. *New York Times* (17 November 1996): p. A3. By 2015, the ten most populous cities will likely be Tokyo (28.7 million); Bombay (27.4 million); Lagos, Nigeria (24.4 million, up from 290,000 in 1950); Shanghai (23.4 million); Jakarta, Indonesia (21.2 million); São Paulo, Brazil (20.8 million); Karachi, India (20.6 million); Beijing (19.4 million); Shaka, Bangladesh (19 million); and Mexico City (18.8 million). "The Mega-City Summit," editorial, *New York Times* (8 April 1996): p. A14.

297  Wealth is already quite unevenly distributed: Paul Kennedy, *Preparing for the Twenty-First Century,* New York: Random House, 1993, p. 49.

297  Put in terms of geography: Paul Kennedy, *Preparing for the Twenty-First Century,* New York: Random House, 1993, p. 53. South Korea, Brazil, and Australia also are affluent nations.

297  In 1986, Rushworth Kidder of *The Christian Science Monitor:* Rushworth M. Kidder, *Shared Values for a Troubled World: Conversations with Men and Women of Conscience,* San Francisco: Jossey-Bass, 1994, p. xv.

297  In a book entitled *The Need to Have Enemies and Allies:* Vamil D. Volkan,

*The Need to Have Enemies and Allies: From Clinical Practice to International Relations,* Northwale, N.J.: Jason Aronson, 1988.

299   In *The Immune Power Personality:* Henry Dreher, *The Immune Power Personality: 7 Traits You Can Develop to Stay Healthy,* New York: Dutton, 1995, pp. 244–247.

303   Vaclav Havel, the former president: Vaclav Havel, on the occasion of his receiving the 1994 Philadelphia Liberty Medal, as reprinted in *New Age Journal* (October 1994): p. 162.

303   If everything in the Universe: Abell, Morrison, and Wolff, *Realm of the Universe,* New York: Saunders College Publishing, 1994, p. 433.

304   It logically follows: Vaclav Havel, on the occasion of his receiving the 1994 Philadelphia Liberty Medal, as reprinted in *New Age Journal* (October 1994): p. 162.

# Index

Grateful acknowledgment is made to the following for permission to reprint previously published material:

*Academy of Chicago Publishers and Gregory Alan-Williams:* Excerpt from *A Gathering of Heroes: Reflections on Rage and Responsibility: A Memoir of the Los Angeles Riots* by Gregory Alan-Williams (Chicago: Academy of Chicago Publishers, 1994). Reprinted by permission.

*Sheldon Cohen:* "Interpersonal Support Evaluation List" by Sheldon Cohen. Reprinted by permission of Sheldon Cohen.

*William Damon:* Excerpt from *Greater Expectations: Overcoming the Culture of Indulgence in America's Homes and Schools* (New York: The Free Press, 1995). Reprinted by permission of William Damon.

*Lawrence Erlbaum Associates, Inc., Aimée Dorr, and Beth E. Rabin:* Statistics from "Parents, Children and Television" by Aimée Dorr and Beth E. Rabin from *The Handbook of Parenting*, Vol. 4, edited by Marc Bornstein. Reprinted by permission of Lawrence Erlbaum Associates, Inc., Mahwah, New Jersey, Aimée Dorr, and Beth E. Rabin.

*Free Spirit Publishing Inc.:* "Making Social Studies Come to Life" (pp. 117–21) from *Kidstories* by Jim Delisle. Copyright © 1991. Used with permission of Free Spirit Publishing, Inc., Minneapolis, MN. All rights reserved.

*Health Communications, Inc.:* Excerpt from "You've Got Yourself a Deal" by Florence Littauer from *Chicken Soup for the Soul: 101 Stories to Open the Heart and Rekindle the Soul* (pp. 281–82), compiled by Jack Canfield and Mark Victor Hansen. Copyright © 1993. Reprinted by permission of Health Communications, Inc., Deerfield Beach, FL.

*Alfred A. Knopf, Inc.:* Excerpt from "No Exit" by Jean-Paul Sartre from *No Exit and Three Other Plays* translated by Sean Gilbert. Copyright © 1946 by Sean Gilbert. Copyright renewed 1974, 1975 by Maris Agnes Mathilde Gilbert. Reprinted by permission of Alfred A. Knopf, Inc.

*J. Michael McGinnis, M.D.:* Figures from a paper entitled "Actual Causes of Death in the United States" (JAMA 270:2207–12). Reprinted by permission.

*Sister Helen Mrosla:* Excerpts and summarization of an essay about seventh-grade students keeping descriptions of nice characteristics about themselves. Used by permission of Sister Helen Mrosla.

# About the Authors

VIRGINIA WILLIAMS, Ph.D., is a historian by training and president of LifeSkills, Inc. She is the author of *Surrealism, Quantum Philosophy, and World War I* and the coauthor of *Anger Kills*.

REDFORD WILLIAMS, M.D., is director of the Behavioral Medicine Research Center, professor of psychiatry and psychology, and associate professor of medicine at Duke University Medical Center. He is the author of many scientific articles and *The Trusting Heart*. He is coauthor of *Anger Kills*.